A VERY SPECIAL CONTRIBUTOR

Roberta E. Young whose constant encouragement, long hours at the computer, critical comments and insightful suggestions helped bring this book to life. She shares my dedication to assist and teach present and future generations of innovators.

Thank you Bobbye.

Guts, Imagination, Vision: Conversations with Innovators-Changemakers
By Shirley G. Schmitz

Copyright © 2008 Shirley G. Schmitz. All rights reserved.

Reproduction, copying, storage in a retrieval system or transmission by any means of contents is prohibited without the express written permission of publisher.

Published by: TechPress, Inc. of Paradise Valley, Arizona USA. Visit our website: www.TechPressPublishing.Com. TechPress, its logos and Marks are trademarks of TechPress, Inc. Guts, Imagination, Vision: Conversations with Innovators-Changemakers is a trademark or service mark of Shirley G. Schmitz and/or Innovators-Changemakers LLC,

First Edition: May, 2008

ISBN - 13: 978-0-9763540-3-1
ISBN - 10: 0-9763540-3-9

Retail Price: $39.95 USD

Cover and inside book design by Norma Strange.

Photographs used with permission of respective contributors or interviewees.

This publication is designed to provide competent and reliable information regarding the subject matter covered. However, it is sold with the understanding that the author, interviewees and publisher are not engaged in rendering financial, legal or other professional advice. Laws and practices often vary from state to state and by country and if financial, legal or other expert assistance is required, the services of a professional should be sought. The author, interviewees and publisher specifically disclaim any liability that is incurred from the use or application of the contents of this book.

GUTS • IMAGINATION • VISION

CONVERSATIONS WITH INNOVATORS-CHANGEMAKERS

Shirley G. Schmitz

AUTHOR'S DEDICATION

This book is dedicated
to all the people who have galloped,
run, strode, ambled, walked
or crossed through my life - -
and especially those who have chosen
to remain there.

Your influence is ever present in my life and work.

PROLOGUE

In 1949, I graduated from Arizona State College and took a job teaching at Mesa High School for the sum of $2,712.00 a year. The $226.00 a month ran out quickly, leaving me with more month than money. Accordingly, I took a commission job in the summer of 1950 selling the World Book Encyclopedia.

My vision had always been to have a company of my own and to save a little and transition eventually from teaching to business. Besides, I had to work during high school and college just to survive. In consulting the help wanted ads I saw there were never meaningful jobs for women. Most always they were titled "Help wanted – male." I needed money so I applied. Over that period of time I held jobs delivering packages for the postal service, washing carrots at a packing shed, and also as a summer head cook at a bar & grill, an evening fry cook, a waitress, a marker in a laundry, commercial artist and a sign painter. Anywhere I could raise a buck, I worked.

So, I figured there were always jobs to be had. Accordingly I began to read numerous books on attitude — the inspirational kind that bolstered my desire for independence. My friends and family thought I was nuts. Business in those archaic times was not the purview of a woman and so I got more ridicule than support when I talked about my goal. While reading about attitude, I came across an anonymous poem that struck a chord — and seemed to talk to me. The naysayers in my life thought I had gone as low as I could when I took the job selling books, but along about the end of June of 1951, my sales began to surpass my income as a teacher. And the poem just said to me — the time has come. Here is that poem:

"Isn't it strange that clowns and kings and fools who caper in sawdust rings

And men and women like you and me

Are makers of eternity.

"To each is given a bag of tools

An hourglass and a book of rules.

And each must build ere his life has flown - -

A stumbling block or a stepping stone."

In July I told my superintendent I was not returning and that I had taken a job with Field Enterprises Educational Corporation as an Area Manager. He wished me well and said I would always be welcome back. While looking back has always been one of my mental tools for planning forward, physically going backward was never an option.

Fast forward: I have had a lifetime of building my future by breaking society's prescribed rules for women. Somewhere along the tumultuous road of building my success, the world began to refer to people like me as ENTREPRENEURS. And we are a pretty important and exciting category of people. We've become the catalyst to a strong economic global world, absolutely indispensable to local communities — large and small.

According to the Oxford Dictionary an **Entrepreneur** is: A person who undertakes an enterprise or business with a chance of profit or loss.

Well now, that describes my life. I call what I do an adventure in developing people. So let's see what the dictionary says about it. **Adventurer**: person who seeks adventure for personal gain or enjoyment.

I believe we are then correct to refer to this literary effort as telling the stories of modern day pioneers who, not unlike those of history who ventured forth to develop a country and a chance for personal gain, now adventure to create businesses for profit. Over the past two years I have interviewed a select group of fascinating people, sorted through the corners of my mind, reflected, mused, pondered and jotted notes, then contemplated what I might share with the readers of this book about these entrepreneurial, adventuresome individuals.

The people featured here are living proof that pioneers and adventurers, creators of commerce and economic value are alive, well and opening up new territories every day. They are willing to expose their failures and highly cherished successes with the goal of helping others. There are light years of difference in the world of business constantly unfolding, but to know what is possible is to visit what is now and reflect on what was yesterday and all the unfolding yesterdays, as they become today and tomorrow. We do that here.

HOW AND WHY WERE THESE PEOPLE SELECTED?

I selected a group of 30 possible candidates representing a wide range of types, ideas, creativity and generations. Through their willingness and my choice the group was winnowed down to the final series of stories told here. This small select group are people who:

- Exemplify dynamic individuals shaping the future rather than waiting to see the shape of the future
- Come from a variety of backgrounds, personalities, temperaments, education and industries
- Vary widely in their interests, ideas, creations
- Possess strong visions and determination to achieve those visions
- Race forward to meet their future rather than waiting to see what the future will be like
- Come from different decades with different sets of circumstances to contend with
- Take risks to achieve their continued success
- Build businesses and enterprises by building other people
- Hold their community interests high on their list of needs
- Possess strong moral and ethical compasses
- Have excellent communications skills and apply them
- Are worth emulating
- Work every day on ways to guide themselves toward keeping their future on an upward curve
- Are largely unknown on a broad geographic scale

WHY AND HOW YOU CAN PROFIT

We are going to invest some time together. I'd like us to part company having earned a profit for that time expensed. So, before we start it would best serve our relationship for me to briefly cover who I am, who I am not, and why this book came to be. My five-plus decades in business were heavily vested in corporate house building, both start-ups and others needing rapid growth, and corporate house renovation for companies needing saving. Some of this experience has been with public companies, one a Fortune 500, and some privately held companies. My passion – indeed addiction – has been and still is finding people with ideas and talent and helping, motivating and encouraging them to harness and use their potential to develop other talents and companies. The past two years have been devoted to writing the stories of a few exceptional people some with good ideas who started and are growing businesses, others who inherited and are second generation entrepreneurs, and still others in the process of grooming a new generation to lead their businesses. Additionally, I seek out young people with talent and extend them some partial support through scholarships, funded by my non-profit foundation. I am constantly looking for people who want to join in this great adventure in the people business, and are willing to invest time and personal resources in building a larger more productive infrastructure of small businesses and supportive enterprises.

I am not an armchair expert. I've lived the adventures of building people and businesses across the North American continent and I've worked with and trained people from other parts of the world. There is a great difference between theory and practical applications that succeed and get the job done. There is a mountain of books that purports to have the "secrets to success". It seemed to me the exciting stories of real entrepreneurs and their successes every day would be an exciting read – real examples of success and the living secrets. I call these people the pioneers of our times, the people much like the indomitable individuals who crossed oceans and continents, reached for the stars and opened the world for others. Your modern enterpriser who daily conquers problems and serves us all is that pioneer in our world today. Thousands of these people migrate every day from unfulfilling careers with painful limitations and risk to build their own futures.

You will be treated to a small sampling of actual stories of these entrepreneurs who largely learned as they performed with successes and failures they are willing to share. These stories are conversational between author and entrepreneur. I want you to feel like you are sitting here enjoying them as a listener, stories that are episodic in nature, people-focused events and programs which convey what these unique individuals feel and are experiencing.

This is not a statistical tome. This is not a how to do it book but rather stories of real people who do more successful than unsuccessful work. Without the candor and giving nature of all these outstanding talented individuals we would not know what a true entrepreneurial experience is all about. Without their willingness to answer personal and sensitive questions and go on to share outcomes – some good, some painful – we could not have brought you such human adventures. These are true unvarnished stories of everyday pioneers who service, repair, invent, delight, and enrich the world they influence. Their stories show and tell how under daily circumstances, they guess right more often than wrong, with more good plans more often than bad ones.

Every story has one or more of the following elements:

- Defining life events.

- Failures and successes as building blocks.

- Lessons learned.

- A profile of the individual as perceived by the author and one by the entrepreneur expressing the type of person he/she believes they are.

- Who they trust and admire.

- Why they became the person depicted in their story. What makes them tick.

- How they respond to society's needs. Their good deeds. Their giving for the future.

- Their vision for their future.

- A chronology of key events, i.e. birth date, education, awards, organizations they belong to, etc.

- Their philosophy.

- Images to illustrate their unique personalities and stories.

You will read great stories of determined people performing superbly. You will be taken inside the sensitive, humanistic world of practical business building and be privy to a conversation between interviewer and fascinating entrepreneurs through words and pictures. Highly personal and informal it is a show and tell that courage is not just the purview of soldiers, athletes, or space pioneers in the traditional sense. That artistry is not just for artists, that creativity and civic concern are all part of the successful business processes of people who start, build and carry on enterprises.

The stories are warm, emotional, sometimes funny and robust. A slice of the people side of many industries and a series of short, intimate looks at adventurers — often overlooked because they are business people.

These are events, movements and forces converging that make this time, the first decade of the 21st century, an unprecedented time to start businesses. Technology, economics, demographics, psychographics have come together to influence the opportunities for success. The Global Entrepreneurship Monitor states that in 2003 one of every nine American adults was involved in entrepreneurial activity. Perhaps you are contemplating starting your own business or know someone who is. These stories could answer some questions or deal with possible concerns.

In the world of the enterprise builder there are no norms or formulas. There are intriguing problems to be solved. There are ideas, human drive, competitiveness, tenacity, bravado, courage, and an ever present desire for the quest. The working landscape is messy, strewn with trial and error, failure, missteps, constant personal aggravation, pessimism liberally controlled by optimism and a refusal to quit. Entrepreneurs subscribe to a motto of "keeping on

– keeping on". Yesterday's, today's and tomorrow's entrepreneurs are our visionaries, possessing the same courage as those who crossed oceans in tiny boats, opened territories on foot, horseback or wagon, and fought nature's unpredictable elements, unknown predators and secretive enemies.

Entrepreneurs, for the most part, are not focused on restrictions, boundaries, regulatory fences or impossibilities. Their landscape is always considered open for going over hurdles, under fences, around obstructions and ignore the naysayers. Their mindsets are not clouded by doubt. The simple track is - "there is a way. I will emerge."

Where do we find these remarkable people? Arts, sciences, technology, agriculture, engineering, finance, teaching, entertainment, construction, and publishing just to give some samples. And, what are they like? These unique individuals come in all sizes, shapes, skills, opinions, backgrounds, and yes - likes, dislikes, prejudices and temperaments. They are alike in that they all possess spirit which is the fuel driving their engine of accomplishment. Innovations thrill them. Failures are just bumps in the road signaling refocus and digging in. Making change is their goal, pushing – their style of operation. You may like or dislike them, but should never ignore them. Challenge is the daily menu. Like them or dislike them – they will change all our tomorrows.

The ideas they generate, the inventions and concepts they produce, the structures they assemble often end up being refined, extended and enhanced by a whole set of other people. Their work makes the world better or more complex.

As our stories will illustrate, some entrepreneurs transition into builders who capture and dominate the market they establish. Some may at some time sell to bigger organizations who move the process ahead, and then go on to create yet another entity. The stories contained here run the spectrum. The successes, failures, achievements and ongoing challenges will entertain you, teach you and inspire you. Enjoy!

DEDICATION

In January 2005 I attended an event that was also attended by several people who had won awards and been recognized for their entrepreneurial spirit. As I looked around the room I remembered them telling their stories of hard work and determination and I was inspired again! As I left the event that morning I mentioned to Shirley Schmitz, a true entrepreneur herself and a leader in the field, that someone should write a book so that the inspirational stories of the entrepreneurs in that room would not be lost but shared with young people and others wanting to start a business of their own.

Shirley spent the next two and a half years writing this book. It reflects not only the entrepreneurs that she interviewed and wrote about but also her unique and compelling spirit. The stories are informal, told in their own style, so that the reader has a sense of sitting with them and "hearing" them share their feelings, philosophy, fears, failures and accomplishments. I'm enriched by their candor and know you will be as well. I'm also extremely grateful to Shirley for giving us this book.

— Verna Campbell Malone
Vice Chairman
Legacy Bank

SPEAK SO THAT I MAY SEE YOU. — Socrates

The following chapters are selected stories of eleven innovators whose entrepreneurial spirits are glimmering lanterns in a world possessed with conformity. These interviews were conducted in informal settings where many of the questions could be classified as highly personal. The interviewees spoke candidly so that you could hear and learn from their efforts. These stories are a treasury of people who touch people for the better, everyday.

Entrepreneurs are addicted to problem solving and search for opportunities that they can capitalize on. Sometimes they are ahead of the population's recognition, sometimes the timing is perfect. They are the reason we have economic miracles. Government and educational institutions have been slow to recognize the innovators who create the bread and butter we all enjoy.

Listen to these everyday innovators, each very different but collectively touching and influencing thousands of lives. Each provides great lessons of challenges faced, problems solved, as they pursued their visions. Along the way each learned about themselves and had the courage to tell us about their journey so far. As they speak, you see the person they are now and a little of why and how they got to this place in life.

- John Ridgway   www.novo.com
- Ananda Roberts   www.nfocus.com
- Gregory E. Torrez   getorrez@aol.com
- Marcia Veidmark   www.sscboring.com
- David Kravitz and Eileen Spitalny   www.brownies.com
- Ogbonna Abarikwu, PE   www.ckengr.com
- Carol Den Herder and Kristin Rezler   www.identitymarketing-AZ.com and www.ourguardian.org
- Eileen Proctor   www.topdogbizboosters.com
- Doug Ducey

BRANDING the WORLD

*I*n the world of movers and shakers, ideas count for little, dreams even less. Ideas and dreams without actions are merely non-events. The old proverb, "Actions speak louder than words," separates the winners from the losers.

THIS PHOTO WAS TAKEN ON SET IN GERMANY WHILE SHOOTING THE TALENT FOR RTL EUROPES #1 (PREMIER) TV CHANNEL.

RIDGWAY: AN AMERICAN ORIGINAL

John Ridgway is a man whose ideating power has attracted talented people. Together they have created memorable images that have added grace and humor to charm the masses. Through dynamic action, unusual images and exciting sound, they have enhanced the critical messages of countless corporations, countries, governments, agencies, charities, entertainment, and individuals worldwide.

He's a quiet man who considers his neighborhood the world which he traverses with ease. He is a man with a gracious manner and thoughtful understated demeanor who possesses a soaring mountain of varied talents and capabilities. He has steely determination to improve his world neighborhood, one country and city at a time.

John is man whose quiet power moved millions of people to reject shackles and choose to be free. Did this man really change the direction of one of the significant nations of the world?

The year was 1993, less than three weeks before a referendum that would either give democracy a chance in Russia or return Russia to the communists. The fate of this nation rested on the people voting, "Da. Da. Nyet. Da." So let's begin with my question to John Ridgway about his Russian experiences; it is a story that has been largely overlooked.

John, I'm going to begin with your Russian experiences of which very little has been known. There is so much I want readers to know about you and we'll get to the rest of your career after this, I promise.

For years my friend Ben Goddard, President of First Tuesday, and I have called it "The Russian Thing." My Russian experiences kind of fall into three chapters and your question is about chapter two. Let's start with chapter one which is when I visited the Soviet Union with a group of other journalists from The Wall Street Journal, The New York Times, The Los Angeles Times and the Washington Post. It was a trip set up to speak with the press there.

We had scheduled meetings with the editorial board of Pravda and it was quite an eye opener because, first of all, just seeing the Soviet Union and the way that communist systems worked in those times was exciting. I had been to China right after China opened, too. I think people never really knew that it was hard to get into these communist systems and people here never really knew how bad they were. They were really awful, just soul-scarring and wretched, the complete opposite of our systems. They were systems that just beat people into the ground. It became very, very clear to me that this was a system that had to go away. I also came out of that trip thinking that one of the real keys was going to be television and communications, a line of work that I loved. I knew that once we could break that iron curtain we would be able to use technologies that were coming, that would allow us to be able to receive satellite transmission. Once those folks got an idea of the way we were living, things were bound to change. The other dynamic was that they could not keep their people from knowing the way the rest of the world was living. I became fixated on that and came back and actually did some work with USA, some pro bono work toward that end.

JOHN WAS A CONTRIBUTING MEDIA ANALYST ON NBC. HE WAS CALLED ON TO COMMENT ABOUT THE MEDIA IN THE MOST EXPENSIVE CONGRESSIONAL RACE IN THE HISTORY OF THE COUNTRY.

"It became very, very clear to me that this was a system that had to go away."

By early 1993, Gorbachev had given it up and Yeltsin was in power, and there still had not been an actual election in Russia. The communists were still waiting in the wings with plans to take power back one way or another, but at this point we were talking about, it was Russia, and Yeltsin was running it. The communists did somehow have enough control, or did control the Duma enough, to put together a referendum that had four questions which threatened to topple the Yeltsin administration, opening the door for the communists to take over again. It was a very cleverly

John Ridgway (continued)

constructed referendum. I mean, we see them in Arizona or California as Prop 103 or Prop 104 that requires only a vote of yes or no.

I have a kind of parallel life in politics along with this, which I stopped doing more or less professionally for money when I went to Los Angeles. I have a very good friend and mentor, Ben Goddard, who is one of the preeminent political media consultants in the country, and when this thing came up, I mean, we became aware of it in the west and began to get some press about a month out. I got hold of my friend Ben and went over and had a glass of wine and a cigar with him one Sunday afternoon and said, "Ben, you know some people in St. Petersburg. I don't think they've ever done television over there for these campaigns and they're headed toward losing this referendum because they have to win all four parts of the referendum and it isn't yes on all four or no on all four." The way it had to fall for Yeltsin was yes-yes-no-yes, which is just about impossible and they had to get over 50 percent of the vote. Over 50 percent of the eligible voters had to vote. The election was to be held on Sunday which is common in many countries and it was not going well. The polling showed him down about 10 or 11 points on every question. The election was about three weeks away and I said, "Ben, you know we could turn things around fast, because I've worked in news and you've done campaigns. If we could get hold of these folks, and they'd just let us do what we do, we could turn this around." I don't know how we'll get them to agree to all of this but they have to let us in. They have to give us access to all the research and they have to agree to run the campaign the way we want to run it. They have to give us unlimited access to the television station called Stenkeno that reaches all nine time zones, has a 50 percent share, and we have to have some cooperation, very quiet cooperation from our state department. We have to hit the ground running. We have to be in production and having our meetings at the same time. We are about the only ones that can do this and we are going to have to pay for it ourselves because we don't have any time to do any fundraising.

Ben said, "Yeah, that sounds cool." That was on a Sunday afternoon and Ben wrote a fax to the people he knew in St. Petersburg that night which was Monday morning over there. Tuesday morning our time we had a fax back that said, can you be here on Wednesday? We took that as a yes to all of our requests. Ben was tied up with something so I got on a plane the

I have a kind of parallel life in politics along with this…

John and Ben await pickup to work on the Russia campaign. Pictured here in front of the Metropol next to Red Square.

next day and landed in Moscow on Thursday. Ben arrived late Friday and we spent the entire weekend going from committee to committee and listening to what everybody in that part of the world had to say on this until we finally got to the one group that had the stack of research papers we needed.

We had to know all the arguments. We knew how everybody in the hierarchy felt and knew what the politics were but, to the Russian people we had to reach, none of that made any difference. We had to find a hot button quickly and get to the people and hit that hot button to get them to respond. They had to respond and it had to happen in a very, very short period of time because at that point the elections were two weeks away. We knew we needed at least a week with two weekends. We had to do a saturation the weekend of the election and we had to do a saturation the weekend before that. We had to do as much as we could in the interim week, which meant we had to do all of our production and have the work satellited in by Friday, a week after we arrived. By Monday we managed to have all the information we needed. We put our "tent" in the Metropol Hotel right off of Red Square and sat in the bar where Ben wrote and I sketched pictures. That's the way we work together, words and pictures. The hotel had a fax so we were able to contact our staffs who were on standby in this country. My staff got all of the visual production work, all the story boards and the information from me, and Ben's staff got all of the voiceovers. A part of this story that never got publicized was that the State Department provided us with the Russian voice-overs that sounded exactly right. This is one of those things that couldn't have any "fingerprints" on it at all. At the time we couldn't tell this to anyone because if it had come out, it would have destroyed the whole campaign and probably caused an international incident.

JOHN AND BEN WORKING IN RUSSIA.

"This is one of those things that couldn't have any fingerprints on it at all."

Our combined staffs worked on production for the first part of the week; the second part of the week Ben flew back to D.C. where we did the post-production to assemble everything. I flew to Paris to be within striking distance, so I could get back to Moscow, but I didn't want to be there because of the possible consequences of losing. There were consequences later on when someone shot up the TV station. But that could have been expected.

When we were ready we went to the TV station and said, "Look, we've got to have your absolute cooperation. You're going to get five tapes satellited to you on Saturday morning and, unless there's something seriously wrong, which we'll fix, you play them as is, and this is when you play them." They'd been given their marching orders as it had

John Ridgway (continued)

gone up to Yeltsin and come back down, that we should get what we needed. So we directed the whole thing from the lobby of the Metropol Hotel, completely unsupervised and unencumbered, until the day before we left. That was a Monday afternoon, and we got call from one of our handlers who said, "There is a black Volvo that's going to pick you up at six o'clock sharp. There is someone you need to meet." We said, "Can we talk about this?" We were told, "No, we can't, because we're on the telephone." Soon the car arrived and we got in. The driver, a big guy who didn't speak any English, proceeded to drive us out of town. We were watching the city go by and thinking, well, this is either a really good thing or this is not so good a thing as we were driven out of town! Finally we were out on the road with nothing but woods. The driver pulled off onto a dirt road and suddenly there was a checkpoint with Russian soldiers. The driver had a conversation with the soldiers, the gate went up and we got in. We got to a clearing where there were cabins, like you see on the lakes of Minnesota, and we were greeted by this fellow whose last name was Burbulis. He was Yeltsin's political advisor and his Secretary of State. He was there with his family barbecuing. He took us up to his study and said, "Now tell me what you are doing." I nodded to Ben and suggested he do the talking.

We were nervous as hell and Ben walked through each spot, what the point was, how we were going to do it, what we had found to be the hot spot. The strategy was to address one of the main problems, apathy, motivating people to vote because we couldn't find anything that would make them vote. You can go out and talk about democracy and freedom until you are hoarse and it would get you virtually nowhere in the communist world of that time. We explained what we had found to be the problems and how we were going to hopefully solve them. The hot button, by the way, which we found in the research material, was that Russian people actually would respond and vote for the future of their kids. That was it. So everything centered around love of kids. He sat and listened to the whole thing and said, "It's great, but I want you to make these two changes." I quite honestly can't remember what the two changes were, but they were very subtle political changes that did not affect the core of our message, so it was fine with us. He smiled and said, "Good luck. I'll never see you again."

Off we went in the black Volvo, back to the Metropol Hotel. We assembled all the spots the next week in Washington, D.C. and they were satellited in. I think there might have been one small technical change because obviously we had to make it look and sound like home-grown Russian wording. We were successful. The election turned around the next week. It slowly began to move in the right direction and, when we did the saturation on that Saturday, it completely moved Yeltsin's way. The communists didn't know what to do because this had never been done before. In that sense it was a very creative thing to do and, in a lot of ways for us, it was an obvious thing to do. You know, it was like we came in with 21st century military technology and blew their doors off. "Da. Da. Nyet. Da." We won the referendum and we all had a little celebration in Malibu. Nobody really found out about it until a month later when we got a call from someone at the L. A. Times who said, "We know about this campaign and we are going to do a story either with or without you." I said, "Well, we'll talk to you because we would rather steer it than not." It was on the front page of the business section. It wasn't quiet, but it didn't attract a lot of notice. So this was chapter two of our Russian affair.

Then came chapter three. Later on in '96 I was asked to go back, this time to re-brand the main TV station where they were conducting the media campaign for Boris Yeltsin's presidential bid and so we advised on that. We didn't do the production at that point, because by now they were able to handle production themselves. They were up and rolling and that one we were very quiet about. There were some other people who were in a hotel talking to Yeltsin's daughter and they made a movie about Yeltsin with her. I got a kick out of it because these guys weren't anywhere around in 1993. The movie was only about the 1996 campaign, not about the referendum we had done in 1993.

The referendum was three years earlier and the only information was the short article in the L. A. Times. What I have just told you has never before been told. If "Da. Da. Nyet. Da." had not been successful, there is every possibility the '96 campaign would never have happened. In the years after the referendum the democracy began to emerge. There weren't ways and systems in place to accommodate democracy. It just came BOOM! There was a huge void that allowed organized crime to move in and take over. Berezhanovsky, a huge Yeltsin supporter with a lot of money, came on strong. He purchased a major bank, the airlines and the television station. When I went to work for them to re-brand the station, I didn't realize that I was working for Berezhanovsky; it only became obvious later on and turned into quite another story. They were supporting Yeltsin through the station and that's how they were controlling the media. I told them we were willing to prepare a campaign. We basically laid out the scripts and directions, discussed how to use them, timing and the like, but they took over from there. I still have a couple of the scripts. At the same time, a firm in California made contact with Yeltsin's daughter who was theoretically running his campaign. They made the movie. I'm sure they gave her some advice that

> "If 'Da. Da. Nyet. Da.' had not been successful, there is every possibility the '96 campaign would have never happened."

THE VOTE: DA, DA, NYET, DA.

John Ridgway (continued)

In the lobby of CBS News in New York.

was probably good, but the movie was more a projection of what they would have done than anything that actually happened, as they were not in the middle of what was really happening. The media portion was going on at the station.

I was working with Yeltsin's #2 guy, Berezhanovsky, who was pretty frightening. I remember getting off the plane just before the election. I got up from my seat, was met at the door of the plane, taken to a room that was like a bar, and served a drink. They went away, came back with all my papers, took me to a car and whisked me away. They just removed me from the system. If you remember, Yeltsin had been put in the hospital for his heart and nobody knew what the hell was going on. I asked if he was alive and was told he was alive, but I had the feeling that he would be elected dead or alive.

The campaign didn't have the frantic activity and energy we experience here in the U.S. Everything seemed calculated and wired. I witnessed the nastiest political dirty trick I have ever seen. The other candidate had a whole campaign he was prepared to launch the weekend before the election and had to pay the station in advance for his media placement. The station took his check to the bank and then on Friday after hours called him up and informed him the bank had put a hold on the check. No money, no media. I learned later the bank was owned by Berezhanovsky. It was pretty nasty.

But the Yeltsin saga is important. I was involved in the referendum drama and the 1996 election. Looking back, these historic involvements were probably the most important in my life to that date. I was given the incredible opportunity to be a major part of a world-changing series of events in which I could apply everything I had learned to change and effectuate the events. I remember sitting in my hotel and thinking, if this works this may be the reason for my life of learning and perfecting my craft. The adrenaline rush – the short time frame – the entrepreneurial spirit. I didn't have to do this, didn't have to generate paperwork that someone, anyone had to approve. We just did it! We helped change a nation. It wasn't pretty. In fact it was nasty and messy, but it did set the stage for the momentous events that followed. We helped change a communist country in its early stages of democracy. In retrospect, I still think about that fateful day in that Moscow hotel where, with my adrenaline pumping, I was thinking, "You've got a week to do all this. Now go!" No one made Ben and me do what was a necessary challenge. No one was paying us. It was just our entrepreneurial souls. We knew we were able to perform because we wanted to.

John, one of the reasons I wanted you to talk about your Russian experiences is because I believe it to be the ultimate entrepreneurial process. Would you do what you did in Russia again if the circumstances presented you with the option to choose?

That's a good question, Shirley, but I venture to say I'm not sure just how to respond. I can say that, perhaps in a more benign way today, I change the world in many countries by my involvement with the communications organizations that seek my help in re-branding and positioning. My company, Via Worldwide, has worked with groups in Poland, Germany, Japan, China, Singapore, Hong Kong, United Kingdom, France and others, besides here in the U.S.A. And our international client list grows daily.

Your story, I believe, provides marvelous insights into the entrepreneurial mind because, John, one of the things that I have discovered is that you are an forever entrepreneur.

A recovering entrepreneur, Shirley.

No, John, you will never recover. You're a creator of many dimensions and each time I look through the material you gave me, I think of those dimensions. I've read the article in Post as well as others, and I have a sense of some of your thought processes and some of the ways you internalize these things before you pass them on to somebody else to get the job done. Any good director does that and then passes it on. In any event, there's nothing you do that's mundane. I'll just say it that way. I know

JOHN'S COMPANY, NOVOCOM, HAS CREATED MANY OF THE BRANDS THAT WE SEE EVERYDAY ON TELEVISION.

John Ridgway (continued)

how you foster ideas; you have a soft way of getting into some of these things and I want that to come through as we move ahead with our conversation. Some of the questions I'm going to ask may seem intimate. They are. They are intended to be intimate because I cannot get into your personality and some of the ways you think and produce without tough questions. Perhaps someone will read your story and say, that's just like me. If he can make it, so can I.

JOHN HAS TAUGHT AT INTERNATIONAL HOME SCHOOL SINCE 2002.

That would please me, Shirley. As you know, I love to teach and would consider that result worth our discussion.

That comment of yours about a soft spot comes up often with my students. I presently teach on and off at three different institutions, two in California, one in Germany and I've requests from other countries as soon as the schedule allows.

Please tell us more about your classes.

I'm on the faculty at the Otis School for Art and Design in Los Angeles and I have taught motion design for film and television in the University of California Extension program at Los Angeles (UCLA) for 20 years. For three years now, I've also taught a class in logo design for the broadcast medium at the International Film Institute in Cologne, Germany, once a year. I've lectured at the Pointer Institute in Florida and I've lectured at ASU. I've lectured for all the major television conferences pretty much throughout the world. I'm one of five speakers representing promotion in North America who lectured at the first television promotion conference in China in November 2006. And I am speaking in Singapore as well. Teaching is very much a passion and I can say, off the record, I may accept a professorship in journalism at ASU. This fits my next dream which is curriculum and broadcast news structure, a very important topic for anyone in broadcast news. The way news is being structured is changing very much right now, both here and internationally and it is having a profound effect on the way we live. I do have an agenda!

John, you and I have known one another for more than 15 years. To tell your story well, we need to go back to the beginning of your entrepreneurial life. Those early years and the productive experiences would be beneficial to the reader of your story. They show how you have been a creative builder all your life.

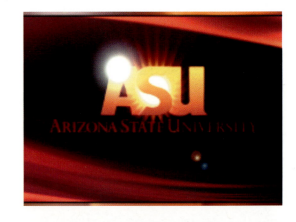

Well, I remember a very insightful comment made about entrepreneurs working from the mind and from the heart. I would classify me to be the latter. I never set out to be an entrepreneur, never set out to take on a particular project or enterprise, or have an agenda or goal for the potential revenue it might generate. I recognize revenue as necessary or, as you so often underscore, a result if the endeavor's saleable.

I am someone who has been very fortunate. I've had a number of interests that I have been passionate about ever since I was 10 to 12 years old. Most of these interests have had to do with communication. Somewhere in high school I discovered the power of the juxtaposition of imagery and typography in conveying ideas. Those years were the late '60s, very tumultuous political times. I found that the contribution I wanted to make, I could best make expressing ideas succinctly through those combinations of graphic design-typography and photography. To that end, growing up in Arizona is interesting because it is a land of opportunity. I am very much a westerner for that reason. What is it that Shaw says, "You see things; and you say, 'Why?' But I dream things that never were; and I say, "Why not?" Growing up in Phoenix, it was often hard to get a job to do what I wanted to do. So, because those jobs weren't there and, particularly they weren't there when I was in high school, I would simply go out and create what I thought it should be. I soon found that if I created it in my mind, or if I could see it in my mind, a real picture of it, and I began to take steps toward it, my subconscious and enthusiasm would get me there. Soon the pieces I was putting into place in somewhat of a "nail" soup progression would actually lead to creating the entity. So I took over a small design club and turned it into a graphic design firm during my junior year of high school and began to create and sell posters to other campus groups. When I came to Arizona State University, I began to look around campus for a group like that and discovered there wasn't one. So I found a room that had a printing press, found out who was in charge and asked if I could I use it. On the weekend they gave me the key to the office in the Memorial Union. When no one was there I turned it into a design studio. I bought second-hand equipment for the drawing boards, gave it a new name, built business cards, printed them and told everybody it was a design group. Then I went to the art department, found students who wanted to be part of a design group and told them they would get paid when we get paid. I've never missed a payroll. So I built a design group in 1970.

JOHN AND MIKEY AGE 5 IN 1957. THEY WERE CHILDHOOD FRIENDS AND LIVED ACROSS THE STREET FROM ONE ANOTHER.

"I am someone who has been very fortunate. I've had a number of interests that I have been passionate about ever since I was 10 or 12 years old."

John Ridgway (continued)

That was at the beginning of my freshman year at ASU. Along the way I was fortunate enough to have mentors who'd been in business ten years who helped me structure the pricing and set up a business. Next I landed at the New Times during the early years of that paper, the very early years. The New Times was just sort of thrown together as the copy came in, so I became their first real art director. When I moved to LA, public television had the same problems. They had people who did a little of everything but no real image plan. So I created an agency for servicing public television for Southern California. When I was sent over to Paramount to work on a new show that was being launched, I had dreams of running their design department and was told they didn't have one. I said, "Well, why don't I create one for you?" And they said, "We don't want one. That's not the business we're in. We're Paramount Pictures, we make movies and television shows on occasion, we don't need an art department. Why don't you just build one and then we'll use you when needed." I agreed, and my first company was formed in 1983.

As I recall, John, that company's name was four letters of the alphabet.

Yes, it was GRFX. That came from one of my mentors who used to write that in the column of scripts; it meant "graphics goes here" to indicate the insertion of a visual. He would write the script and I would figure out the visuals that went in. Whenever he wrote GRFX I had to come up with something to cover the next few lines in terms of the visual. So, that was GRFX and it eventually became Novocom.

That is essentially the progression of my early thinking and why and how I started companies. It was tied into other things I was involved in while in Arizona. When I left Arizona for California, I was actually not considered a graphic designer. I was pretty much known around Arizona as a political activist and organizer. When I left, I had just finished two terms as Executive Director of the Arizona Students Association, representing all the student associations at ASU, the U of A, and NAU to the Board of Regents, the Governor's Office and the Legislature. I had successfully put together concert programs and activity programs at ASU in particular and extended those to the U of A and NAU. It was so much fun to put together these activities and concerts. I brought the first big concert to ASU – Pink Floyd on April 17, 1975. We did it because it was a good branding exercise for the student association and it was an independent revenue stream. Having an independent revenue stream meant we were not under the thumb of the administration in terms of our

Top Photo: Al Senia, Editor of New Times with John.

Bottom Photo: John formed his design group and took over a piece of the Memorial Union at ASU.

views and our activities. So I extended that idea across the state and still don't know why no one's ever thought of this or acted on it. Here we have the best venues in the state for these kinds of shows. There is a built-in group of audiences, the student associations, the athletic department and the whole student body. I was the art director for the New Times so we could tie into that for getting the word out. We put together a block-booking coalition that basically could control all the big shows that came to the state of Arizona. We would get into all the big venues and have them right on campus where the audience was. I actually had a job offer to head up the US Student Association and attempt the same program on a national basis, but I declined and made the choice of communications instead of politics and eventually moved to Los Angeles.

You've done some special work with KAET Public Television with re-branding. Can you say anything about that?

You know, it's where I started my work with public television. The second week in June of 1975, I got a job offer literally five minutes after I walked out of my last critique for my degree. I ran into KAET's art director and spent a year there before I went off to make jewelry, an enterprise that didn't work out. It turned out to be just a diversion. KAET was the beginning of my television career back in 1975. I held it along with the New Times gig and the state-wide student association job.

But John, let's talk about what you did for KAET.

> *I brought the first big concert to ASU - Pink Floyd in '75*

Television is going through a massive change in terms of how it is delivered and how you receive the information and what the entity is from which you are getting the information. Is it KAET? Is it Channel 8? Is it PBS? Who is it? How is it sorted out? How does the viewer perceive it? All of those structures needed to be sorted out and the station needed to be re-branded and I accepted the assignment and carried it out.

So, can you give us a little more information on these changes you made at KAET?

Yes. First of all, what we ultimately will call convergence is the set-up of a brand extension structure to be used in launching other channels and other vehicles, including delivery on the Internet. It's programming what you want

John Ridgway (continued)

when you want it. It's a combination of Internet lean-forward viewing versus broadcast lean-back viewing. When all of those things come together, certain things, certain brand elements, become obsolete, like the call letters, KAET. It becomes Channel 8 for multiple products and delivery systems.

So there needed to be an identity constructed that could adapt to all of the different kinds of products and delivery systems that KAET will utilize. They range from your phone, to your PDA, to the big entertainment center you have at home, to eventually the screen in your car and to your computer. We created a process we called a "Swiss army knife" system that supports all the variations of that identity system and lets the viewer know that they're really getting this from a trusted and known entity, which is Channel 8 in Phoenix. It is at present the fifth largest public television market in the U.S. Quite impressive.

John, I belong to the World Future Society and I've been reading a lot about what you are describing. There are those who believe that the ultimate convergence is man and machine. So when you say convergence, I think of the primitive part of it which is what we are doing now. The ultimate, according to a lot of the people I talk with, is that man and machine won't have many differences between them. I don't subscribe to all that, but there are those who do. I know you've worked on other ASU projects. Can we touch briefly on some?

I think you may be referring to telebusiness. The project is the distance learning project we created as a prototype for the ASU College of Business in 1999. I've had a real interest and love of education for many years because I had so many people get me going through that process and really motivate me. I think that's probably the most important contribution I can make in my life. For the last 10 years, I've had a vision in mind where, to put it simply, universities could be branded and be turned into, effectively, what we would think of here in the United States as television networks. We could revolutionize education in a meaningful way.

John, that sounds like a very detailed process. One left for a longer discussion over a glass of wine.

Shirley, the wine sounds great, but to sum up - using the skills that I've spent 25 or so years learning in Hollywood about making information entertaining, making it appealing, making it accessible is the concept behind what I'm suggesting. It's something that I've been pursuing for years and years and years and something I continue to pursue. Arizona State was one of the first universities to really get this when we walked in the door. I give them huge kudos for understanding the concept. Other universities that I'm affiliated with in California just don't get it at all, yet.

It's a very expensive project. The last few years have not been good years for universities to be going to legislatures seeking the hundred million dollars needed to set this up. But I am absolutely convinced that it's something that is not a matter of if, but when. I'm sure I'm not the only person to think of this, and it will happen, it will evolve somehow. I think there are ways we could accelerate that and I intend to be a part of it.

Your travel schedule is incredible and, I say to myself, how does John manage these sessions of teaching, training and all of that with his travel schedule? What percentage of your time are you on the road? This is someone asking who has spent a big portion of her life on the road, so if you can give us a little bit of an idea we'd appreciate it.

Well, first of all you're right, constant travel of any kind is grueling. I started traveling internationally about 25 years ago. The fax machine had been invented which made so much more possible. It is much easier now than it used to be. Communications makes even more possible now that we wouldn't have even dreamt of attempting before. And even in the last two to five years, the advancements in what we are able to do with the Internet have made working, while thousands of miles from home base, like being at one's home base.

SITTING OUT ON COUSETTE IN CANNES, FRANCE.

I think the real key to it is integration. I don't particularly compartmentalize running the business in Malibu versus seeing a client in Dubai versus teaching my class in Germany. I integrate them all because my value added, which is what it's all about to my clients, to my students, to my fellow co-workers, is really that integration of developments. For my classes in particular, I am able to construct a curriculum, start to go through it, give out assignments, and explain to the students what my concurrent assignment is right now. This is what my client is asking me to do. Every time we sit down with a new client there is something different. Everything is custom-built. So I try to integrate my client consulting with my classes with my time at my studio in Malibu. And the other thing that I've accepted and now live with is that I operate on a 24-hour clock. It is one o'clock in the afternoon right here in Arizona, which means it's five o'clock in the morning in Singapore where we have production that will be starting up there in three or four hours for a show that's going on in Hollywood. We have clients in Hollywood who we're hopefully talking to

John Ridgway (continued)

John in his Malibu studio.

right now about things that we are planning and doing for them. Anything that's going on in the East Coast, where we have some appointments, our sales executives are hopefully wrapping up as we speak. It is 10 o'clock at night in Central Europe where we've received probably the last of the communications for tonight from our producers over there who are juggling two clients, one in Poland and a new one in Paris. They're setting up appointments there that will happen in October, so I will stop getting emails from there within the next two hours. I will start getting emails from Singapore in four hours. In India, meanwhile, it is the middle of the night where we have a legal matter going on, so I won't hear about that for awhile. In Dubai, where we have ongoing work with a couple of clients, it is pretty late at night so they're quiet for the day. What is it they say? It's always cocktail hour someplace.

I've wondered John, how do you keep a 24-hour day?

We do have downtime. For example, let's look at Singapore. They work Saturday mornings, which generally starts midnight on Friday, Pacific Standard Time and lasts until maybe Sunday morning if there's any downtime at all. Often we work on weekends too, but what I try to sort out are the certain times when I rest. I do shut down and when I do I let them know when there will be no response. I always adapt to the time zone that I'm in immediately, go to bed when everybody else goes to bed, get up when everybody else does and make that time my time and adjust the 24 hour concept accordingly. Once you can get a picture in your mind of all of these projects that are going on and where in the world they're going on, it's kind of like a three-dimensional chess game. One leads this life where there is morning, afternoon, and evening all together. All the activities we're talking about are going on all at once but in different time zones. Businesses have marketing, finance and production as three components for example. Well these components that we are talking about here – education, client relations and production – are components of my business. So they all have to be coordinated and they just happen to be in different parts of the world in separate time zones.

They all have to work together, John?

Right. I hope that wasn't too long an answer.

I know the readers are going to want to know what and how and why you got to where you are, and I'm going to get a little more personal here. Would you describe for me, and that's for the reader as well, the type of person you believe you are?

I want to be someone who puts back more that I take. That's important for me. I guess we won't know if I've succeeded until the end of my days, but that's what I strive to do. I do like to visualize concepts and make them happen. That's exciting for me, just to say "why not" and "let's do it" gets my adrenaline flowing. The Russian experience was one of those. We imagined it and we did it. I've tried to be the antithesis of other people, making sure I was not like them. I've had some influences in my life from very negative people, so I have really worked to not be negative. I've worked to lead my colleagues and employees optimistically and not with fear. I believe in getting the best results from people and environments through encouragement and positive, realistic thinking. I come from a family of CPAs. For a large portion of my early life, some of my more creative ventures were criticized as pathways that would not accomplish much in my life.

> *I want to be someone who puts back more than I take.*

It's not that I don't want to be or resent CPAs. I happen to think that finance and accounting are arts and oddly enough, I rather enjoy both. I build my own management and finance systems. I don't build companies that are based on fear of taxation, I build companies that are optimistic about revenues.

Those are good points, John.

I remember when I was eight years old on a family vacation; we stopped for lunch during a road trip at a park in Fargo, North Dakota. I announced that I wanted to be an artist and was told that would be unacceptable because I would never be able to make a living. For a curious youngster that was a bit of a "downer."

Given the accomplishments you have had, John, you must have had a lot of determination to prove that threat wrong.

Or you could say that for part of my life I have been pretty angry at the negative comments and I enjoy making points which deflate the naysayers.

HIS DOGS ARE NAMED AFTER PRESIDENTS AND SPORTS FIGURES. SHOWN HERE IS FRANK AND MICKEY. NOT PICTURED ARE ELENOR AND HARRY.

John Ridgway (continued)

Let's move on to my next question which could be considered stage two of what drives your success. Please talk a little about some of the highly personal principles that you have followed and that have made a difference in your personal life.

IN FRONT OF HIS SELECTION OF EMMIES AS HE LAUNCHES HIS DIGITAL DIVISION.

Well, I'm not a terribly religious person in terms of organized religion. I have, more or less, your midwest Protestant background, but through several different directions. I have grown to realize that I tend to believe in a lot of the basic concepts of doing unto others, particularly treating others well. It has served me well in life and business. Take the simple concept of treating people with respect – a lot of people say, how do you work with all these different cultures? And we do work with hundreds of different cultures. The simple answer is to treat people with respect, to listen and to be polite. I believe that is a principle. I think being honest in transactions is an important principle. For me, it allows me to live with myself and it makes for good business. It makes for return business and a good reputation. Through good times and particularly tough times, which my businesses have been through in the last few years, this has carried the day. I try to remember the objective is to provide real value and try to understand why people are interacting from a business standpoint or in the educational area. For example, I'm working with ASU now in the educational area determining what they will need, and the principle there is to deliver what they need and then secondarily make it fit my grand scheme. I believe those are all real principles. Through my media relations firm I worked for awhile with Dick Lippin, who owns a firm in LA that represents the Academy Awards. He walked into my office one day and said, "Tell me what you do." So I told him I provide branding design and music for television stations, shows and news projects around the world. He said, "Well, that's fine, but what I think you provide is value for your clients. You ideally create a balance sheet item that is vastly increased when you are finished. That's what you do." I think, in terms of my own values, if I am doing that for other people all the way from interpersonal relations to working in education to business, then what comes back to me is always worthwhile. Those are my core values.

Your life has been productive and varied and I'm going to ask this question and see how you feel about this. What has been the most defining moment in your personal life, not your business life?

Well, that's a hard question because there has been more than one. Probably, the answer is dealing with and finding a way to handle personal betrayal.

There was some genesis to that, John? A story behind that episode?

Yep. It ties business and personal together. I was defrauded by a family member in my business in the year 2000.

I see. Do you want to talk about it? There would be no names needed.

There's a lot of picking up pieces to be done after an event like that and it is defining. I had no choice but to deal with it. Unfortunately, it's a rather negative defining moment, but it forced me to really go back and look at those key things I was talking about. What is my value added here? Let's get back to the core of it very quickly, because that is how one begins to reassemble and go on. Obviously, it affects your outlook on all the different emotions personally and professionally.

That leads me to a more positive question. You have many extraordinary achievements. Perhaps you will share with us three or four you are most proud of. I assume your Russian venture has to be number one?

That's pretty high up there, yeah.

So, let's talk about a few more.

Well it's hard to choose. In terms of events, there have been quite a number so choosing a singular striking event isn't easy. There have been some other achievements like winning my first Emmy. That was a pretty big deal and winning the second one and the rest of them in news and documentary meant a lot because that's the area that I'm most interested in. Just having the industry and your peers say, yeah, you've done something important here, you've made a contribution and having it recognized, there's a lot of self-satisfaction in that. In terms of things that we actually achieved, I always had a dream of having a worldwide reach

ABOVE: STANLEY DASHEW AND JOHN. STANLEY INVENTED THE CREDIT CARD MACHINE.

BELOW: JOHN'S MOM HAD A GREAT IMPACT ON HIS LIFE. SHE PASSED AWAY IN 1992.

John Ridgway (continued)

and thinking in a worldwide way. I take "domestic" out of the vocabulary of the company.

The United States is just another country, John?

The United States is just another country. And when we do our sheets, our case study sheets, it'll say whatever the country is. The most exciting achievement was when our operation reached the point where the sun never set on our work or operation, when we were on the ground across the globe and had become truly a global company. We are sitting in Tempe, Arizona right now and it is the middle of the day; next up is Singapore, and it will be the middle of the day there. I've got a woman in New Zealand right now bugging me for my outline for my talk in China around the second week in November. It is the middle of the day there.

I've been looking at some of your sell sheets and other portfolio material. It seems hard for me to select any one because they are all eye-popping.

Well, in terms of other specific projects, I think of the successful re-launch of CBS and all their products at the point when Walter Cronkite left CBS. This project stands high on my list. I had always wanted to be involved with the major networks. There's an interesting twist here. They came to me. The story behind my selection goes back to Cronkite's recommendation that CBS had to change, that they should take some pointers from highly successful shows and he singled out "Entertainment Tonight." I worked with the original team in the launch of ET and have done all their subsequent design work for 18 plus years. So CBS called me and brought me into New York. The CBS newsroom was called the fish bowl. It was a round room and all the producers' offices were around the edges. Dan Rather's office was upstairs and so was the executive producer's office. The broadcast set was in the middle of the room with the control room off to the side - it was a very, very intense place. There was one vacant office and CBS said, "You can set up in here and use the office as long as you want." Most of these production areas are kind of skuzzy as they are strictly work areas with no decorations. They're pretty worn as they are in use 24 hours. Well, the office designated for me had a little plaque on the wall; it had been

Edward R. Murrow's office. And, I said to myself, don't screw this one up!

What I did on the CBS assignment earned me my first Emmy for news. Another unusual part of this first Emmy was that it was presented to me by Victor Posner, a very key figure during the fall of Communism. I don't know if you remember but, towards the end of the Soviet Union, Phil Donahue had a series of interviews with this very articulate Russian, Posner. Having him present my Emmy to me was exciting.

I note, John, that you have impacted the branding of stations across the globe with offices in Europe, the Americas, Asia, the Mideast and Africa.

Yes. We are always extending and expanding, for example, designing the brand extensions system of STAR which is Rupert Murdoch's empire. One of the major components of STAR, which is based in Hong Kong, is satellite and it's kind of like combining FOX and Direct TV. Its footprint is north to Korea, south to Australia, east to the Philippines and west to the Mideast. We designed the branding structural system so that they could pull everything together and use it in all those different countries, making it recognizable and interchangeable from a recognition and production standpoint. You know, the fun there was a few years ago when I had a speaking engagement in Bombay, riding through those awful streets where everything's a mess, except for those big billboards up there with my logo on them.

John, now I'm going to focus on you as a person rather than the Via Worldwide John. When you play, what do you do?

When I play? Hum. Well, I've been working on defining play, because what I've been describing has been my play. I love what I do, so I do what I love. The people in my life question why I work all the time. They insist I should take a vacation, but my home in Malibu is where I would vacation, anyway. I'm incredibly blessed to have two acres overlooking the Pacific Ocean, four dogs, and a beautiful studio and a vineyard, so I love being home. In the last few years, I've revisited my other interests. I've gone back to jewelry-making and learning to bake. I've been working on my baking skills for the last three to five years. I've always had an interest in cars, so I have a minor car collection that has ranged from nine at one point, down to six cars now.

THESE IMAGES REACH ALL AREAS OF THE WORLD - HONG KONG, PHILLIPINES, MIDDLE EAST, KOREA AND AUSTRALIA. OVER 3 BILLION PEOPLE RECOGNIZE THESE SYMBOLS AND ADMIRE JOHN'S WORK WORLDWIDE.

John Ridgway (continued)

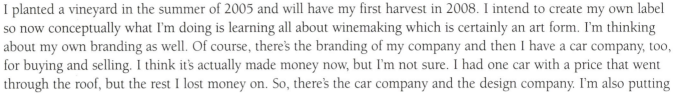

From his classic 1970 Olds 442 to his sporty Jaguar, John loves his car collection.

I planted a vineyard in the summer of 2005 and will have my first harvest in 2008. I intend to create my own label so now conceptually what I'm doing is learning all about winemaking which is certainly an art form. I'm thinking about my own branding as well. Of course, there's the branding of my company and then I have a car company, too, for buying and selling. I think it's actually made money now, but I'm not sure. I had one car with a price that went through the roof, but the rest I lost money on. So, there's the car company and the design company. I'm also putting together something for my jewelry. I realize the pressure of making money on jewelry can destroy the creativity, so I want to put together something where I can reproduce some of my good pieces. I'll have the vineyard and I have a music company now, as well, which we really haven't gone into.

That's the one in your sales packet that does the music branding?

Yeah, Via Music is a partnership and a subsection of Via Worldwide. We've been operating jointly for five years, but it's a music branding firm. And I am kind of busy in my own mind creating my own umbrella brands. The wine will be Ridgway Malibu Estate Winery. Because I'm a branding guy, I'm going to go into major branding mode on this and I've already heard that the Wine Spectator wants to talk to me. So I'm working up the story there. There is a very good chance I'm going to make my wine exclusive to Australia for the first few years because I have a distributor down there who feels they would know exactly what to do with it. I can only produce 150 cases so this is a project in which I've got three years to learn what to do, three years to "first, do no harm," as this will be an organic wine. I integrate everything. I'll walk through the vineyard to look for weeds and to see if there's something eating the plants while I'm on the phone handling business.

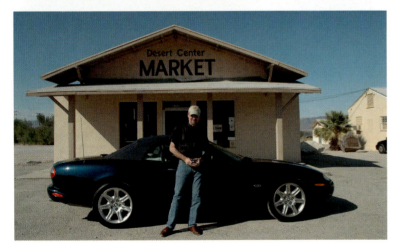

So these ventures of yours, John, can also be hobbies that can develop into businesses, right?

Yeah. but I don't want to start them out as branded businesses. First I want to perfect them, enjoy them and be proud of them. I believe the money will follow. If it doesn't, I will still enjoy the venture and try not to lose money on them.

Do you do any sports, John?

I don't do much. I hike, that's about it. I have a very severe case of scoliosis and had surgery in 1967. They put in a metal rod so there are not too many physical activities I can do. I stay as active as possible.

Okay, I'm going to ask you a very critical question that goes to your legacy. Your talents are far-ranging, John. You have created some incredible programs, moved a nation, taught throughout the world and your creations have earned you more than 150 national awards of which 14 are Emmys. Additionally you have been a nominee for more than a dozen more Emmys. If you were to disappear tomorrow is there anyone in the wings who would carry on what you started?

That's a very good question and one I put a lot of thought into. The answer is a guarded, yes. But in this business individuals create, they have a learning curve the hard way. Everyone's creativity is individual and unique – their approaches to design, color, sound – all their own invention. One cannot simply transfer a portfolio or sell one. When someone's buying the services of Via Worldwide at this point, they're really buying my services and have been for years.

Yes, I know. Then maybe I should ask, is there anyone who is understudying you, if that's the proper term?

Yes, Shirley, there is an understudy system which, if it falls in place the way it's supposed to, will produce a number of possible candidates. My first candidate is a fellow by the name of John Griffin. He's from Minneapolis, but he's lived in Singapore for the last 15 years. He's a designer/art director, very good with clients, knows the Asian market and the U.S. market, as well. He's someone who could step in, who's had a great amount of experience with the Via Worldwide portfolio and what clients use. The plan presupposes the possibility of my disappearing tomorrow. Here is the concept of phasing in a team. I'm in my 50s, Griffin is in his 40s, and I've got another person in his 40s in place. He's a top producer but I needed a creative director, which he is. We then need someone in his 30s which I haven't filled yet. I had someone in his 20s but he left to find another position, so I'll have to replace him. I also have an intern system and that has been successful. I've brought some of our staff in through interning.

John Ridgway (continued)

Is part of what you are doing with these interns at ASU a part of the system?

As a matter of fact, yes. I involve my ASU interns with the work I do here in Arizona. They come and work with me over the summer and then come back here with internships that work into jobs. I have a number of clients here in Arizona that provide challenges and experiences, under my guidance, for these exciting young novices. If something happened to me tomorrow, I can't guarantee that this is exactly what these people would want. I can't control from the grave, but the plan is set up and funded to work. Why am I doing this? Legacy. I want to leave behind a solid working program. If all goes well the plan has a chance to fulfill and prosper.

Well, how would you assess the viability of your understudy and internship strategy, given the volatility and sensitivity of your product? Art, craft, design, plays on stage – all involving the emotions of both the designer and the client. Pretty creative. Pretty personal.

Well, you know, you are questioning how important that continuity is. You know, it's really only important if other people want to carry on and I think there are people who will carry on. You had asked, what would you tell people to do it they were starting up a company? I remember something I was told and ignored. That was to come up with an exit strategy. Always have an exit strategy! You know, there really is an exit strategy with my company, which is ideally to sell it and make it part of another company that does what we do on a broader spectrum. I want to be in a position to say, "It's good if we do it, good if we don't." Hopefully, that's a win/win. I've talked to the other big groups about buyout before. All these big agencies and big groups are all owned by about two or three companies, Omnicom and WPP for two examples. So I could sell to them, but I know if that happened they'd want to keep me around for three years and maybe it would go well. Maybe, but I doubt that I would do well in captivity. And once I leave, it would change and they would little by little take it apart and merge it into other things and it would disappear and I'd hopefully walk away with my money. So there are different plans for succession. For anyone contemplating starting a company like mine, it's very important for them to have plans in place for all kinds of reasons. Last summer I ended up in the hospital for a month. And that was just boom, out of the blue. You know, you've got to have people who can step up to it. I fortunately had staff who could hold everything together.

John, would you sum up your advice?

We talked about entrepreneurs from the mind and entrepreneurs from the heart. I'm a firm believer and have discussed this with all my students and my nephew who is going to school at ASU. I really firmly believe that you've got to pursue what you love. That's number one and an important track to stay on. I think if you do that with excellence, good things come out of it. In terms of starting a company, it's having an exit strategy, be it succession or selling or both, and thinking about things like capitalization. There are a lot of basics to think about and one can't assume that the market that is out there today will be the same one that will be out there tomorrow.

Those are good suggestions, John. Is there more?

In a sense, reverse engineer it. Don't think about what's good for you but what is it that's good for your client. Determine the value you create for your clients and then that'll tell you all about what to build. Entrepreneurs of the mind, with no criticism from me, are more like venture capitalists or something like that. It's a different kind of thing and I'm not in any way condemning it. Maybe that's what people are interested in doing. But that to me is almost a different kind of entrepreneur. That's someone who's a financial entrepreneur in a sense. He's looking at creating because there's a need. That's sort of putting money into something because it's going to get a monetary return, not because you have a burning passion to create.

"I really firmly believe that you've got to pursue what you love."

John, you mentioned venture capitalism. Venture capitalism doesn't exist in this country anymore. All that exists today are people with money and they want a return. And that's not venture. Venture capital is being prepared to risk and, if you lose, walking away. That's venture capitalism. If you win, whoopee! If you lose, you lose.

John Ridgway (continued)

ABOVE: JOHN IN FRONT OF FUGI NEWS IN JAPAN.

RIGHT: JOHN SPOKE AT THE FIRST EVER DESIGN CONFERENCE IN CHINA.

That's an interesting topic, Shirley. One of the mistakes I made along the way with my first company called Novocom had to do with how I financed it. You'll recall my earlier comment about being defrauded by a family member.

That was Novocom, right?

Yeah, that was Novocom, and in hindsight, I would have been much better off with a bank where the rules were very clear, than with somebody I thought was a deeply interested venture capitalist, who, when the times got tough, spooked and ran. And then you're dealing with trying to run the company the way you know it needs to be run, versus someone who is interfering. It could become a disaster and it did.

With Novocom and the forming of Via Worldwide, I assumed there were some differences of opinion.

Yeah, yeah, very big differences of opinion.

And yet it was your company, right?

It was my company and that's where the fraud part came in. My company was literally stolen while I was out working hard to bring in business and wham, there was no company.

I gathered that it was a sensitive issue.

If I can I'll make the story short. Starting in the 80s in the U.S., television went through a huge boom and changed with everything from the technologies to the deregulation of markets. In Europe and in Asia you could go to countries like Germany where there were only two government stations, and then, boom, it opened up. But this boom had to slow down eventually and that was a component. There was also the technology that changed and became available suddenly to everyone. Where we used to have to spend a million dollars to build a specially equipped room to produce for television, radio and film, it was getting to the

point where anyone could afford to do it without all the asset investment. Still we prospered. Our value-added was always that we knew what to do and could do it better than anyone else. Our flair, special effects and creativity won clients across the world. We were the best and everyone recognized that. But then came the late 90s and a recession took hold. From our business standpoint it was a perfect storm that hit. We knew costs were high, partially done big orders were cancelled, there were too many players, dwindling orders. I traveled across the world working to find clients and save clients. While I was out along with others of our staff, the business skies got darker at home base. Unknown to me, the financial supporter we were counting on bailed out and took the remnants of the company with him. I found ways to survive as my reputation was basically intact, but most of my former competitors are gone. I susrvived because my clients trusted me.

John, I remember calling you to get some answers and you assured me you were okay. But what you said to me at that time resonated in my mind when I got your new card which read Via Worldwide. You said, "I know what I do well and see no reason to find a new career."

You further said to me, "My clients everywhere in the world trust that I will be there when they need me. And so I will be there."

I also mentioned before, Shirley, that failure is not an option. My client base never abandoned me, even in sensitive economic times and condition. Setbacks are part of the learning curve. My own branding, as always, is simple, direct

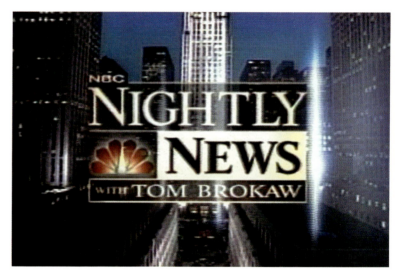

More evidence of John's branding work.

John Ridgway (continued)

John in Martha's Vineyard sporting his New York Yankees sweatshirt.

and positive. We were here yesterday, we're here today and will be here tomorrow. Each failure and each success brings opportunities to improve what I do and causes my creative juices to flow. We work hard and persist and prosper.

I want to add my latest defining moment. It represents my steadfast positive approach to adversity. The fateful fraud took place about six years ago and I have done what I tell clients to do – persevere and rebuild. In the meantime the person who stole the company, Novocom, had fallen on hard times, tried to sell and found without creative growth there was nothing to sell. When they stumbled this year, I was there to catch the company and legally reclaimed Novocom. The strategy I've employed is the founder of Novocom returning to rebuild for the future. It thus becomes a wholly owned subsidiary of Via Worldwide. Deep in my heart, I believed that one day, Novocom would again be a part of my organization. April 19, 2006, a Tuesday, we legally assumed control and made a seamless conversion as a part of Via Worldwide. We announced the celebration of Novocom's 25th Anniversary; founded in 1981, it became the oldest company in broadcast design in the world. .

We launched the new look "Brand Structural Solutions" and "Music Branding" services for our clients. Via Worldwide's Novocom will specialize in design and production of motion graphics for the global broadcast industry. I persuaded Jon Teschner, who was a part of the early stages of Novocom to return to a newly created position of Executive Vice President. I know you remember Jon from your work with us back in the late 90s. Since leaving Novocom in 2000, he has created concepts for motion picture organizations, Academy Awards, CNN and 140 or more U.S. TV stations. Jon will oversee all of Novocom's production and creative work to ensure the expectations of clients are met.

John, being a part of your dynamic career over these years has been a privilege.

Shirley, I've considered you a mentor. When you told me in 1998, I was to be the recipient of The Spirit of Enterprise Award, and that I would have to speak at the luncheon group of outstanding guests, I felt challenged as to what to say. Then you said, "They will want to know how you achieved – what your past was like." You launched me toward understanding my past and how it positioned me to achieve. In the industry I'm always thrust into the future because the problems my clients need to have resolved are problems of their future. I know now their future problems are influenced by their past activities, so that often is our starting point.

"Failure only comes when you decide to fail."

John, thanks for the compliment.

You are in my mind and experience a true entrepreneur. You have built a new enterprise based on the positive foundation of your passion. This is a very special message to anyone seeking to start a business. You represent my best example to those who seek advice, a true entrepreneur who understands that success is based on the attitude of, "Keep on keeping on." Failure only comes when you decide to fail.

AT TBS IN JAPAN IN 2004.

ChaNGiNG the WORLD

Ananda Roberts is insightful and often eloquent, thoughtful and pensive, driven to excel, energetic and responsive. Her answers to questions reveal a creative and inquisitive mind. I first met Ananda in September 2003, when she received the prestigious Spirit of Enterprise Award. Over several months we met occasionally and discussed issues relating to her expansive, determined vision. I found her to be generous and giving, caring of her employees who both like and admire her. She in turn inspires them to share a vision - CHANGE THE WORLD FOR THE BETTER, ONE COMMUNITY AT A TIME.

Fast forward to August 2005 and a comprehensive interview designed to tell the story of this unique entrepreneur. I found her to still be on vision and willing to share her personal story - her quest. In September 2006, we met again for an additional interview to further explore areas of her career only touched on initially.

In order to set the stage you need to know about her company, which is nFocus Software. Since 1984 they have worked with nonprofit organizations and government agencies to provide unique products and services. Their software applications enable public sector organizations to better manage data for trending, analysis and reporting. They serve national, state and local public organizations including the military, schools, children's organizations, and police departments in the United States, Canada, U. S. Virgin Islands, Puerto Rico, Japan, and Great Britain, just to name a few. In addition, they have selected Fortune 500 companies as clients. How Ananda and her team do business is germane to her attitude, character and the success of her enterprise.

What do you most want a client to remember about you and your business? What makes you different and why choose this particular business and client base? What products/services do you provide?

Thank you for the honor of selecting me for inclusion in your book. I will try to answer these questions to your readers' satisfaction. We welcome inquiry calls as well. I want our clients to remember the level of care we take with each of them. Our products are built specifically for the needs of the public sector. We deliver unique products and the best support possible, which in turn allows our clients to deliver an even higher level of service to the public at large. Our vision is to **Change the world for the better, one community at a time.** We believe that the level of service we provide and the quality of our products assists both our clients and our company in doing just that.

We are different because our systems are cutting-edge and we take advantage of the latest technological advances in order to deliver more efficient solutions for tracking and training. We also bring a level of compassion and direct, personal service to each and every one of our clients.

I started my company in college, raising money for nonprofit organizations and I saw vast levels of disparity between the haves and the have-nots within the public sector. I wanted to be able to "level the playing field" and I felt the best way to do that was through the use of technology. Our clients can accurately tell their stories through data that truly reflects the impact they are having on the communities they service.

We write tracking solutions which are web-based allowing organizations to track the efficacy of the services they provide to the general public that increasingly demands accountability. These systems are used by the United States Army to track the training and career paths of all the individual soldiers in the Army. This allows our nation to deploy more effectively during wartime and to train more effectively during peacetime. Nonprofit organizations and public schools can track the impact of the social services they provide to youth. In our country, we spend billions on programs and services to youth, expecting better grades, higher levels of graduation, lower drop out levels, less gang violence, etc. The nation's investments have not delivered results commensurate with the investments because without accurate data only non-objective perception prevails. I believe perception and anecdotal data have been driving the development and delivery of social services to youth for so long, that an accurate picture of what really needs to be done has not been fully developed. nFocus products can and do provide the accurate data needed, so that effective decisions can be made. These decisions can begin to correct the problems witnessed for far too long in America. We are a software company, so we always have products being refined and new ones

Ananda Roberts (continued)

developed. For example, we blend our military product with our youth product, so that a child will be able to manage his/her entire school career from a website much in the same way we manage the financial performance of our retirement portfolios.

Ananda, give us some insights into the type of leadership you provide and whether you have always been that type of person.

Whew! I believe I am very direct, and open. I don't think there are any questions I would avoid. I strive to be honest in my assessments of situations and people so that I can be forthcoming in my opinions of those situations. I tend to be compassionate when it comes to understanding why people think or feel a certain way. I also try to bear in mind what is for the greatest good, not only for the organization but also for everyone involved. So, decisions are often not always in my personal best interest, but are in the interest of what I sense is the greater good. I think that I also try hard to make certain that I live up to the value system that I put in place for the company, understanding that no company can be any greater or better than its leadership. My personal task is to grow myself as an individual thus setting an example for our team.

ANANDA'S FIRST GRADE CLASS AT SILVER SPRINGS ELEMENTARY IN MADISON, WI.

Have I always been this type of person? Well, looking back to my early years my dad and mom expected and encouraged that kind of behavior from me. I was expected to care about my value system - even though it was not called that when I was a kid. At our home honesty was the policy. I had those elements and qualities my parents exhibited to build on and refine as I matured. They were good role models and encouraged me to make enduring choices. Sure, I often stumbled and fell but there was always the encouragement to try again. So, I guess those refinements became personal integrity, openness, compassion and a belief that all of us, as individuals, have a calling to do something that goes beyond what our individual needs are. Because of my guidance at home, I grew up knowing what I wanted to do.

Okay. If you were starting your business all over today, and your life – I think they both go together – would you change some of the actions you took initially and if so, what would those changes be and are they based on what you estimate to be wrong or unproductive?

You know, there are two thoughts on that ... two theories and I really don't know which one is correct. There is that line of thought that says, at least from my perspective, that God doesn't ever give bad gifts. So there are lessons that I had to learn along the way that I could have certainly done much better. I can tell you that starting the company in college there was a lot more kindness and forgiveness extended to me. I could have been a little more compassionate which would have advanced me much more quickly as an individual and as a business owner, but I had to learn those lessons. I wouldn't be where I am today had I not gone through those early trial and error steps. There is the line of thought that says okay, what did I learn? I think that looking back I could have been so much more strategic. And, so much more intelligent about the decisions and the relationships that I pursued or didn't pursue. I would change many of my snap reactions, so many of the words spoken in haste. I'm philosophical. On the one hand, you know, everything is always in perfect alignment. It is God's world and we are just playing in it. That would mean there is perfect alignment and you wouldn't go back and change a thing. But, when you do look back, you know, there were those situations that you would have handled so much better and that was possibly God's will as well.

Is it a process of having more information about the world you are in and yourself, both of which come with time and experience?

Well, I used to believe that having the best product and being the strongest competitor I would always win. I have learned that absolutely is not the case. But it took me so long to learn that because when I started the company in my 20s in college, it really was the case for me. I was just extremely competent at what I did. So in my mind it meant that all I had to do was be the best and everything I wanted to do would follow. When I moved the company to Phoenix 14 years ago and converted from fundraising into a technology firm serving the public sector, I learned that the appropriate relationships play such an incredible role in business. This is a perspective I did not have at all. It was such a shock to me to come to the understanding that centers of influence were a critical piece of doing business. It has taken all of these years to fully understand what a strategic role that plays in not only the evolution of the business, but in my own, personal evolutions.

ROB FULLMER, MANAGER, DESIGNED THE CORPORATE LOGO AND HAS BEEN WITH THE COMPANY SINCE 1998.

Ananda, what one, or collection of events define your life and directions?

One is hard to select. Every day our business presents defining occurrences, some personal, others impact on nFocus' business in significant ways. I'll start with a highly personal event, which influenced my development. I'm a firm believer that God places opportunities in our way. We just have to respond. The first one that comes to mind

Ananda Roberts (continued)

occurred when I lived in El Paso doing charitable fundraising. This was the pre-curser company I formed that transitioned to nFocus.

TARA ROCHELLE TAYLOR AND ANANDA SPENDING TIME TOGETHER.

I noticed a lot of inequities in the health care system that were funded by public dollars, especially those impacted by poverty, child abuse and the like. On the southeast side of El Paso, there is an area called Colona. It is part of America, but there was no running water and no sewage disposal. It was my first experience with the reality of the less educated you are, the less likely you are able to take advantage of primary health care. The same is true with dentistry. At this time El Paso was considered either the poorest or second poorest city in America. So, I was always clear in my fundraising that what I raised money for had to provide a direct service. Those were the only clients I would take on. Some of these clients were having very little success in getting the funds needed. That is really why I came up with the idea of creating software to track for them the level of success they were having with such direct, targeted assistance. I believed that tracking would help organizations prove the efficacy of the money they raised.

But during that time many of these clients' heart-breaking experiences touched me personally. One of profound influence had to do with a young child named Tara who had terminal cancer. Her mom had eight children, all by different fathers. Her mother paid no attention to her and one of my clients asked me to drop by and meet Tara. So, I went to the hospital, and there she laid, covers pulled up over her mouth. I talked but she did not answer. I stayed about an hour but had to leave for a fundraising event. When I got up to leave Tara asked, "Are you coming back tomorrow?" Honest to God - it struck me in the heart! A simple, brilliant comment. She really didn't know how to express herself during my one sided conversation. Interaction with people wasn't something she had ever experienced in her environment. I said simply, I don't know if I will be back tomorrow, but I promise I will see you again. I didn't want to make the tomorrow commitment and not fulfill it.

Well, I did go back the next day. She was supposed to have about three months to live. I was with her a part of almost every day for the next 17 months. I often slept in her room at night, got up at 5 a.m., and went home to shower and go to the office. My sister, mom and my brother-in-law would also go to the hospital when I was unable to be there. She began to call me mom. I mean, I felt like she was my kid. It was the most enriching experience I have ever had in my life.

When on occasion she would be able to leave the hospital, she was with me. Her mother and her siblings paid no attention to her. The mother basically extracted cash from me to pay bills and allowed me to keep Tara. I wanted Tara to have that quality of life she had never experienced. I was in my 20s, doing fundraising and driving a Cadillac. To Tara I was rich like the people on the Dynasty show. She told everyone I was her mom. I would take her shopping and tell her to pick out what she wanted and I'd buy it. I also influenced her life positively in other ways.

When she was in the hospital all day, I would call her from the office and we would talk. On one of those occasions, I asked her what she was doing. She said she was watching soap operas. I said, "Tara turn that trash off. That's lazy. You need to read the books I gave you. Right now, do so and write me a book report. I will be there at 6 p.m. tonight and will review it with you." When I hung up I thought, oh my God, she is terminal and why should she do these things? But, you know what? She lived longer than they thought she would. And, I treated her as though she had a full life ahead. We shared an enriching life experience together in a short period of time.

> *We shared an enriching life experience together in a short period of time.*

A month before Tara died her mother called and told me she was moving the family to Jackson, Mississippi. Dr. Sweeney, Tara's oncologist, told us she could not possibly survive a trip on a bus that far. Her mother said, "I don't care, we have to move." Tara was in the ICU at the hospital when I went there to say goodbye. When Tara arrived in Jackson, she was rushed to the hospital. She immediately had them call me. That was 19 years ago.

I would call her three times a day after that. During that time we talked about death and she knew what was happening to her. The day soon came and I received a call alerting me that time was short and I should get on a plane and get there. I said tell her I'm coming, because I know she will hang on till I get there. She lasted about a week after my arrival. We had our goodbyes. Her family never showed, never came to say goodbye. The doctor said that for indigents cremation was the mode of handling the burial process. We agreed with that.

A week later, I received a box with her cabbage patch doll and this little heart with these arms that said, "I love you this much." I had given her that doll. The nurses had wrapped the package and sent me a wonderful warm letter with it. They had tried to reach her family and no one had ever showed up.

ANANDA ROBERTS (CONTINUED)

I flew back to El Paso and immersed myself in my work. Celebrity golf tournaments, concerts going on, a million things to do. One of the last things Tara said was, "Mom, we need peace." I remember that well.

That was not the end of this story. In mid-2006, Oprah Winfrey opened a Boys and Girls Club in Mississippi where she was born and our software was installed into that facility. I went there to make sure everything was running okay. When I told my mom I was going to Jackson, she said to me, "You haven't been there since Tara died." It hit me like a ton of bricks. I got emotional. I had thrown myself into work and really had never dealt with her dying.

Oprah's facility was about two hours drive from Jackson. I stayed in the area for the grand opening along with our client, Ralph Whitney of General Dynamics, and his communication director, Fran Ford. Fran and I knew one another from the El Paso days. I had told Fran about Tara and she knew how emotional I was. She suggested that I stop at the hospital and walk in. I hadn't planned to, but said I would. With a lot of mixed emotions and hesitation I did go in. The pediatric oncology unit was not there now, so I went into the chapel for a couple of hours. It was about midnight when I left and Fran called me on the car phone and talked me through my emotional letdown, my coming full circle in my grief, and the brilliant comment by a dying child, "Are you coming back tomorrow?"

Tara has had lasting influence on my life and seventeen months with her taught me commitment, total love and acceptance. I know that keeping on, not giving up, is the legacy of this child's gift to me. Here is this little baby who cut through the world's crap to express all that mattered to her to someone who cared for her. I will never forget that moment. In her simple way she was a very cool little kid.

Ananda, you said the Tara part of your life was highly personal, emotional and indelible - it changed you as a human being. There has got to be something that caused you to abandon a successful fundraising business and start a technology company.

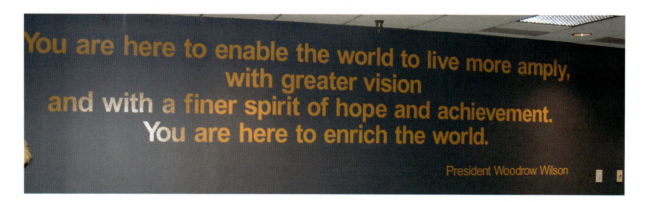

Yes. I concluded that fundraising and other social efforts and public issues and needs lacked ways to prove their success or failure. Through software, you can track what you are doing and measure outcomes against what you expect to get. And that was really the motivation behind creating software that tracks.

Okay, but why did you come to Arizona from Texas?

Well, I knew that for a technology company, I needed to be in an area that had a Microsoft office and that meant either Dallas or Phoenix. I love Dallas and Texas but Beth, who has worked for me since I started in business and is my right-hand assistant, had two sisters living in Arizona. She knew nothing about Dallas, so I thought Phoenix would be an easier change for her. The other thing, is I am extremely loyal to American Airlines. And while their base is in Dallas it is easier to book flights and less expensive for me to fly out of Phoenix on American Airlines than it is for me to book flights if I were living in Dallas. Saves a heap of money for the company as I travel a lot.

> *"Your self-worth is never in question. It was granted to you the day God created you!."*

BETH FINGER AND MICHAEL KOLB ARE LEAD DEVELOPERS.

I moved here to Phoenix and thought, "give me a year and the company will be doing a million a year in revenue - easily." Youthful, positive enthusiasm! The first eleven years were, to put it mildly, difficult. Every day produced another challenge in spite of all I knew was right. We had the best product, worked hard, made calls, trained our team and kept their spirits up. We provided service better than others and kept thinking it will all come together for success. I was 33 then and began to feel trapped. Since I started my company in college, I did not have a reference point for how other companies functioned from an internal level. Everything about my business was very personal to me. When the company was doing well, I was happy. When the company was not doing well, I was not happy.

One day, while listening to the radio and changing stations, I came across a Christian talk show and heard a gentleman say, "Your self-worth is never in question. It was granted to you the day God created you!" At that moment I began to understand that my value as a person was not based on my company's balance sheet! It hit me like a ton of bricks! My self-worth had moved up and down like a roller coaster, tied directly to the ups and downs of my business.

Ananda Roberts (continued)

While it took me a few more years to disassociate my personal worth from that of the company, I can truly say that this step toward understanding, has made the second most significant contribution to me personally, as well as to the company on a professional level. nFocus is a separate entity that I created and I have been fortunate to have the opportunity to live out my dreams of growing a business through my work. The company, the work I do, does not define my self worth. Even if the company grows to the size of a General Electric - or conversely if it fails - my self-worth is not in question. Coming to grips with this reality was a defining moment. The change in my attitude - the way I felt made an impact on those around me whose enthusiasm soon caught fire. Now I am able to count my blessings and daily say - wow - how fortunate I am to have my work and all its character building challenges. This is now the kind of playground I get to enjoy.

It sounds like you have become more spiritual, Ananda.

I think I always have been a very spiritual person, but there is always that adage that you go to God when life bottoms out. That is when everybody turns to God. I am serious. Looking back on it now, I wouldn't change those 11 years, as hard as they were. There were plenty of times I thought I was going to lose my business and as hard as it was, I absolutely needed to be refined through those situations. I needed to understand how difficult it really, truly is to have an idea and take that idea and see it through to fruition as a business. I did not have that experience in my 20s. I made a lot of money and I did very well and I was good. And I just thought that was business and it was going to keep happening the rest of my life. So I had a lot of growing to do as an individual. While I felt compassion toward people while I was growing up, I never expressed it. I can now really understand. I used to have a very Darwinian view of life. You know, survival of the fittest. And these last years taught me a lot about looking at situations and understanding why they occur. It is not always because someone isn't as smart as they need to be or as capable as they seem to be. There are a lot of factors that play into people's lives that create the situations they experience. Being able to understand where someone is in their life and why they are in that place, I would have never, ever cared about until I went through this learning process. Seeing how tough it really can be makes you a better leader.

18 MONTHS OLD AND LATER TAP CLASS RECITAL, ANANDA ENJOYED SHOWING OFF AND PERFORMING AT AN EARLY AGE.

Ananda, so far there have been references to your early life and the start-up of your business in college. Let's shift gears and give you free reign to explore more in depth your early life, the influence of your family and other special people who influenced you.

Family? I am the oldest and I have a younger sister. I guess my father, who was an entrepreneur wanted a boy. It just didn't happen so he focused on me. He took me with him to business meetings. Before I started to school, if he had people come to the house, he would have me walk around the room and shake hands, introduce myself, but also remember each person's name and say it was very nice to meet them. It was hard, when you are three or four years old, but he expected that. He used to take me with him in the car and talk to me about business and assumed that that was what I was going to do. There are times I am grateful for this early training - and also times I feel that he should have left that open for me. What might I have done with my life? But then you go back and think there were no mistakes and this is what I was meant to do with my life.

My father traveled all the time. I remember thinking, I am going to do all these important things like going to meetings, traveling on airplanes and meeting important people. I never really played with dolls. I made goal lists when I was a little kid.

"I drive down the street and analyze businesses."

I love business. I drive down the street and analyze businesses. I pass the dry cleaner on the corner and wonder how he markets his business, does he make money? Why doesn't he have a drive through window, how hard is it for people to park? There is a gentleman I see every morning. I stop at McDonald's and get a Diet Coke and he is sitting there. He is homeless - seemingly has nothing, so I always try to give him something when I see him. He always says, "thank you and God bless you." He looks peaceful. I look at people around me and think - did their lives turn out the way they wanted? Did they have a dream they never got to realize? So when I look at my life, I feel so fortunate to have had an entrepreneurial father.

Though I didn't recognize it in my youth, my mother also influenced my life and still does. Yet, all my very young life, my father seemed to be the one. He died about the time I graduated from high school. Dad and I were very much alike and I believe he knew that. My mom and sister are much more generally outgoing. More outwardly compassionate. Like my dad, I can be outgoing all day in business, but going to a gathering or cocktail party is the last thing I want to do. I hate the small talk of such venues.

Mom and my sister have always been very good in that social side of life. Consequently I was just more comfortable with my father. I always thought that he was the one who

English riding lessions in Madison, WI.

Ananda Roberts (continued)

PAINTING BY ROBERT CARLSON, INCLUDES ANANDA'S FAVORITE PEOPLE AND HER MYTHICAL BOARD OF DIRECTORS.

gave me all the strong characteristics I have as an individual. A few years ago I realized that my strength, commitment and ability to follow through really came from my mother. It was an emotional waking! Looking at everything she has done with her life, all the ways she made all our lives better, her strength, follow through, and determination was always there. I didn't see it - but the osmosis process was at work. She stood strong and always kept life on track with her steady commitment to overcome adversity. I really benefited from the best of both my parents.

Of course there are other special people who have influenced my life, some I even try to emulate. In my 20s, I read something that said when you are struggling with an issue or a problem, you need to find the people, living or dead, who you believe are brilliant and personify everything you want to be. I chose five. This reading went on to say, "Have a board meeting with them!" Try to envision how they would answer questions or advise you. My first four were Albert Einstein, Walt Disney, Abraham Lincoln, Gandhi and the fifth was the man I was actually named after - YOGANANDA. He came here from India in the early 1900s with the goal of blending the spiritualism of the East with the materialism of the West. My parents heard the meaning of the name Ananda, which is eternal bliss and happiness. They loved the meaning of it. They had been trying to have kids about seven years before I came along. My sister is two years younger and they named her Susan. Go figure! So anyway, having been named after him, I read a lot about him.

A friend of mine who is an artist actually painted a picture of the five people for me. It is in my office at home. I've added Tara in a corner of the picture. So those are my board members. I would sit in my office, at home or whereever I was, close my eyes and imagine they were all there meeting with me. I would say, okay, here's the issue. I would try to figure how each would answer, having studied their careers and life contributions. Einstein would say, "Information is not knowledge. That is what your products provide." The other thing he would say, "Think like God.

Everything else is just a detail." When he formulated the theory of relativity, he was asked how did he come up with it. He said, "I envisioned myself sitting on the end of a light beam." He had the incredible ability to get rid of all human parts and go into that space today we call "the zone." He had the ability to release his mind into a space that allowed him to understand how the universe worked. Using that I could say, look at only the issue.

Disney who was turned down countless times by banks when he wanted to build Disneyland, would say to me, "be persistent." Disneyland - just a brilliant idea. The happiest place on earth sprung from his mind and heart.

Lincoln. You know he lost many political battles and races. He could have quit but didn't. His ability was to understand what was right for our nation. Again, he got rid of human-ness. He got rid of the baggage of dissenting individuals and sensed what was important for the greatest good and then he took his stand and was steadfast through all the ridicule. He withstood the thunder of complaint over the massive loss of life during the Civil War. He asked God to guide his thoughts and decisions. He disregarded what history might say and stuck to his conviction that his course was right for our country. I heed his advice. Make a well thought-out decision, implement it and stay the course.

And, there is Gandhi. I love his quote, "Be the change you wish to see in the world." He led the most populated nation of the time and took it away from the British without firing a shot. He never lost his temper. He changed the course of the entire nation of India by peaceful protest. He teaches us how to achieve through peace. He got up at 4 a.m. and meditated, walked and spent quiet time and moved the hearts of both the Indian and British nations. His formula applies and works for business as well.

COMPANY AWARDS ARE ON DISPLAY FOR ALL TO SEE AND SHARE IN THE VICTORY. THIS INCLUDES THE ASU SPIRIT OF ENTERPRISE AWARD.

Then Yogananda, whose value system blends Hinduism with Christianity. Discerning what is the right course that follows a moral value system. Whether it is right for you, the decision should be what is right and good for all. Forget what lies in front of you - the issue. The greatness of a decision depends on what you've got inside of you. You have the ability to do anything you want to do. Yogananda's story is powerful. When struggling with problems and choices I think of it. He would say, "There is fighter A and fighter B and they are challenging one another. Fighter A is down on the mat. Is he out? Up to him. He says if I can get up and throw one more punch, it could be the winning punch. Many people stop short - throw in the towel - when with a little effort they could get up and throw the winning punch." I heed that advice. When in a bind, I think of those five board members and bring them into my mind to debate the solutions that lead my team to persevere.

Ananda Roberts (continued)

Actually, Shirley, before you came to interview me you asked 24 tough questions you wanted answered ahead of time. They made me review a lot of my activities so I would be ready for your visit. This was not the first time you acted as a catalyst that provoked pretty deep retrospection on my part. You know when I first met you, Shirley, was after winning the Spirit of Enterprise Award. You and I had lunch. And you were really adamant about vision, mission and values. And while I had the vision statement for the company and I had a mission statement, they were the kinds of things that I had put words to because businesses are supposed to. And, I hadn't even put words to it until maybe four or five years before that. But those words didn't make my heart say, "Wow!" And, so after talking to you then and when you came by the office a couple of times and we kind of drilled down on this, our company vision statement became, "We are changing the world for the better, one community at a time." And, I believe that, with all my heart.

"We are changing the world for the better, . one community at a time."

It is absolutely critical that accurate data regarding what is going on with kids in school and after-school programs, and accurate data regarding career path and training for our military is put in the hands of people who can make decisions - to take both of those groups to the next level and assist them in being the very best they can be. And if we can catch kids before they fall through the cracks, we can make this world a much better place. We can change kids' lives. We can give them the ability to understand that there is more for them than poverty or the cycle of violence they may be growing up in, both in America or around the world.

One of the interesting things we are doing with our military software is giving the soldier the ability to log on and manage his entire career path, somewhat in the way you manage your financials. There are charting and graphing functions and he can move his money around, sign up for classes and do a wide range of activities in a visual setting. Military leaders at the Pentagon and elsewhere have the ability to hit a button and select, for example, the 200 top-trained soldiers on the patriot missile system. Typically, a military only fights and trains. Previously they would deploy, and this is still going on, but it is starting to refine itself because of our products and what we are doing with the army right now. Soldiers were deployed more on a geographic basis. If we have soldiers here and equipment here, we are going to deploy them together. Soldiers are constantly being moved around the world to different posts. All of the soldiers who are here geographically may not have been trained on the equipment they are being deployed with. And we fight very, very high tech wars now.

The military has high-tech equipment that is going out with these soldiers. So what our systems do is track all that training so the deployments can be much more effective and appropriate. And to give that information to people who are making those decisions is just a phenomenal benefit to our nation and to the world. We save soldiers' lives and the military large amounts of money. That I even get to play a tiny role in helping both our youth and the military means a great deal to our employees and me. We know these two pieces ultimately will lead to saving lives. These make us proud of our vision statement.

I still feel today, that in order to be the best nation we can be, it is imperative that we understand what truly works in America in the areas of public sector programs and services. The public sector touches each of our lives every moment and not only touches the lives of Americans, but the global community as well. It is important to me that I do everything possible to make the world better through effective decision making, which can only be accomplished through the use of accurate data. Our systems provide the kind of data necessary to make the informed decisions that affect agencies that deliver services to the public. Through our efforts as a company, we are being the change we wish to see in the world.

Ananda, will you pursue some of the problems and situations that you had to overcome to get to where you are now? Perhaps also some of the failures or temporary set backs that influenced your direction? How did you cope?

Well, some of the problems are like other businesses and some unique. Access to capital - all small businesses face this issue, the answer for me was to tighten our belt and make it happen each and every day. There are days when you feel as though you may not make it through the end of the week financially, but better allocation, coupled with willpower, the drive to succeed, sheer persistence wins every time. We were going through one of our worst financial crises when you and I had those sessions in late 2003 early 2004. As Disney would say - persistence. And I would say that is number one, two and three. It is that ability to say I am not going to give up. And I might say it sometimes, but I know in my heart that I am not giving up. It is kind of attitude over reality. I remember one of the days you came into the office. Our plight was so bad - you can't imagine. Every account was late in paying us. I had payroll due. It was just a horrible, horrible time. I'm sure you remember. We discussed it - but when you left, it was still my nightmare reality. It was just beyond anything I could imagine living through. And I walked into the office that day and I shut my door. I said, "You know what, God? If this is what you want me to do for my life, then you need to give me some kind of sign. If you want me to walk away from this, I will. Really and truly. If you want me to

NFOCUS' GOAL IS TO HAVE THEIR TOOLS USED BY ALL PUBLIC SECTOR AGENCIES. THIS SOFTWARE ASSISTS AGENCIES IN MEASURING THEIR IMPACT, THEREBY ASSISTING THEM IN DELIVERY OF THEIR MISSION.

Ananda Roberts (continued)

shut the doors and walk away from this, I will do it. You need to tell me today. I need some kind of indication that this is the work I am supposed to be doing."

A COMPREHENSIVE END-TO-END SOLUTION FOR SCHOOLS AND AFTER SCHOOL PROGRAMS.

In the back of your head, you know you are not going to shut down, but you need to relieve your tension by discussing it with yourself.

So anyway, the next day I came into the office and three things happened that made me laugh and say, "Okay God, I got you loud and clear." A CFO of one of our major non-profits called my office and wanted to sit down and discuss a relationship. A check was delivered via FED EX on an account that covered our taxes and payroll and I had some good projects finished on time. So I just cracked up and said okay, suck it up and put a smile on your face, gal! Get out there and get with it. There are always solutions. When you deal with governmental bodies, non-profits and the like, they are often slow to pay. It does cause periodic cash flow problems. Another problem closely related to serving the public and non-profit sector is access to the appropriate people - a major small business issue for those of us in this sector. We needed to get our products in front of the United States military and in front of school districts across America. For several years I made appointment after appointment and nothing seemed to pan out. I could not figure out how some firms could make such astounding progress and how we could make so little progress in getting through to the top levels of organizations. However, while working to extend our reach at the top levels, we also continue working at the grass roots level. This approach assisted us in building credibility for our products and services amongst a variety of organizations across the county. Now, as it has become easier to secure meetings with top level individuals in the Federal government and within private enterprise, we have references from over 3,500 organizations nationwide that assist in telling the story of our products for us - people who provide feedback in many areas. These people include Marty Bell, Deputy Superintendent of Schools for Jefferson County Schools, in Louisville, Kentucky. Of the more than 18,000 school districts in America, Jefferson County is the 27th largest. There are 20 or more organizations all very different that we are working with to develop programs and systems.

Another challenge was changing from a fundraising company, which is what we were in Texas, to a software company and moving to Phoenix. To understand my frustrations, I need to take you back to my early careers. You see, when I started college I also started my entrepreneuring. There was a succession of small businesses. There was a marble import business and a seafood business. These were reasonably successful and paid a lot of bills in college and after. I just expected everything I would do would be successful.

When I first moved the company to Phoenix, to change it from a fundraising company to a software business, I encountered setback after setback. There was not a day during the first five years that I didn't question the move to Phoenix. I thought what we were doing made sense, unfortunately, it only made sense to me in the early years. Now, times have changed, even President Bush says, "If an organization can't prove positive impact, they will not receive Federal funding." This is what our software is all about, the collection of accurate data that tells a story of efficacy and impact. Again the lesson, at least for me, has been persistence. Keep going – if it makes sense to you and you believe that what you are doing is the right thing to do, then you must keep moving forward, regardless of what anyone else is telling you. But believe me, it has been and still is a challenge.

DON PRUITT, VP, STANDS FOR THE COMPANY MISSION AND DEDICATION.

But here you are, in business about 12 years and you have been the recipient of several significant national and state awards. You certainly have met your many challenges and unique problems with success. What else is there?

We take pride in our successes. Persistence and attitude are the keys that I believe are the essence of success. I have met brilliant people who did not succeed in achieving their goals, I have met people who appear to be less than brilliant who have succeeded, mainly because they kept at it. As Abraham Lincoln said, "Always bear in mind that your own resolution to succeed is more important than any other." In business and in life, this is the key.

Every employee is involved in the growth of nFocus Software. They each feel that they are running their own business within the company. Each individual has goals and standards to meet every month, quarterly and annually. In addition, we have awards that include monetary rewards for ideas that positively impact our products and services; we also have internal annual awards that carry monetary rewards. They are:

Ananda Roberts (continued)

a. Whatever it Takes
b. Above and Beyond
c. The Gold Star of Excellence

The qualifications to win each of these awards includes exhibiting the core values of our company, dedication to the work we are doing, dedication to our clients and a true belief that we are changing the world for the better, one community at a time, supporting our clients in achieving phenomenal results. We also have an award called the Innovation Award. It carries a monetary benefit for anyone who is able to do something that significantly changes the company or one of our products for the better. It is awarded whenever someone contributes something incredible - something that everyone agrees creates a step to the next level.

The company has received many awards, including the 2003 ASU Spirit of Enterprise Award; KPMG Fastest Growing Company in Arizona; White House Small Business Advisory Council and many others. I have not used these awards to enhance the company. Winning any award is valuable for a variety of internal reasons - including the pride everyone feels, the morale boost that occurs from an outside source telling you that you are doing a great job, the validation that comes from others looking at your business and placing value on your beliefs as a company. The external reasons are something that I have not actively chosen to capitalize on.

Their corporate headquarters is inviting to visit and the encouragement is on all of the walls in the office to keep visitors and employees encouraged.

Our innovative employees are a great part of our success in solving problems and meeting our challenges. As I stated before, each feels that this is his or her business. In addition we reach out to people who have ideas and philosophies that support and enhance our knowledge and work ethic.

I see your efforts in the office environment, Ananda. Open space, color, art with amenities and comfort in so many accessible places. Especially small private seating areas.

Thank you, Shirley. Meeting with people who understand what we are working to accomplish is always wonderful. It is easy to be enthusiastic when you feel that you are making a difference and when others validate that for you. I also have some of my favorite quotes posted throughout the office on walls that everyone can see. When you look at the difficulties that Edison, Einstein, Lincoln, Disney, etc. had in working toward their goals, it is easier to look at your situation and smile, knowing that it is all part of the path that must be walked in order to reach the goal.

In addition to all the motivational activities, amenities, rewards and incentives what else contributes to your longevity and success?

We believe in staying ahead of the industry and provide both an in-house training program that is ongoing as well as outside resources of significant variety so that our major asset - our people are the best they can be.

Tell us more about this people aspect of your business.

My most important efforts and influence are on my employees. I really believe in an open-door policy. And if we had 20,000 employees, I would still believe in an open-door policy. I think that openness and honesty are absolutes. I want people in our company who share my value system. That requires openness and the ability to talk with me. When we have that relationship there is less friction, backbiting or gossiping. Skills go without saying, but what we boiled down to nine years ago is that it is really about heart. If a candidate for a position evidences a really pure, clean heart and we sense it when we interview them, we want them. Then we know they will be good on our team here and do what is right for our customers. We also emphasize the ability to communicate. Even if it is something that is going to cost us a lot of money. If a team member makes a mistake, they know they can walk in and talk to me about it - apologize - and fix it. I love being here and being around all of our team. They get along and love being around one another. We work at this compatibility every day.

Stephen Barry our Network Systems Manager, has been with me for several years. Before he joined us, he was on the team that went into the New York Stock Exchange right after 9/11 and was involved in getting the Exchange back up

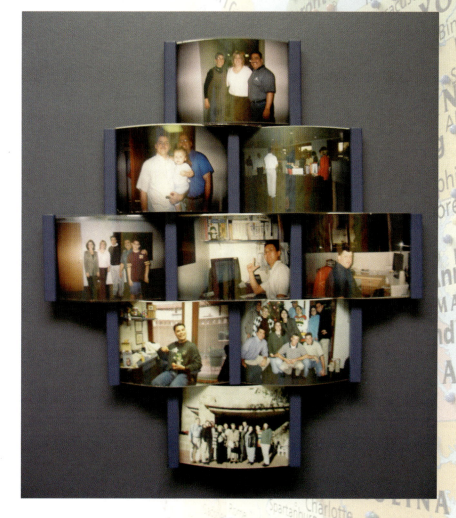

CREDIT IS SHARED WITH A QUALITY TEAM OF SUPPORT. THIS IS A COLLAGE PHOTO IN THE HALL OF THEIR WALK OF FAME.

Ananda Roberts (continued)

STEPHEN BARRY AND VP DON PRUITT.

and running. As a symbol of American economic power it was critical to our nation that it be back up quickly. After he had been with us for awhile, he sent me an email one night that made me cry because it was so sweet. He said the difference in being at nFocus from there after 9/11 was that when he was helping get the stock exchange up and running they didn't know what they were breathing in at the time. No one knew how dangerous it was down there. There were still fires at the Trade Center and the Stock Exchange sits across the street. He said it was uncomfortable and they were in there working day and night; all the officers, VIPs, exchange president and others were in conference rooms elsewhere talking to one another. During that time, not one of those people took the time to come and thank us. Then he said – Ananda, I know if you had been there, you would have been working with us side-by-side, bringing food for us and taking care of our needs.

Making it possible for our nFocus team to go to the next level, supporting them and giving them a platform to do their best work is my most prized job. I used to do everything, but now we have some top notch operational people. It is my privilege to make the conditions right for them every day, to know their personal goals and what special needs and dreams they have. It is my privilege to lead the way to make sure the company is strong, stable and moving in the direction of growth from both my personal and management perspective. That is my obligation – my personal mandate.

When it comes to our community, the ground rules are harder to define because we have clients all around the world. We are also in almost every city in the U. S. as well. I love living in Phoenix and the Valley of the Sun, so living here means providing a strong business that employs talented people, interacting with other business leaders and supporting the activities of education here. Arizona has tremendously complex educational issues. I am working to get our software put in place so that issues and kids with special needs can be tracked before they fall through the cracks. I am also a board member of WIPP – Women Impacting Public Policy, a national organization that works to support women-owned businesses through public policy initiatives at a national level. Since our client base is global, our staff is involved in projects and support services to our clients in a variety of ways. Community involvement to us means communities around the world.

Ananda, share with us specific the unique focus of your systems and why they are so needed.

The problems we face as a nation boil down to both the state and local community levels. Our nation's approach to education was developed during the

Jeffersonian era and an agrarian society. It was accepted that kids needed an ability to read and write, but they were needed out in the fields or working in the family business. Our nation's systems, timing and methodology haven't been modified nearly enough in over one hundred years. Change is needed and can be done incrementally. That's where our youth-based products can remove barriers and supply consistent, accurate data. We can enable decision makers to base their planning on accurate information which they really haven't had access to before. We can cut through habitual perception and anecdotal information when it comes to education. Oddly, the same problem causes many businesses to falter or fail. These same difficulties plague governmental bodies and systems as well. Our strategies have been to work with key people at all levels - local, state, national and international. We find those who sense change is needed and are open to examination of possibilities and exciting transformations.

"The problems we face as a nation boil down to both the state and local community levels."

Ananda, you have effectuated an exciting relationship with General Dynamics. Can you talk a little bit about this interesting relationship and how it came about?

Yes, some because we are evolving now. I characterize the relationship as a protégé relationship. I met with them in 2005 and we explored what that relationship would be, its possible value for both our organizations.

How did this opportunity come about?

Well, there is a group of women here in the state that have come together to begin to develop the next generation of women leaders. I was asked to participate by Barbara Ralston. Each of us had to tell the group what our business was all about. After the meeting one of the women, Diane Mitchell, who is with General Dynamics came over to me, asked for my card and said that her company should be doing business with my company. I said to myself – sure – but like all these possibilities, most never happen. Surprise! That night I received an email asking me to send information on the capabilities of our software. I did. Nothing happened.

Ananda Roberts (continued)

Two months went by, and I got an email from Ralph Whitney, one of their business development people who wrote in caps, WE ARE VERY INTERESTED IN TALKING WITH YOU. We had lunch and he explained they had researched my company and they were serious about working with us.

Talk more about how this affiliation works, Ananda.

You explore with them every area where mentoring will assist your growth and they designate the people within General Dynamics who will help you and your teams. They work closely in our activities. At the present, we are proceeding to become CNMI level 5 certification which sets up managing best practices within our industry. About June of 2006 we submitted the paper work to the Department of Defense, which opens up a huge potential market for us. It requires comprehensive reporting every quarter. This will be in effect for the next three years. It could contribute significant growth to our business.

Is that similar to ISO 9000?

Actually, software companies can be both ISO 9000 and CNMI. CNMI is really a quality and process management piece that lets the government know that at every moment they are getting the highest level quality product. General Dynamics will assist us and support us in six areas, including product development, finance, public relations and more.

My travel schedule is horrendous. I've been to Washington, D.C. a number of times, the White house several times, with Oprah Winfrey when we placed our youth software in her Mississippi youth center. In Atlanta because we are partnering in a project for United Way of America, plus many, many other military, educational, health care and non-profit organizations throughout the country. I already mentioned Jefferson County Public Schools and now Humana based in Louisville where they are creating a model to track education as it relates to childhood obesity.

Rich, significant contributions, Ananda. You are on an amazing venture. How can you keep up with the inside work?

I couldn't if I didn't have an amazing and dedicated team here on base.

You are tackling markets that are complex, many slow pay - especially the government, whose demands are often unreasonable! A lesson in tackling risk.

You don't know how many times I think - am I the biggest dummy on the planet? Who picked these markets? You have to be absolutely beset with self hatred that goes beyond reason. But, I say to myself, yep, we are going to make the world a better place.

Ananda, your story is a marvelous lesson in courage, persistence and commitment. Knowing you, as I do - they put WOW in your life. You well may be a legend in the making. Now, Ananda, I'm going to change and get personal. Are you cool with that?

We'll start with easy stuff. What do you like to do best? How about hobbies? Sports?

What I like best of all is to shop. I love to shop. And I have actually read a couple of books that say that shopping can be addictive. I really thought that through pretty clearly. I just genuinely love shopping. I don't go out and buy things and feel remorseful, I just think it is the biggest kick in the world. I get excited when I am driving down the street and I see a Neiman Marcus logo. It is such a stress reliever to me. I know a lot of the folks at Neiman Marcus here and at Saks. They are like - my friends. I enjoy going in and shopping with them. I admire the artistry of a designer who has an idea for an outfit or shoe or whatever that captures my fancy. It becomes art to them. It is just beautiful to look at that. The one thing that I laugh about, but I really ingrain this in my head is they are going to make new stuff next week. And in my head it is like they are constantly rolling out new things, just for me. Shopping is complete and total relaxation for me.

> *What I like best of all is to shop.*

Sports, no. I have never been involved in sports. My sister was a very good tennis player. She was the athlete in the family. Several years ago I started painting pottery. So, I do that. I haven't done that in quite a while. Growing the business has become increasingly demanding. I love to read. I love to cook. I think that cooking is so creative and business is very creative process as well, so I think that they tie into each other.

Your early efforts started in 1984 while you were in college. You started working on your present business and came to Phoenix as a software business in late 1993. In 1994 you were a company of one - you. Now you have a top team of 35 super people. You were a daring restless spirit, Ananda. Awesome. Tell me a little more about these early beginnings which you mentioned earlier.

Actually, I first did an imported fish business only about a year and a half when I got a good offer and sold that business. For my next and profitable business I did fundraising for non-profits and eventually formed the business

Ananda Roberts (continued)

we are now in. I just loved creating businesses. When I was a kid, I read a lot about people who were builders, mostly business builders. I don't remember how I got the books, but I did. Never read the usual kid stuff. One book was about Rockefeller who started Standard Refining. It was just an idea no one else had at that time. I started thinking about the power of ideas and that everything starts with an idea. I began writing my ideas down. Some were screwy! But the Rockefeller story just fascinated me. When we drove by a Standard station, they were always on corners, I thought wow. I think I was all of eight years old. I still write down things, ideas and even routine stuff, like doing the laundry, shopping, etc. Some of my ideas seem absurd.

Einstein was one of your special "ghost board". Did you know he made a habit of writing down his ideas so he wouldn't forget them? He is quoted as saying, "If an idea isn't at first absurd it isn't worth considering."

> *When I was a kid, I read a lot about people who were builders.*

Ananda, in all these years I have known you, you have spoken eloquently about your love of our country, its systems, and its gifts. I have heard you speak about our obligation as citizens to provide support and solutions. You obviously study our history, which I too, believe should be everyone's personal mandate. This is a good place to change pace and have our readers learn more about what makes Ananda, the person, the entrepreneur she is. Are you game?

Yes! I want to start with the present as a point of reference, because we are now and have been for several years in an era of great tumultuous events. It absolutely hurts my heart when I think that there are terrorists and irresponsible people who have entrenched themselves in our nation and are here to harm and kill. We are in a very intense time in our history. But there have been other traumatic and precarious earlier times. The Revolutionary War to free us from the control of a greedy king. The creation of a constitution to build and govern a free and independent republic. It was controversial. A second war with the British to preserve our independence. Having said that, history tells us that our Republic has weathered many huge times of growth and turmoil. The Civil War - the bloodiest in our history. More loss of lives than all our other wars in total, to hold our nation as one. Participation in two World Wars to save the world from domination by violent dictators. Korea, the Cold War, The Vietnam War and now the War on Terror.

So, I care very much about our country and every day count my blessings of having the opportunities to contribute to its greatness. At nFocus, we have developed systems to help improve the approach to the education of our youth. I'm proud we have tracking, testing
and training software that takes the chaos and guess work out of education. Our analytical tools have helped our customers achieve phenomenal results. I'm, very, very proud of the systems we have provided to the military that help save lives, educate troops and keep track
of their needs.

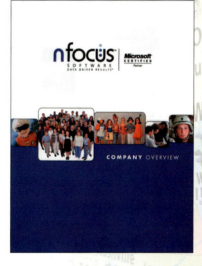
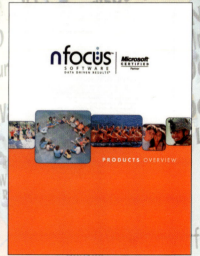

What you are describing is what I would say 99 percent of the people in this country do not realize – that we are inveterate nation builders. We not only are persistent in how we are building our own nation and risking and making mistakes, but that we are inveterate builders of other nations as well. One of the things that characterizes this country and you are describing it very well, is that we want to right wrongs, help build nations, help free people. When you designate that as your goal as a nation, you are continuously involved in controversy and that will go on and on and on. But there are always segments of people who want to withdraw. Your description is very good indeed, Ananda. Your brochures and other ancillary literature emphasizes that the world is your community and that the United States is just a part of that greater community. Perhaps you can elaborate more on this dichotomy.

I'll try. The world is interdependent whether people realize it, everyone in every part of the world has contributed to the global culture and what the world consumes. We sell products and raw materials to one another, although we Americans are the largest buyers. From time to time we are enemies, but everyone is interdependent. Pepsi, Coca Cola, McDonald's, KFC, Wendy's are on corners in most every part of the world. Automobiles are totally international. Airplanes are totally international. People can turn a computer on and tap the Internet everywhere from the tops of mountains to the depths of oceans. Capitalism in one form or the other has taken root across the earth. Even countries that bear hatred for the U. S. sell copious quantities of products to us. International hatred is generational. We think our tracking systems like KID TRAX could be used to effectuate a small amount of incremental change. It is working in our country where it is most used. We are finding children who have been falling through the cracks and our systems are making it possible to intercede to help them.

ANANDA ROBERTS (CONTINUED)

Her dad was a big influence on her early understanding of business. Her mom continues to work closely with her today.

What about legacy? If you were to disappear, would your business survive?

Absolutely. This team has our vision ingrained in their minds. They come in every day excited because they know what we are doing is making a substantial difference in lives and businesses. Each knows he is important and contributes as if this was his own business. We have a back-up plan and designated leadership legally drafted.

What advice would you like to share with the reader of your story?

My company has grown, and is succeeding more everyday and is doing well and it will continue to do well. I think the biggest piece of the puzzle or what I would want someone to know who was reading this and thinking about starting a business or just wanted to read about a variety of people who are in business is that it is never easy. I once read a statistic that half a million people are going to open new businesses in America each year, but what we fail to look at is that half a million businesses or more will close every year. So I think that the reflection of business is a reflection of your life as well. It is that ability to be persistent and to learn from the things that other people look at as failures. To be able to take those hits. I mean, you know, when we say that little kids are mean on the playground, you know they are mean to other little kids. Those little kids grow up to be mean adults. It doesn't go away. And it is tough when people look at you and they want to tell you that what you are doing doesn't make sense. You really have to have conviction in your heart for what you are doing. It doesn't matter if it is motherhood. It doesn't matter if it is business or school. You just have to have conviction in your heart that what you are doing is right for you and for others whose lives you touch. It really doesn't matter if you have lived your life based on what everybody else thinks, you haven't lived your life. You have reacted to other people. In the end, the only thing that does matter is did you do what you felt you were meant to do in your life?

I met a gentleman named Mike Warner on an airplane about five years ago. He was the president of a large IT company and he told me, "If you will operate your life as if there are no secrets, you will always win." When he said that, I thought well, I do that. But you know you really have to think about it. How many times do you tell someone don't repeat this or that? He said to me, you have to just be - what you see is what you get, always. Always. It can't be hit or miss. It can't be sometimes. Operate your life as if there are no secrets and you will win. What he said really had a big impact on me. I think about it all the time. I think about it when I am talking to someone and thinking I would rather they didn't repeat that. Then I think, don't say it. That goes for business and in life. In software language it is called a "wysiwgy" (pronounced whizzywig) which means what you see is what you get. Everybody should operate at that level, you know, and you can tell people who do instantly. I have had a few people kind of hoodwink me over the years, but it is pretty seldom.

If you plan to start a business, make sure you are certain it is what you want to do. People assume that owning a business means you can do whatever you want, you have lots of money, etc. While these things are the by product of a successful business, it takes a lot of sweat equity as well as money to get to that position. It takes a tremendous amount of work, late at night, weekends, holidays, whenever the time is needed, to ensure that your business will be successful. Anything that is done with less than 100 percent commitment may be successful for a short period of time, but it will not thrive in the long run. Your business becomes an extension of who you are. Every decision you make affects the lives of others and has an affect on your clients as well. You must be both thorough and thoughtful with each decision. You must also understand that money is a byproduct of success, it is not the goal. The goal of any business is to have customers and in order to do that, you must provide a valuable and lasting service that will keep them coming back and will make them want to tell others about you.

ANANDA'S BABIES. INDIANA NAMED FOR THE STATE. EMERSON NAMED FOR RALPH WALDO EMERSON.

Let's talk about the future, Ananda. Where do you see your company both in the near future and out say ten or more years?

You ask a lot Shirley. I'll tell you some but not all. Trade secrets, you know!

First we see the foreseeable future as a huge, as yet untapped, market for our existing products. Enormous here and in the world. Massive opportunities in great populist countries like India and China. Near home, Canada. We are there but there is more growth to be had. We have two offices. Here, which is headquarters and Texas. We have our eye on Washington. That is logical. More as they make sense. We are interested in acquisitions, probably a training company. Any company that brings content to the table. Perhaps another software organization.

You are a GOOD MAN, SON

*I*n September 2003, I met Gregory E. Torrez, his brother Raoul, and sister Royna when they were awarded the Spirit of Enterprise Family Business Award. I was impressed with Gregory who took the lead role in representing their company, Azteca Wedding Enterprises. He intrigued me and I made a mental note to follow up on our brief meeting. I did so in April 2004, at which time I visited AZTECA and spent time touring and visiting with Gregory.

Gregory E. Torrez is an expressive, impressive man with a deep, warm respect for family and tradition. The eldest son of Adolfo and Kay Gasink-Torrez, who founded and built the highly successful Azteca Wedding Enterprises. He admired both parents for their different sets of talents and business sense. Gregory says of his parents, "My dad was president, my mom was secretary, treasurer and everything else. My dad got ideas-my mother influenced them, and then made them happen." Gregory has wisdom, foresight, creativity, passion and steadfast persistence. He is on one hand, competitive and a master salesman. On the other hand, he sees potential in others and respects people for what they are or what they contribute. A sensitive, empathetic and loving family man, he's been married to wife Josephine for 36 years and has four children and 10 grandchildren.

He is recognized as one of the top influential business people in the greater metropolitan Phoenix area. He presently serves on six boards and commissions, has seven business affiliations and memberships, and holds partnerships with 22 community organizations. He has received more than 15 significant business awards and recognitions for his community activities and business success and serves as an advisor to the governor of Arizona.

Torrez' impressive list of business and volunteer relationships include:

- A one-third partnership in the Azteca Wedding Enterprises
- The presidency of Torrez International LLC, a company he founded
- A partnership in Paradies-Phoenix, a joint venture in 15 retail stores at Phoenix Sky Harbor International Airport
- A joint partnership in Arizona ShuttlePort, the transportation system that serves the car rental organizations at the airport
- CPLC (Chicanos Por La Causa);
- Integrity Parking
- A relationship with Veolia Transportation System, an international group out of France that manages 62 busses to and from the airport to rental car companies.

RIGHT TO LEFT: BROTHER RUPERT, FATHER ADOLPHO, GREGORY, WIFE JOSEPHINE, MOTHER KAY, SISTER ROYNA, ELIZABETH ROSELL, BROTHER ROUAL, UNCLE ROBERTO AT THE OPENING WEEK OF EXPANSION IN 1985.

End of story? Yes and no. The exciting story is how he came to be the impressive man he is, the accomplished 2nd generation entrepreneur he is today. It is the multigenerational story of a father's and mother's success in starting and developing businesses, but, more importantly, their success in molding their children, in this instance, Gregory.

Gregory will tell this story mainly in his own words and style, a story that is intimate and showcases the impact of his father and mother, two towering, successful entrepreneurs whose simple backgrounds reflect the world of early Phoenix and Arizona. It is a slice of history.

It is a rich history of involvement in the local community and the foundation of his character as he grew up experiencing life and the family values of his parents.

He was taught well by his father and mother, both dynamic and entrepreneurial. His father Adolfo was abandoned along with his brother in Winkleman, Arizona, as preschool children and were raised by grandparents who brought them to Glendale, Arizona. Adolfo boot-strapped himself from field hand to shoe shine boy, to owner of the shoe shine

Gregory Torrez (continued)

business, to pool hall owner, to owning a restaurant step by step with wife Kay, to the impressive city block of the Azteca Wedding Plaza Enterprises. His mother, Kay, was a professional photographer who became a well-known expert on labyrinths, an author of two books on the subject, and the builder of labyrinths in the desert. She was an active humanitarian, a brilliant and dynamic manager, politically active as an advisor to elected officials, and socially responsible in taking on the causes of the less fortunate.

"It has been a process of understanding and starts with learning to like and love who you are."

Gregory possesses the best of both parents. He is a kind and gentle family man who has taken what he learned and inherited to new significant levels of achievement. He's very proud of his heritage and aware of the family tradition of community responsibilities, a determined entrepreneur who is building his own legacies.

MOTHER KAY'S QUEST TO EGYPT TO EXPLORE HER PAST. SHE BELIEVED SHE ONCE LIVED THERE IN ANOTHER LIFE.

The interview begins: the story of two generations, mostly narrated by Gregory.

Gregory, I came away from our meeting in 2004 impressed with your amazing track record of accomplishments. Please describe the person you believe you are today and how you got there.

Shirley, I think about that often. I believe I'm a guy who cares for others, not just his family, himself or business. It has been a process of understanding and starts with learning to like and love who you are. That may seem to border on arrogance, but how can you care for others if you think you are not a good person? You have to respect yourself and be willing to share yourself if faced with that opportunity. All this comes with the challenges of growing up with two driven parents, and certain personal events and life challenges. I have learned from these life lessons how others perceive me but not deceiving myself. Those events molded the man I am. I have this rolodex rolling in my mind: encouraged to be a priest, but deciding for myself that it was not for me; falling in love with my angel Josephine at 16 and marrying her at 18; having four children, the youngest of whom God decided would lose his vision; searching for how to help him; helping the church by buying a banner they needed, cleaning their linens, buying flowers for the altar; simply making a difference and not looking for recognition. My mother set a great example because she never sought reward or recognition, and neither do I. Everything evolves. We are not born just to live and die but to make differences in this world through positive contributions and continuous involvement with others.

Gregory, you are running quickly through some life events. Perhaps you can share more of these defining moments.

Shirley, as you know, I refer many times to my mother and my father's beliefs and teachings. They really started me thinking about my future – what would I be like, would they be proud of me? One of the most memorable and defining events occurred when my mother was on the Phoenix Elementary School Board. I went with her to an important board meeting and while sitting in the audience, I became concerned because people began to stand up and yell at my mom, blaming her for their problems and the schools' performances. Mom served on the board because she cared about kids, being the responsible person she was. I almost got into an altercation with one of the men because he was using abusive, vile language about my mom. Mom gave me a look like she always did when I was about to do something she considered wrong, so I sat down.

Afterwards, I said, "Why did you put yourself in this position?" She said, "Mi Jo (son), somebody has to care. There are events and circumstances that happen in life and you have to decide whether you care and, if you do, how you can help. It could be ideas, relationships or terrible events." Then she said, "I could not stand by and turn away from these responsibilities. I felt I could help. I had a passion to help students and their parents make a better future for those to come. When you are confronted with responsibility you have a choice to walk away or volunteer to help." She continued. "You will soon have events that will happen to you. Some will bring joy, some will require you to decide your role. Your decision to accept or walk away will come soon enough."

From that time forward, I began to pay close attention to events and causes and how they influenced me and/or how I could influence them and help people in the community. My father's thoughts and teachings took me in a different direction. His mind-set was always business-focused. I guess it came from a man whose background stemmed from a struggle from poverty and only a third-grade education. He would say to me, "I own a business. People work for me and I pay them." He had this attitude his whole life. That was his mind set. I thought about that and the differences between him and my mom.

GREGORY'S MOM AND DAD DANCING.

Shortly after that, I sat down with my dad and said "Do you realize that you impact the lives of 50 individuals here? You influence their families, so that is like 150 people a year. The dollars you pay them go back into the community. You influence churches and their ability to help their parishioners. Without realizing it, Dad, you help the lives of 10,000 to 15,000 people as the money flows out." I asked him to think about that and told him he was an incredible man and I was proud he was my father.

Gregory Torrez (continued)

Gregory's mom and dad enjoying life at a young age.

Gregory, let's go back to events with your mother. She seemed to have a profound effect on your moral, ethical and social conscience.

To be very honest, that school board meeting with my mother, watching her being attacked and criticized for issues and events totally out of her control, was a painful shock and it really stuck in my mind. Perhaps the timing was right. It made me understand what it is to be a good person. I realized that life is not just about making money, and not just about power. It was at that moment that I realized that I had been blessed with a mother who truly cared, not just about her children but about other people as well. I knew then I had an obligation to carry that legacy forward.

My learning curve was further solidified in 1976. We did a program called "The Renewal of the Spirit of '76" which was centered around getting the vote out. At that time she was involved with Terry Goddard so I was able to be on the front lines helping in the project. This took a lot of time and, quite frankly, my father was upset as we were not taking enough care of the family business. I realized that he had a point as well, that we all have an obligation to care for other people, but to also care for our own family as well.

Gregory, we've talked some about your mother's influence on your social, moral and ethical development. I'm intrigued by the few things you've said about your father's influence. I'd like to know more about this extraordinary man.

Shirley, my father taught me about business, about working hard and smart. He was truly an entrepreneur. He knew instinctively how to build a business, how to sell, how to be a tough-minded manager. He taught me some great business principals for example, putting a deal together. He said, "Son, when you do business, do you want a great deal or do you want a good deal?" I said, "I want a great deal." He said, "No, no, no. You want a good deal. In a good deal, you get what you need, I get what I need and we leave something on the table for future opportunities." So, as my dad taught me, that is the thing I say to everybody I have done business with. What I want is a good deal. To the people who then say they want a great deal, I thank them, shake their hand, and go do something else. I have really seriously turned down some great opportunities but it was because they didn't have any social, moral responsibility to the community in which we do business.

In a good deal, you get what you need.

What I need to do is profile my father for you. You understand he was a self-made man. He worked in the fields, was a shoe shine boy, ran a pool hall, and had a shoe shine stand. As a young man he frequented the clubs, bars and gatherings of a rousing city center and became a well-known inhabitant of the city. He knew Frenchy, the Chief of Police, back in the day when you had to know the Chief of Police to get special attention and consideration.

When Dad was seven and my uncle five, they lived in Winkleman. Their father, my grandfather, was a wildcatter, a gold and silver miner, a drinker and a womanizer. He abandoned the boys, who had to survive on their own. They were eventually brought here by their grandparents. Anyway, the pool hall owner, a Chinese man, eventually gave the pool hall to my dad, who now owned both a shoeshine stand and a pool hall. My dad eventually gave the shoe shine stand to another young man to concentrate on the pool hall.

When he was 15 years old he came to Phoenix, and while walking downtown, he came to an old shoe shine stand located near the old Luhrs Building. It had 25 seats in it and was owned by an African-American man who said to my father, "Hey, boy, you want a job?" Dad said, "Yeah, I want a job." He showed dad how to shine shoes. Well, shoe shines were 10 cents and boots were 15 cents, a 50% margin. So Dad went downtown to the old courthouse, walked up the steps on the west side and bumped into this big, burley guy with a mustache. He looked at Dad and said, "What do you want, boy?" "Shoe shine, shoe shine," my dad said. This guy walked back with him to where the patrol officers worked. In those days, they all wore the big boots. And Dad thought, here is the opportunity for a lot of boots. So one of the men gave my dad a pair of boots, Dad ran back to the shoe shine place, shined them and then returned them to the man. Pleased, he introduced my dad to all the other police and said, "From now on this boy is the only one who will shine our boots." The big guy turned out to be Frenchy, the Chief of Police. When dad was 18, the shoeshine shop owner died, and he left his stand to dad. A year later, Dad got an extra job at a pool hall, sweeping and cleaning. There was never enough money, as he had his younger brother, Uncle Chapo, to support as well.

GREGORY WAS DESTINED TO BE A STRONG LEADER. ABOVE HE SITS WITH HIS SISTER ON HIS FATHER'S LAP.

INNOVATORS - CHANGEMAKERS

Gregory Torrez (continued)

My dad was now 24, back from military service, and the relationship with Frenchy again came into play. Frenchy was a rather powerful individual in Phoenix. Dad wanted to expand the pool hall with a little extra gambling but if you didn't get Frenchy's blessing, you couldn't do it. So he took his proposal to Frenchy and, long story short, Frenchy gave his blessing for Dad to have an 8-ball game, but cautioned, "That's it!"

Brothers Adolpho (R), and Rupert (L).

There are so many other stories I want to share with you about my dad in those early years before he met my mom. He was truly a driven personality. While he got the shoe shine stand and pool hall because the owners liked him, around 1930 he also bought into an unusual business. Dad cut melons and onions in the fields in Glendale on a ranch with a big plantation-style ranch house. Dad didn't speak much English but always managed somehow to be understood. He got to know the woman who owned the house and fields and asked if he could have some melons. She asked, " You work for me boy?" Dad said, " Yeah." Field hands had to be pretty humble in those days. She said, "You can have what's left after the fields are picked." So, Dad went to the junkyard and bought two junked Model T trucks for a total of $40.00, and fixed them up. After the fields were cut he got a couple of guys, loaded up and took the remaining produce to the market, which in those days was in downtown Phoenix. He made $800.00 in three days on those melons. From then on my father decided he liked owning his own business and didn't want to work for others.

I would like to say that my father's whole life presented me with defining moments, as did my mother's life. But that's not reality.

My mother and father met in 1946 when my father had come out of service in World War II. It was at the time he owned the pool hall. Mom's dad owned a night club photography business and she worked for him. My father had been married before and had two small sons, Adolfo and Eddie, ages three and five.

They met when my mother was taking pictures in a Phoenix bar, saw him through the lens of her camera, and asked if she could take his picture. He agreed but added he wouldn't pay for it. My father had a reputation as a ladies man and my mother was attracted to him. They were subsequently married and Mom agreed to raise my father's children by his previous marriage. Mom and Dad were from opposite worlds and environments. Dad had been abandoned when he was seven years old and raised by grandparents and had only a third grade education. Mom came with her family from Fargo, North Dakota, graduated from Phoenix Union High School, and became a professional photographer. These two opposites were attracted to one another. They married and divorced more than once and remarried each time, destined to be together. The first business they owned together was the Azteca Café, followed by the Torch Bar and the Flower Shop. Six years after their marriage, Royna was born, then me, and finally Raoul. Dad passed February 4, 2002 and my mom died October 17, 2000.

Knowing the legacy of my father's early life presented me with the obligation to fulfill what I believe to be family legacy. I determined to personally have a company with the Torrez name and that need compelled me to found Torrez International L.L.C. I am the President/CEO and certified DBE-MBE (Disadvantaged Business Enterprise).

Gregory, you have discussed some key moments linked with your mother and father. I'd like to switch our direction for awhile and ask you to go back again in time. Readers will want to know more about your interests when you were young. What were you like in grade school, high school and then as a young adult?

Well, in my grade school years, I was going to be a priest. I was influenced by a priest name Father Aloysuis from Immaculate Heart Church, a very reverent holy man. Parishioners are currently working to have him canonized as a saint. That's how holy this man was. I had a shoulder twitch when I was a young boy, up until I was about 7 or 8, and the doctors couldn't fix it. Father Aloysuis laid hands on me and it went away. I was an altar boy at the time, and served mass almost every day until I was in eighth grade. It was a prideful thing. I was driven by the emotion of being wanted. You have to understand, I didn't like or love myself when I was a kid. I didn't understand that because I was always trying so hard for other people to be my friends and to like me, the typical things that all of us want. So I was kind of lost, you know. Being an altar boy gave me a direction and it gave me a position of pride because nothing moved until I gave the priest the wine and the host. I served mass at funerals when I was asked by the head priest. When priests traveled from other parts of the United States, and even outside the U.S., they would ask for me to serve because of the way I served mass. So it was a prideful thing and I was a part of something very special. I was sent to Coretian Monastery in Los Angeles when I was 13 years old and in the eighth grade. My mother thought I should be a priest. My father thought I was crazy.

Gregory Torrez (continued)

Everything was going along fine, but then St. Mary's Girls High School came to play volleyball with us. The girls were beautiful and I thought, wow, I can't spend my life without being with girls. Well, the priests tried to get me to stay, but two weeks later I came home. My dad said, "Good!" Mom said, "Are you sure?" I explained how I felt, so she was okay with my decision.

I went to high school and, to be very honest, I really didn't have a good time. It was St. Mary's High in Phoenix and I was not comfortable with the inside crowd. I just didn't fit in. Freshman and sophomore years were hard. I tried out for football but it didn't work out. I would go to school all day, go to football practice after school and then work at the store when I got home.

My father had a simple philosophy. When I was 12 years old, he took me to the bathroom at one of our stores, the flower shop. He had a bucket, Comet, a toilet brush and a mop. He said to me, "I am going to teach you a job so you will never starve." He showed me how to clean a bathroom and then put me in charge of the bathrooms. So now I would finish school and football practice each day and come home to clean the building. I was the janitor, right? He just saw it as my doing my part. I just couldn't do it all, so I quit football. My responsibilities started when the school day ended. I had made a commitment to work here as long as my parents were alive and so that became my driving force.

High school for me was really 'go to school, come home to the job.' In my junior year came a life-changing, defining moment. God blessed me and gave me a direction that would go with me for the rest of my life. I found my angel, Josephine. Her brother came in to get tuxedos for his wedding and I heard he was short one guy in his wedding party. I said, " You know, sometimes people ask me to be in their weddings because they need an usher and I have my own tuxedos." He said, " Why not!" So I went to the wedding and, as I was leaving, I looked across the room and saw this beautiful girl sitting under what looked like a spotlight. She had a glow around her. She was with this older man who had his face in his plate, eating.

ABOVE: Josie, Gregory's wife, at her brother's wedding the night Gregory first met her in December 1969.

RIGHT: Sophomore high school picture of Josephine.

I love to dance, but I hadn't danced that evening yet. I saw her and said to myself, "Wow, she is so beautiful." I thought I'd like to dance with her but figured she'd say no, but I asked her anyway. I walked up and said, " Would you

like to dance?" She said, "Yes." There was a Motown song playing (I love Motown music), but it stopped and a slow song started. We looked at each other, and I just swept her into my arms. I kissed her on her forehead and she said, "Wow, you're fast."

She looked up at me and I said, "I have to be home in 20 minutes, but I wanted to meet you." Long story short, I asked her if I could take her home because the wedding was over at midnight. She said, "You have got to ask my dad." Being from our culture, I understood the respect of that request. So I said, "Sure." I didn't even hesitate. Luckily for me that night, her father was drinking, so he was in a very good mood. I walked up to him and said, "Mr. Leon, I would like to escort Josephine home if that is okay." He said, "Sure." Josephine looked at me in shock, as did her mother who was standing next to him. I thought I said something wrong. I later learned that it was because she had never been out with anyone previously. This was the first time.

We left in my 1950 Plymouth station wagon which I still have and plan to restore. I had my 8-track tapes playing Motown. My car was baby blue in color with black interior which she really liked. I stopped at Reddy's, corner of 16th Street and Jefferson, which was like a Circle K back then, and bought her a strawberry pop. I just fell in love with my Josephine that night. For two years my life consisted of high school, seeing Josephine, and my job as janitor in our buildings. I was making $35 and needed most of it to buy things for her siblings. I saved $5 to buy gas, and the rest went to others who accompanied us on dates. We were never alone together during our courtship.

After high school I wanted to marry Josephine but my father and mother wanted me to go to ASU, so I enrolled to please them. In the meantime, I went to Josephine's father and asked for her hand in marriage. He became angry and abusive as he had been drinking. Josie suggested I leave, which I did.

Next morning while driving to ASU with my sister Royna, I made my mind up that I was going to marry Josephine. I stopped the car at the ASU campus and asked Royna to get out. She was shocked and asked me why. I told her I was going to get Josephine and ask her to marry me. Royna said, "Mom and Dad won't like that." I said, "All I know is, I can't live without her and I'll make them understand."

LEFT: Junior prom photo of Gregory and Josephine.

ABOVE: High School Graduation 1971 at St. Mary High School.

Gregory Torrez (continued)

Royna went to class and I drove down to South Mountain High School and found Josephine dressed in her leotards in dance class, along with a lot of other girls. They all looked like gazelles floating around. Josephine was sitting on the floor, and as I stood over her I blurted out, "I'm going to ask you one question. Will you marry me? I want to spend the rest of my life with you, but you have to come right now." She stood up and started crying and all the other girls were crying, too. Josephine went to the locker room, got her clothes, and we got in the car and drove off.

She asked, "What are we going to do?" I said, "All I know is, I can't live without you and we'll work out what's to be done." We drove to the Plaza here to see my mom and dad. We walked in and I told them that Josephine and I were going to get married. My mother was upset, but Dad was different. He respected my decision. Mother said, "Are you sure?" I said, " This is what I want to do."

Everything moved then at warp speed. Mom quickly got a pretty dress for Josephine. I put on a new white shirt, we all drove to Las Vegas that night. We stayed at the old Landmark Hotel, got up the next day, went down to the courthouse and got married. Royna was the maid-of-honor, and the bellman at the Sahara was the best man. My dad was a friend with him when dad came to Vegas, so he was happy to help.

We got married and here we are. I've worked out the rest. As a quick recap to my early life, I was going to be a priest but it didn't work out. I was going to be in business and play football and that didn't work. I fell in love and that worked, but I didn't finish school. I tell everyone I graduated from the U of A, the University of Azteca, our family business. I got married and that's worked well. My angel Josephine and I have been married 36 years, we have two daughters, two sons and 10 grandchildren. I hope all this answers your questions about my early life!

Rupert and Adolpho in front of Azteca Restaurant. The wedding plaza is named after this early business.

Gregory, let's get back to the building of your parents' legacy, Azteca Wedding Plaza. When we first talked together in 2003, you told me a little of the story of this unique enterprise. I need for you to expand on what you told me then.

To tell the story right, we again go back in time. My parents were married in 1946. In 1948, they opened the Azteca Café and Restaurant in downtown Phoenix, on 3rd Street and Washington. That area now is the Civic Plaza, just where you go under the bridge. My parents went to look at the building to rent it and Mom said, "What are we going to call this?" While they were standing there, the owner went inside and turned the lights on. They looked up and the neon light said AZTECA. It was right across from the old Azteca Theater. Perhaps you remember it?

Yes, I do Gregory.

Well, when they opened, it was 65 cents for a taco, tostado, enchilada, rice and beans combination plate. You can imagine how hard they had to work to earn enough to pay the rent and support themselves. Once they got going, Dad acquired the old Torch Bar next door. He sold long-neck beers for 10 cents a bottle, which improved their income. They had the restaurant and bar for quite some time. They still had it when I was in my teens. I remember thinking how out of date it looked and decided to make a suggestion to my father to update it and make it look as stylish as other businesses in the city. So one day while at the restaurant I said, "We need to have glass, marble and chrome, Dad, it's the style today." Dad just looked at me and told me to go down to the White House, a little department store next to Skaggs Drug Store owned by an elderly gentleman. Dad said, "Buy a pair of Stacy Adams black and white wing-tip shoes, size 12." He gave me the money, I went down, walked in and asked for the shoes. The old gentleman walked to the back of the store, returned and handed me the shoes. I paid for them and returned to my dad with the shoes. He took them and asked me, "Was his store clean? Did he have a lot of merchandise? Did you get what you wanted?" I said yes to all the questions. Dad asked, "Did he have glass, marble, fancy trimmings?" I said no. Lesson learned. We went on with our business without all that froufrou.

There were many other lessons he taught me, timeless lessons that I apply to my business and personal relations to this day.

SIDE VIEW OF AZTECA IN OLD PORTLAND HOTEL.

"My dad taught me many timeless lessons that I apply to my business and personal relationships to this day."

The most important of all decisions pertained to Azteca Wedding Plaza. They already owned the name Azteca. Dad wanted to start a funeral parlor because there was no Hispanic funeral parlor in Phoenix, and he thought it would be a successful business. Mom was opposed. She thought death was not a good business. She wanted a wedding business which had more class than a funeral business, a business of life and growth. Mom won. Looking back, she set the stage for the most ambitious and successful venture for our family.

Gregory, the Azteca Wedding Plaza became the major legacy of your parents' exciting and colorful entrepreneurial career. I'd like to pursue its evolution with you. Since your mother persuaded your father to pursue this course instead of the funeral business, I assume she had a strong hand in its subsequent development.

Yes, she did but, in his own way, so did Dad. I sometimes think about the decision. Do you know, there is still not an

Gregory Torrez (continued)

Hispanic-owned funeral business; at least I've not been able to find evidence of one. However, let's pursue Azteca as it soon began to evolve.

Stages of Azteca building over the years.

There was a process to get the business underway and to produce value for the family. And I believe we were truly blessed. Yes, it was, and still is, the work ethic and efforts of our family and all our employees. We truly came along at the right time. Mom and Dad bought the property on Washington Street when nobody wanted to buy property in the late '40s and early '50s. They were able to buy this first piece for $5,000 because nobody wanted it. At that time, the city, the downtown, was starting to go away. It started in the late '50s and by the mid-'60s, or right about then, the downtown was gone. Phoenix began to fall victim to the migration of the population to the suburbs. First it was Christown Mall, then Thomas Mall, and one strip mall and shopping center after another following the local migration, and then the influx of the new people moving to Arizona after World War II.

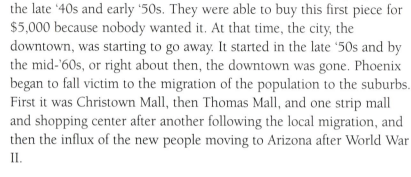

In a way, we were lucky nobody wanted land here. The business grew because we were different, one of a kind, a well-displayed and stocked wedding business. Nobody displayed like we did. We grew and grew with the great ideas from Mom and Dad. In the wedding industry, the godsend is that women will drive to Timbuktu to look for the right dress. We have also attracted that same interest from men as well. We are further helped because we are now selling dresses to daughters and granddaughters. We are helped by the best advertising of all, word of mouth. We are a one-stop shop for everything needed for a wedding - clothes, flowers, cleaning, accessories, invitations, gifts, etc. Every time an opportunity presented itself, it was driven by an idea from my dad and evolved into a business. So we would tear down a wall to create another room or build another building - so then we were in another business.

HOW THE AZTECA GREW AND GREW

My parents took a huge leap in 1984. They borrowed $1.4 million, added on 35,000 square feet and soon needed more space. I remember Mom became her own contractor. She went out and found the best bricklayers, plumbers, electricians and the like, and told them what she wanted built. She would be doing sales in our first building and word would come from construction that there was a problem. Mom kept a pair of mud boots at the door, so she would ask the customer to wait a few minutes, put on her boots and go to the construction site. She'd wade through the mud, assess the situation, come up with a solution with the workers, and tell them to continue. Then she would go back, take off the boots and continue with her customer. We had nice business. Thank the Lord, we had enough to support the $16,000 a month payments, because my mother wanted it paid before she passed away. When we began this in 1983, my mother was 61 and Dad was 68. You have to understand my father was partially paralyzed on his left side from an accident in 1979. So you think about all the hurdles they went through, and all the sacrifices they made for us. Now we have 130,000 square feet on three acres of property with 45,000 square feet of building.

Gregory, you've alluded to your father's accident and it seems it was a life-changing event. Would you tell us a little about that?

Yes. He was almost killed in 1979 in a head-on collision. My eldest daughter, my wife Josephine and my mother were with him. They went out for Christmas dinner and, as they were going down 44th Street, a woman in a Ford Falcon Fairlane, one of those big monster cars, had a heart attack and died. She rammed head on into my father's '79 El Dorado and the whole front end caved in. Both of the ladies in the Ford died and my dad ended up paralyzed. My wife, daughter and mom were ok.

They put a halo on Dad with six screws in his head. Most people would have given up, but he kept asking Jesus if he could just sit in a chair, and he not only got in a chair but out of it. He started walking and eventually driving again. That is when I realized the mental power and greatness of this man, my father, what it means to be a man. I think about his strength when I'm having a bad day. I guess you would call this, also, an important defining moment in my life.

There have been others, Gregory?

Yes, my mom was intent on having all the family in one place. So we

Gregory Torrez (continued)

ended up with Mother and Father buying the rest of this city block. We now sit on five acres, own all the buildings, and own everything on the land. The business area is Washington on the south and Van Buren on the north between 9th Street and 11th Street. Directly behind the businesses is the family compound which fronts on Van Buren. Every day we walk to work and when we finish we go home. We are truly a family business.

GREGORY'S MOTHER KAY AND NURSE HELPING FATHER ADOLPHO RECOVER FROM AUTO ACCIDENT IN 1980.

RIGHT: 1985 CHRIST IN THE GARDEN OF GETHSEMANE WAS BROUGHT TO THE AZTECA PROPERTY.

To Mother family was everything. She had foresight. She bought a family cemetery plot in Saint Francis Cemetery under a tree. There were 14 plots at a cost of $37,000. I asked her why she was doing this. She said, "I want a place all you guys will come to see me." In addition, she paid $2000 extra for a marble bench under that tree. I said, " Mom, we'll always come to see you." She said, "When you come to see me you'll stay longer if there is a place to sit." I remembered that because the day we buried Mom, I sat on that bench and remembered what she had said. So, now when I go I sit, talk to my mom and dad, ponder my life, and think about my family.

My family means everything to me. The car I drive today, the '99 Tahoe was my father's car. The wheel has a special knob on it for the physically challenged. So when I need to think and get some balance in my life, I simply walk out the back door, get in his car, put on the music I enjoy, take a drive, hold on to the knob and reflect on my life.

There are many remembrances of my mom and dad that keep me from going crazy in our crazy world. They never talked about legacy, never defined what they did other than they wanted all of us to have the best they could build for us. They also insisted it was ours, when they were gone, to do with it what we wanted to do.

They only asked us to preserve that little garden that sits in front of our plaza, created as a replica of Christ at Gethsemane. Both Mom and Dad insisted that the garden be maintained in perpetuity, no matter what else we determined to do with the business and property. We have pledged to do everything in our power to be sure their wishes are honored. As to the business, my parents built this successful beginning and we have the challenge to take what they built and carry it on to the next level of success. When I was 12

years old, I made the decision that, as long as my parents were alive, I would always be here to manage or work in this company on their behalf.

Gregory, we've come full circle. The influence your parents have had on the formative years of the Valley of the Sun, their enormous influence on the boy you were and the accomplished man, business leader and humanitarian you have become. We couldn't have gotten to the nugget of who you are without your parents' story. Now we need to pursue your story, present and future. Let's start by getting some specifics on you as a person. When you want to relax, what do you do?

Well, I love to play golf. In 1960 at 58 years old my father took up golf and became a minus two golfer. When I was 12 he took me out to play at a little golf course in Tempe. Afterward, he said I was on my own. I love to play golf even though I'm not an exceptional golfer. I play using my father's 45 year old golf set. Tiger has no worries.

My wife and I are really movie people and we go a lot. Holding my grandchildren is the most wonderful and relaxing part of my life. There is a wonderful exhilaration about sitting down and having my 10 grandchildren, from the little two-year-old to the 15-year-old hug and kiss me. That's unconditional love and very relaxing.

No hobbies. My uncle tried to interest me in fishing and hunting. It just didn't fit my lifestyle and I didn't find other interests. I'm really a people person and that is great for me.

Gregory, what do you believe are your greatest strengths?

Definitely number one is respect of all people. I approach every interaction with another human being in an open way. In that 15 to 30 second moment of truth, I know whether we will be friends or have differences. Either way I respect them no matter what my impression of their ways of life, philosophies, or businesses.

Number two is compassion, even if our philosophies differ and the individual displays uncomplimentary actions.

Number three is the capacity to love.

GREGORY AND HIS CHILDREN.

Number four is passion, passion for life and all living things, passion for ideas and causes that benefit the many, whether those causes are family, work, ethics, morality, my faith, or my promises and commitments.

INNOVATORS - CHANGEMAKERS   PAGE 79

Gregory Torrez (continued)

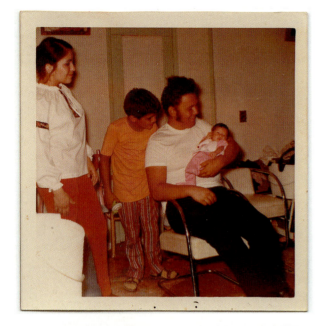

I am wealthy because of the children I have.

Number five is hope. We all have challenges and sometimes at the end of a day there is only hope.

These are all very important strengths because I love to help people, and to do that respect, compassion, love, passion and hope are needed. I live my life this way as an example for my family.

People say, sure you can do that, you're wealthy. I say no, no. I am wealthy because of the children I have. I have four beautiful children who were created with my wife and they like and love themselves as much as they can as young people and they treat others the same. We are the wealthiest people in the world because of what they will now manifest to mankind. You see it in my daughter. She wants to be a teacher and open her own little school. My other daughter is the director of Tumbleweed, the youth-at-risk program. It is amazing. Tumbleweed has wealthy, affluent kids who tell their parents to "jump in the lake" and now they are out on the street. She helps get these children back on track. That takes heart. That takes passion. My son Gregory took on the challenge of raising the six daughters of his sister-in-law because she had drug and alcohol problems. He fell in love with these girls, adopted three of them and is now responsible for the youngest and oldest and is getting ready to get the sixth one. That wasn't driven by anything except his heart. And his mother, Josephine, and I are there helping this initiative. They're six of the prettiest angels you have ever seen in your life. So my kids have heart. They have passion. I am successful. I have done my job. So people need to try and understand what is success, what is power, what is greatness. It is not driven by buildings and the money.

The most profound emotion in my life came shortly before my dad passed away. His comment to me, the greatest compliment of all was, "You are a good man, son." That hit me hard. It still does, because there were times I thought my father didn't like me, but he really did! I knew he loved me because a man doesn't work as hard as he did for his family if he doesn't love them, but I needed him to like me.

I describe myself as an individual who was fortunate enough to be raised by two loving, caring parents who taught me the business and life skills and how to help others by helping myself. That I believe is my greatest strength.

Gregory, there will be people in family businesses, and some who will want to start a family business, who will read your story. I'd like to pursue the present structure of Azteca Wedding Enterprises and how and why it is structured the way it is. There should be lessons here that will help others.

Well, as I shared with you, we have probably a one-of-a-kind structure because when my mother passed away, my father was still president of the company and, while he was at limited capacity, we would not change or challenge that. All day-to-day operations were handled by Raoul, Royna and me. At one point my mother wanted to set up some structure to transfer ownership and we went through four attorneys. The first three told her she was trying to control from the grave. The fourth one was wise enough to ask her what she was trying to do. She told him she was trying to ensure that her children would have the business. In the document there were structures that kept us from selling our ownership to anyone outside until we offered it to the corporation. There were other items on our ownership documents, but they didn't work out the details on how to best ensure we could execute Mom's wishes. That poses problems.

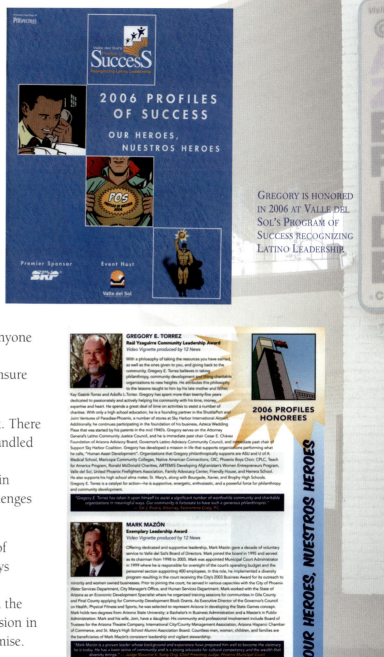

GREGORY IS HONORED IN 2006 AT VALLE DEL SOL'S PROGRAM OF SUCCESS RECOGNIZING LATINO LEADERSHIP.

When Dad passed away, as the eldest boy I proposed that I become president. There was disagreement and the attorney ended up suggesting the presidency be handled in a rotation. There was a name drawing which resulted in Raoul serving as president in 2002, Royna in 2003, and me in 2004. It rotated back to Raoul in 2005, Royna in 2006, and me in 2007. Frankly, there are many difficult challenges in such an arrangement.

Given the fact that neither my father nor mother were educated in the ways of business structure and the subsequent necessary management, Dad was always president, Mom secretary-treasurer and everything else, and we each were management, not owners. We had no infrastructure, nor did they understand the concepts of having a president, CEO, COO and other kinds of titles. The passion in our family business enabled us to handle most problems, usually by compromise. No one was designated to take the lead. We each had 33 1/3 percent of the company. So the rotation is the outcome.

It takes two thirds to vote in any changes. At the same time safety measures were put in place to protect us from ourselves. Any major financial decision over $50,000 requires a unanimous vote.

I believe my mother wanted some structure but she passed away before it could be worked out.

We have been discussing where we should go from here so that the business can continue with third and subsequent generations. The challenge is to build this into a business plan. Our parents went only to the second generation but without a plan to accommodate us. The difference is adding the third generation and that is the greatest challenge. For now, we are successful because as a family we work together for that success. We are presently working with a counselor, not a consultant, to facilitate the dialogue that my mother and father could not bring. My hope is we can communicate to come to an understanding to include the third generation. The way it is now, we cannot embrace the third. My oldest and my middle child are involved in the businesses and have strengths and attributes and great selling abilities. We need to cultivate their talents. They certainly have the desire to be a part of the business, but they need to know where they fit.

What is the situation with Royna and Raoul? Is this also true with them?

Royna's oldest is an attorney in Maricopa County. Her other two sons have recently graduated from ASU and are searching. One studied production management, the other general business and they are working here at present. Raoul's boys are still in high school and grammar school.

What are the three you of trying to effectuate with the counselors?

You understand we have a lot of dynamics going on. If you think about it right now, we own these five acres of land, own the buildings, own everything. We have a family business. And every day we come to work, we do our job and we go home. But the planning for this - where does it go? What happens with this land? I am 51, my sister is 53, and my brother is 48. We're not ready to retire. You have to think, in 10 years what is it we want to do? At 62, you might not think the way you do today. So we are barely in the planning stages now. I hope we can come to that answer because I would love my grandchildren to have the opportunity to be part of something that their great grandparents began. I would love that. The challenge for the three of us is how to get there.

Gregory, is this process working? Are these counseling people able to facilitate family counseling?

They are asking a lot of questions and giving us a lot of information about future activities and changes for Phoenix, and for this area where we have our family business. For example, the light rail system will run right down Washington Street in front of us. From their studies of other light rail systems they know what went right, what went wrong. They want to help us know what to expect and give us ideas to help us survive. They want us to know the challenges we will face and they gave us their best take on how to potentially get through all of this change.

The counselor, who has no emotional connection to us and is driven by numbers, suggests our decisions should be driven by economic questions: Do we need the area for wedding invitations? Do we need a thousand square feet or could we put something else there that gives us more dollars per square foot? Do you even like this business? Do you want to be located here? Do you want to have a board of directors and have managers running the business? That is the structure of a typical corporation. But we are not a typical corporation.

Gregory, do you have any people from outside the family here, right now, who are in management roles in Azteca Wedding Enterprises?

From the outside, Shirley? No.

Are you thinking at all in that direction Gregory?

Well, no, we have not been considering such a strategy. Again, the counselor asked these questions, and I thought they provided outside insights. For example, he asked if we ever thought about leasing the whole thing out and just being in charge of leasing property. He is looking for areas of interest, for our strengths and weaknesses. I believe he is trying to bring some outside intervention to get us to discuss possibilities that look to the future.

GREGORY'S SON, GREGORY JR., IN THE TUXEDO SHOP AS THE BUSINESS SUPPORTS THE THIRD GENERATION.

Gregory Torrez (continued)

Gregory, such counseling is done in a lot of ways. I am curious on where you stand. My role is not to impact on what you do but to find what you are doing because that is a big part of your story. You all three have a critical job ahead of you to resolve your future.

Well, Shirley, I believe my mom and dad are watching, so I believe we will come to the right decisions. That's pre-destiny and my mother believed in that.

Gregory, whatever happens here, you have been resourceful in building your own businesses. You are in that degree very much like your father and mother. I'd like to hear more about these entrepreneurial activities. There are three, I believe?

> *My next step was to become a certified Disadvantaged Business Enterprise (DBE).*

Shirley, I have to step back in time to the events leading up to these other companies of mine And which are not a part of the family business. Up until 1996 I worked for Azteca along with all the family. Mom and Dad were still alive so we all worked here. But I was becoming very frustrated. When I was 43, I began questioning and soul searching about what I would do to be my own person. I went across to the Immaculate Heart Church where I served as an altar boy and said, "Lord, I'm feeling unfulfilled and need to know what direction I should take." I sat there a long time running my life inside my head. I made a physical and emotional decision to end my frustration and follow the path my mother taught me, that you must find out what part you can play that suits your life.

Chicanos Por La Causa and City of Phoenix Minority Enterprise awards.

February 1997, I got a phone call from a good friend Ricardo DeLeon. He asked if I knew anybody at Basha's Supermarkets. Coincidentally I knew a young man, Raoul Ayola, who worked in the graphics department. He had worked for me 20 years earlier, I was just about to become the godfather of his child, Alexis. I put Ricardo on hold, called Raoul and explained to him I needed an appointment with the buyer of paper products. He put me on hold, comes back and he had made an appointment with the head buyer, Dale Scholoss to go to lunch. I got back to Ricardo and told him we had the appointment. Ricardo picked me up and between then and our arrival at Basha's he briefed me on the special toilet paper he had and wanted to sell. He had a marvelous price point of 39 cents on an end cap. Ricardo gave me a lesson, by the way, in the time it took us to get there on the language of retail in a supermarket environment.

We walked in, met Dale, drove him to lunch. I took the four roll pack and set it on the table. A long story short, we made the presentation and sold him three truck loads. Ricardo was grateful as he told me I had just made several thousand dollars. I refused and told him the money was his. Now between the time it took to get to the car, my brain started working and I thought maybe this is my sign to take this new direction.

When we got to the car, I called information on my cell phone for the number of Southwest Supermarkets. I called them up, talked to the paper buyer and made an appointment for a courtesy call. I informed him we had just sold three trucks to his competitor, and explained the great 39 cent deal on an end cap four-pack, a great loss leader. That afternoon Raoul and I sold another three trucks of toilet paper to Southwest Supermarkets. So the light bulb went off in my mind. I thought this is where I am supposed to go, a way to put my ideas, concepts and dreams to work, to take my ambition and energies to the next level. Within two weeks, I formed Torrez International, LLC, my first business and the opportunity to give my family name a future.

My next step was to become a certified DBE (Disadvantaged Business Enterprise) which would give me access to contracts with local, city, state and, eventually, national entities. We quickly started selling product to a bunch of different companies, but my challenge was that the producer was in Mexico and we were dealing with the problem of getting timely delivery. After about a year and a half, in August 1999, I struck a deal for the company to buy out my contract which freed me to seek other businesses.

In September of '99 I got a phone call from Greg Paradies in Atlanta. He owned the Paradies shops, a family-owned business since 1960. They were looking for a DBE partner and had heard of me. After considerable discussion, I became a partner and started building the footprint. We built several new

Gregory Torrez (continued)

ABOVE: 2003 Spirit of Enterprise Award for Family Business

RIGHT: Mother Kay meets President Clinton as nephew Jason stands by.

FAR RIGHT: Mother Kay with Terry Goddard, Gregory and wife Josephine.

retail stores together that solidified our relationship. We now have 15 stores at Sky Harbor International Airport.

In November 2003, I got another call from a company called ShuttlePort, a sub-division of Van de Aa Mobility Group, a huge transportation company across the U.S. After considerable negotiating, I agreed to take on the challenge of building an operation here at Sky Harbor. We were successful and have been awarded the contract to do bus transportation for the entire rental car facility. We operate 62 buses running between the three terminals, moving nine to ten million passengers a year.

I prepared myself for opportunity, and my many years of building marvelous relationships in the community prepared me to become a go-to guy. I continue to strengthen those relationships and look for logical next steps for Torrez International, while at the same time managing my responsibilities in the family business at AZTECA. We each have an area. Mine is the tuxedo and dry cleaning business, Raoul does miscellaneous, and my sister bridal.

Of course, I also pursue all my community, state, educational and philanthropic responsibilities, as well as some select national commitments. These follow in the model my mother taught me.

Gregory, you have a rich history of combining many obligations, talents and challenges! Perhaps you have some advice you would give to the readers of your story who may be budding entrepreneurs.

I see so many people who are sad, living lives of quiet desperation, people who have money, position and recognition but are miserable. They've never learned to like or respect themselves, but they have to start there. They need to find what gives them passion and pursue it while being respectful of others in the process. They must be aware that entrepreneurs are a combination of risk taker, gambler and

humanitarian, with a level of community involvement. They need to understand this, as there are dark hours. Nothing is a slam dunk.

They must have a business plan but be aware that even the best plan does not have all the answers, and can fail in spots. My definition of an entrepreneur is an individual who can create or grasp new ideas and handle challenges and problems as they arise. They understand to never, never, never quit! They must find some device or attitude to lift their spirits when they're at the end of their rope. For me, I think of my family and grandchildren. I use my music to keep my rhythm in place. I reach out to friends via phone, cards, e-mail. I pray and work out, read or listen to some motivational person. Finally, I think of all the people in my life, and my employees especially, who are depending on me. I accept there will always be setbacks, but they will continue to develop character and stamina in me.

I take my own advice as it relates to Azteca's present and potential future. My mother would say, there is a solution, you just haven't let it occur. I believe so much change is taking place that we must do our research, develop options, select the best, and then set aside our differences and take action to accommodate our third generation of ownership. To do less than this is to fail our parents and lose our destiny. I serve on so many boards and committees searching for the greater good of others. I cannot shirk my obligation to those closest to me. We must secure Azteca's future for the generations to come.

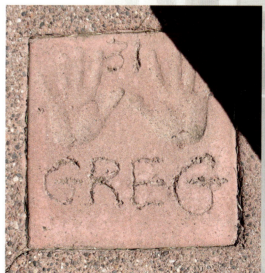

Ribbon cutting of major expansion, June 1985. Gregory's handprints are in the concrete at Azteca as he leaves his mark on business for all in the future to see.

I DIG the FUTURE

When describing Marcia Veidmark, the terms faith, family, honor and responsibility come top of mind. She is a kind and caring woman with a firm sense of ethics and moral practices. Marcia is the president of Specialized Services Company (SSC). Known to be a strong leader with a sense of structure, her successful long-term planning capability is based on a clear understanding of the lessons learned while building her company and of the future of her industry. She is a risk taker, decision maker and builder. Marcia's business is one usually considered the purview of men. SSC specializes in horizontal and directional boring, large diameter tunneling, pipe ramming and bursting, utility pot holing, sub-surface utility engineering, consulting and shoring. SSC is a family business and Marcia is currently mentoring her sons to assume the business in Arizona, while splitting her time between Arizona and Maui, Hawaii where her husband is based and is developing the next iteration of their careers.

I have known Marcia for several years and knew she would be in the final cut of the stories I wanted to tell. Our interview was exhilarating with her flow of boundless energy, agile, organized mind and her ability to anticipate the direction my questioning would take. Marcia's story provides marvelous insight into the entrepreneurial mind. She is comfortable with introspection as a way of solving problems and has a natural inclination to be empathetic. She looks at problems and setbacks as a part of life and is determined to resolve them through positive actions, setting plans to overcome and proceed with life. Her optimism has carried her through the hard challenges of early family life and continues to support her as she faces the challenges ahead.

Marcia was born October 20, 1948 in Clark County, Missouri the fourth child of seven. Born on a farm with the assistance of a neighbor, the doctor showed up just in time to cut the umbilical card and check to see if mother and daughter were okay. The doctor was paid for his services with 30 chickens – killed, hand-dressed and packaged by her mother. Times were difficult and for the first five years, Marcia lived with family friends Myrtle and Mannie Baugher. Although hard, this is a time Marcia remembers as the best. The Baughers gave her unconditional love and guidance. Today, Marcia attributes her balanced self-esteem to this important period in her life.

In 1953 her family sold their farm and moved to Phoenix, Arizona due to her mother's and baby sister's severe asthma. Just four years later, her father was killed in a terrible accident, leaving her mother a single parent with seven children. Marcia says of this period. "I watched my mom take this huge assignment with courage and obvious reliance on God for the strength it required." Summers between 1953 and 1961 were spent back with Myrtle and Mannie on their farm. "They played an important role in my early life as I handled all the farm chores during those summers," says Marcia. She returned to Phoenix and city life for schooling each fall. When Marcia was ready for high school, Myrtle and Mannie again helped her set a different course; they paid her tuition to Phoenix Christian High School. This gift, in its own way, continued to be instrumental in her future.

MARCIA IS COMFORTABLE OVERSEEING ALL ASPECTS OF BUSINESS EVEN ON CONSTRUCTION SITES.

At this point I would like to share my interview with Marcia so she can tell her story in her own style. We will at various stages have the privilege of handling some intimate insights into the philosophy and activities of this unique personality.

Marcia, your years at Phoenix Christian High School were very good and included being crowned Homecoming Queen. That must have made your mom, Myrtle and Mannie very happy. Where did you go next?

I went away to Azusa Pacific College in California. My freshman year was great! When it was time to return for a second year, Mom had some major physical problems with my siblings and asked me to stay at home to help her through the difficult time. I did, and found full-time work at a downtown Phoenix law

GRADUATION FROM HIGH SCHOOL AND OFF TO COLLEGE IN CALIFORNIA IN 1966 – GREAT TIMES!

Marcia Veidmark (continued)

office. As time permitted, I picked up college courses at Phoenix Community College and Western International University.

Marcia's wedding day — June 28, 1968

You obviously had difficult times and disappointments at a young age. Would you describe the type of person you believe you are and the personal principles you have followed that have made a difference in your life and allowed you to persevere?

I am extremely optimistic. I don't have to work at it. I am courageous because I believe courage is a choice. How much of this is DNA I don't know, although I watched and was privy to my mom's example. I know God has had a hand in my performance and beliefs. The Bible and its messages are giant to me. They give me peace, optimism and hope. My faith helps me believe I will succeed and do what is right. It is sticking with these principles that have brought Specialized Services Company the successes we have enjoyed. Even with the stressful times we had in the '70s and '80s and more recently the 9/11 period, our faith in God, our can-do persistence, inventiveness and creativity have brought us though.

Marcia, I'd like to go back and catch up with the young Marcia. I understand you first met your husband at Phoenix Christian High School when you were just a freshman and he was a senior. You had dated only once when he joined the Marines and went off to serve in Vietnam, correct?

You're right Shirley, and I did not see him again until he returned in 1968. Our romance grew, we were married and shortly thereafter decided to attend Northern Arizona University together. On my husband's birthday, May 27, 1969, his parents came to Flagstaff to visit us and presented us with the idea of the four of us going into business together. In August we moved back to Phoenix. Just four months later, December 13, our first son, Arvid L. Veidmark III was born. These were amazing experiences for me at just 21 years of age.

At the same time, Specialized Services was born and incorporation was finalized in February 1970. My husband, his parents, and I were learning to work together. The complexity of family-owned business had begun. From 1970 to 1975 we were thrust on the front lines of owning and operating a business. I learned new skills of bookkeeping, taxes, payroll, employees, etc. from my mother-in-law who had handled these for previous small businesses started by my father-in-law. We officed out of their home as building SSC consumed our lives 24 hours a day. Our second son, Aaron, was born April 19, 1972. Our growing family and our dedication to keeping Sunday for worship did add some balance to our lives. Sometime during this period Mom and Dad

Veidmark left SSC and built a dairy in Phoenix and then moved on to build an even better one in McGuireville, Arizona. These facilities were state of the art. My father-in-law was truly an entrepreneur. In 1973, I returned to school to learn how to better operate the business. I started with classes at night and on weekends at the local community college. I'm an ardent advocate of life-long learning.

Marcia, these all seemed to be defining moments in your life.

Yes, Shirley, they were. You asked me in an earlier discussion for the ONE most defining moment. I told you then, there was more than one. Each has been, when it occurred, life changing, and the summer of 1975 was no exception. I cry even today as I think of that tragedy of giant proportions.

MARCIA'S MOM, HER HERO AND ROLE MODEL FOR LIVING LIFE WITH A POSITIVE OUTLOOK, GRATEFUL ATTITUDE, PERSEVERANCE THROUGH HARD TIMES, STRONG AND GROUNDED IN FAITH. SHE DIED OF PARKINSON'S DISEASE AT THE AGE OF 78.

BELOW: THE FAMILY GROWS AS THEY HAVE 3 BOYS.

My father-in-law was scheduled to undergo a triple by-pass. The Sunday afternoon prior to his surgery we had a water skiing trip planned for Lake Pleasant with Dad, my brother-in-law Bill, my husband and our two sons. I was actually pregnant with my third son at that time. Bill had recently returned from service in the Air Force and had purchased a ski boat. Our afternoon of fun ultimately turned into death. The two brothers, Bill and my husband, were double skiing. Bill fell and my husband dropped fairly close which is standard when double skiing. My father-in-law drove around to pick Bill up first and as he got close he hit the throttle forward too hard and the boat ran over Bill. I heard him cry out as the boat ran over him. I ran to the back of the boat and saw blood filling the lake behind us. He had been sucked up into the prop and his upper legs cut open. My father-in-law went numb. I shut off the engine and called out to my husband floating in the lake. He told me to take the wheel and pick him up. I did and once he was in the boat we circled and pulled Bill into the boat. He was alive and crying out, "Jesus, sweet Jesus." My husband went top speed to the dock. I held Bill's head in my lap as his father tried to get to the artery and stop the bleeding. Bill died. My father-in-law underwent surgery four weeks later and due to complications came out of it blind. December 9, 1975 our third son, Abram Paul Veidmark was born. He shares Bill's middle name. His birth added joy again to our lives.

In 1978 tragedy struck again. My in-laws had been living in McGuireville building their second dairy. It was almost complete, ready for the grand opening when Dad got

Marcia Veidmark (continued)

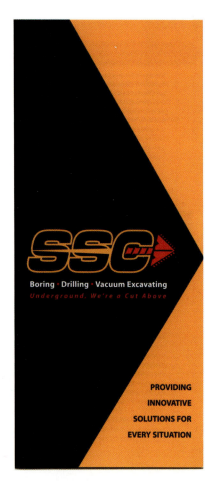

caught in some fencing and was knocked down by the cattle. He hit his head. He had torn tissue and was hemorrhaging around his brain. The doctors tried surgery to relieve the pressure but were not successful. Dad died during the procedure.

My mother-in-law was now part owner of a giant dairy about to open and did not know how to handle the role. My husband stepped in as her replacement on the board. As I attended the large-scale board meetings, I did not like what I witnessed happening. The dairy got hit with an IRS tax lien. It was scary! My in-laws' partners were crooked and had not paid federal and state payroll taxes. Our own business was now under attack. It took 18 months for me to redirect the lien to the guilty individuals. It was a painful business experience but it helped me develop. My husband and I began to refine our roles and soon our company began to grow and form.

It seems to me, Marcia, that starting your business with your husband and his parents presented challenges to relationships. How did it affect you?

Well, going back to when we returned to Phoenix from Flagstaff, we lived with my in-laws initially and had the company office there as well. The four of us had to learn to work together as well as live together. It was an arrangement that lasted four months at which time I cried "uncle" and asked for our own place. We moved to an apartment within walking distance so I could walk to work at my in-laws'. This experience taught us both what not to do when starting a company.

SSC evolved into what it is today over a 38-year period. We started as a basic excavation company that performed standard open cut type work with backhoes and trenchers. There were many such companies in 1969 when we began. As years passed we saw the low-profit-margin business as a problem. Our main customer, US West, was always seeking low bidders for the contracts, so we knew it was time to seek out a specialty type of underground work.

We made changes constantly to improve our position. We wanted to do the kind of work that we could actually make a decent profit for our company. We decided to do horizontal boring. There were only two other companies in the state that performed this kind of work so we decided to take the leap and become number three. The other two companies were not happy about it since we had used them as subs previously. Fortunately, these rifts did not cause long-term damage. Eventually, one of the other two left the business.

During these years, I grew in confidence and inner strength through the many, many backpacking trips we took as a young family. Abe, the baby, was only 10 months old when we took our first trip with him strapped to my back as we hiked Havasupai Trail. For 10 years we aggressively packed and hiked the Grand Canyon wilderness areas and the Idaho Sawtooth Mountain range. I stretched myself physically and mentally each time and grew to see just how much I could do beyond what I originally thought possible. Backpacking memories continue to be a source of courage for me when life has thrown me curve balls to deal with. I recall the feeling of "victory" over the high summits and the ability to keep climbing-often with injuries and great pain. These experiences were amazingly building my inner being of "self."

What do you want your clients to remember about you and your business?

Well, we have always had good relations with our competitors because they are often clients as well. We want them to remember that we give excellent performance due to our extensive knowledge of the industry, that we are skilled and that we have above-average employees who represent the foundational core values of our company.

In what other ways are you different from your competitors?

That would be the multiple types of underground construction work we perform. Most of our competitors are strictly focused and perform one type of underground service. We currently provide five types of underground construction service and plan to keep adding more in the future. We are also known for our market strength in "innovation." When a customer asks if something "can be done," we do our best to find a method to make it happen-no matter how unusual the request may seem. Things are never boring at SSC. No pun intended!

ABOVE: GRAND CANYON BACKPACKING AND OTHER FAMILY OUTINGS ALLOWED US TO RELY ON ONE ANOTHER FOR SURVIVAL, ASSISTANCE AND FUN. MARCIA CREDITS THIS ERA FOR HER PERSONAL DEVELOPMENT.

FAR LEFT: FROM 1984 - 1994 THEY LIVED AND WORKED SEASONALLY AT LAKE POWELL WHILE LIVING AND WORKING IN THE PHOENIX CONSTRUCTION BUSINESS. THEY SOLD THE LAST HOUSEBOAT AND CLOSED THE LAKE POWELL BUSINESS IN 1994.

Marcia Veidmark (continued)

Were you involved in other companies or did you start other businesses, Marcia?

Yes I did. In the mid '80s we took our foremen and their families to Lake Powell for a weekend of fun and celebration and became hooked on a new venture. So enter another "defining moment." We decided to begin a private, multi-ownership household boat program that would allow us to own the majority of the new company and invite our fellow business friends to purchase a percentage of a houseboat. Creating this second company filled my life! As a majority owner, we managed the company and established the guidelines for maintenance of boats, collected revenues, etc. We grew to four houseboat corporations within four years and had approximately 75 co-owners. We operated this company for 14 years and closed it down in 1998. Running the construction company while still creating, growing and managing this business in Page, Arizona and, at the same time raising three sons was a giant growth experience for me.

BELOW: Valerie Manning, Greater Phoenix Chamber of Commerce President, celebrates with Marcia at the awards ceremony.

During this period we also purchased a nearby automotive repair shop that was in our complex. I did not want another business but I saw that the current owner wanted to sell and we hoped that he would become employed at SSC to manage our mechanic shop. He did and this worked great for five years. He then moved on and a new manager was hired to fill his position. I learned how to handle inventory and learned customer service for a retail customer base where as SSC had only utilized a commercial customer base. These were very different challenges to learn to work with. Great success came as the automotive repair shop grew by 400 percent. Unfortunately the repair shop also gave me the unwanted opportunity to experience big-time embezzlement, done by a manager at the shop. He stole so much money I finally quit counting. We took care of the problem and finally sold the shop at a nice profit.

RIGHT: Abe Veidmark, Aaron Veidmark, Marcia and Arvid Veidmark III were all thrilled to be honored at the awards ceremony.

Marcia, you mentioned living through some difficult times in a talk you gave during a Phoenix Chamber of Commerce awards program. I was impressed with that talk. Would you comment on these challenges?

The Greater Phoenix Chamber award was for Response to Adversity. Wow! This was a huge boost to my self-confidence. I needed to have this outside affirmation that what I had endured was truly "giant

and hard" and that we had done a great job of not only surviving but in re-creating our company to make it through the economic hardship. We had also created a new and better company with the new divisions we added. Once again, my inner strength grew and our company prospered due to this honor. I am so grateful to the Chamber and everyone inside and outside of our company who made it happen.

Marcia, I'd like you to review more in depth, some of these especially painful business experiences. I believe these would be helpful for other entrepreneurs or those contemplating starting businesses.

In the 1980s the construction industry hit bottom. We were so slow we had to lay off personnel and were thrilled when on occasion the phone would ring and a potential job was on the horizon. We learned to try different avenues of work just to create work opportunities and we tightened our belts so tight it was truly painful. Money was so short that we had to move out of our office into a construction trailer we were given by a customer who could not pay his bill to us. The great thing from this era, which lasted a number of years, was that I saw we could endure and continue to exist even when the economy got really bad. This first-hand knowledge helped me a lot when we hit the most recent economic crisis in our country - 2002 and 2003 following the September 11 tragedy. I knew we had to act quickly to find new revenue streams and that we had to move fast so our lack of revenue from our normal line of work would not create such a great deficit that it would be almost impossible to recover.

"The great thing from this era, was that I saw we could endure and continue to exist even when it got really bad."

The memory that we had made it through the '80s helped me a lot in continuing forward in 2002 and 2003. My faith was critical to my believing that God was there with me, to give me courage and provide for me one day at a time. I constantly reminded myself that He saw us through the '80s and I could believe we would endure and make it through the latest test. Truly, my faith is the source of my courage, strength and wisdom.

Marcia Veidmark (continued)

While I have my faith to cling to, there were other people who had faith in me and helped in these trying times. They deserve mention and credit; Rena Huber; Sandy Kolberg; Diane Geshwind; Jill Mapstead; my attorney, C. Richard Potts; and my best friend from grade school, Dr. Sherry Schauer. These people have been with me on this journey of hardship and growth. They have helped me develop the ideas I had in my mind and needed to get onto paper and into action.

Your husband retired, I believe in 2002, and is now in Maui. You took full charge as president of SSC and won the Spirit of Enterprise Award as Emerging Entrepreneur that year. Tell us about this unusual progression.

Ah yes, The Spirit of Enterprise Award for Emerging Entrepreneur. This public affirmation of what I was doing at SSC as the sole leader after my husband's retirement was a true 180° turn in my inner "belief" of myself and my skills as a leader. This award was truly prophetic as we were labeled a new, emerging business even before I saw clearly what was happening. I needed the boost in confidence and I needed this huge "pat on the back" from such a prestigious organization as the ASU Spirit of Enterprise.

Receiving the ASU Spirit of Enterprise Award was instrumental in propelling SSC to the next level in business operation. We succeeded an economic downturn and created new divisions of our company to create revenue making us a larger and more solid business moving forward. Marcia is pictured here with her two sons Arvid and Aaron and ASU's Mary Lou Bessette.

To others this may seem unusual but to my husband and me it was a new iteration of our partnership in business. My husband and I have a separate LLC which owns the building and property SSC leases to operate. There are also other tenants in the building who have been leasing from us for more than 15 years. These are long-term relationships. We began to consider opportunities available in Maui that could prove good financially as well as open a new door for business in that area away from Phoenix and SSC. Exploration of the area began and we purchased the first property there. Our LLC has also purchased land in El Mirage for future growth opportunities for SSC as well as to build commercial office/warehouse type buildings to lease out to future, unrelated tenants. The LLC has also branched out to purchase other residential property in Maui for the purpose of improvements and leasing. The market in Maui has great potential for investment appreciation at this time and we hope to capitalize on this opportunity. My husband has overseen this operation since his retirement from SSC in 2002.

Our challenge has been the task of moving into the "succession process." This has included my husband's retirement in 2002. When family members and a company are all going through growth pains, it really hits from all sides. It has been five years as we have all moved forward and into this new era of our lives and our company. I am happy to say we are successful in the process but it has not been without a fair amount of effort. On the bright side, our Maui efforts have been exciting and successful as well.

To aid in the succession process, I returned to school at Western International University. This was a HUGE and important step for me to "get back on track" to work to complete my bachelors degree in business administration. I met a professor who recommended I apply for the APS AAAME program. How interesting when people like this are put in our lives just to "direct us down a certain path." I applied for and was accepted into the APS AAAME program. I asked to have my two sons who were to be the company successors also attend. My oldest son, Arvid, and I attended the program and graduated.

This was the year I hired our first sales manager at SSC. Our son, Abe, was working in Maui at the time and he heard I was looking for a sales manager. He had recently married and with a baby on the way, he wanted to be back home with family. Abe is a terrific salesman and he fit our job description, so he came back to join SSC. He was and is a huge help in finding jobs we can bid on.

RENA HUBER, ARVID III AND MARCIA AT AAAME GRADUATION IN 2003. MARCIA CREDITS RENA FOR AMAZING GROWTH, BOTH PERSONALLY AND FOR THE BUSINESS, IN THE AREA OF LEADERSHIP AND DEVELOPMENT.

Marcia, this was 2003 when Abe joined and it was during that tough period of time for SSC. Can we touch on the circumstances in a little more depth?

We were hit financially with the 9/11 disaster. In 2001 we had contracts and work on the books that took us through 2004. In 2002 there were almost no jobs to bid because the federal government stopped developing the United States and focused on defending it. Thus, in 2003, we had very little work. Living through this long two-year, fearful period as the leader of the company called on everything I had as a business leader. I had to rally our employees and convince them that this time would pass. I knew we would survive and we would come out stronger, smarter and better so that when the economy did return we would be poised to maximize the work and profit. I promised that we would share that profit with them. They believed me and trusted me. They stayed and we pulled together by cutting every corner we could and did jobs bid at 30 percent below normal bid-just to get the jobs. How rewarding to me that the people stayed!

That same year I negotiated a purchase for three acres of land in the West Valley. It was tough, but we had a serious need to find a new place to store all our large equipment. Our current rental yard was not renewing our lease due to a residential developer who purchased the land and we had to vacate. I knew that I had to step to the front and take this assignment, ready or not. I was stretching again and it was hard. I learned lots. I oversaw the development of land in a fast track manner by calling on all contacts I had met over the many years in the construction business in

Marcia Veidmark (continued)

the Valley. When we moved onto the lot with our large equipment and iron it was one of the greatest personal victories I have experienced as a business woman. It also brought a more efficient and profitable operation for the booming West Valley work that we have been able to bid successfully. That was part of my vision and it proved true. Confidence in my own judgment grew.

Marcia, what special ways have you involved your employees in growing the business. Do you have incentives?

The main tool we use to involve our employees is conducting regular meetings with the entire group at SSC, a group of approximately 30 people. We call these OPS meetings and T&D (training and development) meetings. One of our company values includes the development of employees and ourselves. We strive to build community among our employees by encouragement and assisting with good communication and open discussion on various topics that our employees care about. Sometimes we have a housekeeping section in our meetings when we talk about the little "grains of sand" that are bugging one another. We encourage an open format where the topic/issue is presented, after which I pull them in from the floor and they begin talking between themselves as a group. We end up finding an answer to the problem or issue the group has created. It builds team spirit and relationships.

> *We created a game to show how profit is created or diminished.*

We also have fun together with at least one annual company event each year. We choose to have a fall picnic and bypass the busy Christmas season for a party. Our party includes the entire family and thus the picnic setting. We play great games, have awesome gifts, bar-b-que and incorporate a fundraiser for a local community where the employees compete to raise food, money or school supplies for kids. Lots of good comes from this annual event.

Special incentives for all of us would mainly be our profit sharing plan. We made the 2002-03 promise "dream" a reality in 2004 which was an excellent year. In previous years we had a 401K plan but I could seldom get the employees to see how this was a great perk for them. Our company matched 30 percent of their personal contribution, but even with this match only a handfull participated. I had to finally close it due to "top heavy rules" with so few employees being in the plan. Happily, in 2005 we were able to give our employees the same generous contribution in profit sharing. I concluded that the only effective incentive I could offer was fully "free and given" money via a PSP (profit sharing plan). So, that is what I strived for and finally accomplished in 2004 and 2005.

In order for our group to understand that we all had a role in how successful and "big" our PSP contribution could be each year, we created a game to show how profit is created or diminished. I used the game of monopoly as my guide and tailored it to our company. It was a huge success in getting the message across to our group. They all strive to see the year-end PSP pot is as big as it can so we can all share it. Retirement money is something very few small companies provide. It is especially true in the construction industry where they are seldom found.

The other non-tangible incentive for our employees is the message of personal pride that we speak of, promote, and show by example. We encourage our employees to take great pride in the work they do. We brag on them constantly. We ask them to make their company, SSC, stand out to our customers and to our community. A few get this message and benefit from it with energy and compassion. Others do not understand and are merely along for the ride of a job. We work on converting these people as well.

In 2005 we added a new HR consultant to our advisory board and completed a new employee handbook that was well received. And, we also have an employee tuition reimbursement program for classes taken outside the company in trade schools, colleges, universities, etc. One of our core values is continued development of employees in both their personal and professional lives. We understand that employees who are constantly striving to grow and improve themselves bring great value to the company. We want to be part of our employees becoming "More tomorrow than they are today at SSC."

Marcia, you mentioned involving your employees in some elements of community service. I know this is very much an integral part of your concepts of community involvement and stated in your vision. Could you tell me more?

My vision sees SSC becoming much more involved in our community via participation in various organizations and direct charitable giving. I see SSC as a great addition to our local community, to the state and the world as a whole. We have three main projects at this time. One is incorporated with our November company picnic and will provide school supplies to children in low-income schools in the U.S. as well as all over the world. This is called "Operation School Box" and is administered by World Vision. Another is a continued partnership we have with Desert Mission Food Bank, a local food bank in the neighborhood of our main office. We are contributing money to a fund that accepts "only cash" so they can shop for and provide a full array of dietary needs to low-

Marcia Veidmark (continued)

income families in the Sunnyslope area. You cannot give food to this fund, as they have to actually purchase the fresh foods, etc. with the cash donations.

And, lastly, we have a program called "SSC Employees Care and Help" in relation to the Hurricane Katrina disaster. Our employees are contributing personal checks to either the Red Cross or the Salvation Army and SSC is matching their contributions 100% with a donation to each of the two organizations. There's a neat story on this one, Shirley. Our oldest employee is Clyde Webb and he is about 70 years old. He has been with our company for 16 years and is awarded 10 days vacation each year + 16 days off with pay (1 day for each year he has been a part of our company). He came in and asked if he could give 6 of his paid vacation days to the Katrina victims program. WOW! That really made my heart skip a beat. What a huge and generous offer from this man.

Throughout the year we contribute to multiple organizations that cross our desk via mail, employees requests, various organizational involvements, etc. The Spirit of Enterprise is one of our core interests each year. We also support the Phoenix Chamber Small Business Awards event, the Susan B. Komen cancer walk, the AZ Foundation for Women, etc.

Marcia had the honor of hosting a group of Afghan business women as they visited the U.S. This was a milestone in Marcia's life as she treasured the few days they had together.

One of our goals as a company is to include our employees' interests in our charitable giving. We want to create a culture where our employees (especially the core group) feels like *their* company is giving to support the organizations and programs that matter to them. Our goal is to reach the day when 10 percent of our annual net profit is earmarked for charitable giving. Many employees support their individual church's various functions and their children's school fundraising events. Other employees run in cancer races and outdoor trail maintenance programs. We also have others in the National Guard.

Marcia, what about your vision for the company? How has it changed? What about where you see yourself in the future.

That is a pretty broad series of questions, Shirley. I'll give it a go!

Has my vision changed? I think it has become larger and clearer. There was a time when I was younger when I was satisfied with just getting through the day. I am not sure I knew how to look broad and big. Now I look to the future and all that is possible and I strive to accomplish that which I see. Every day I look at what we have done, achieved and have yet to achieve. As days and events occur, we change to better our goals or reshape by both circumstances and perceived new opportunities. You can see by what we have in process that we are focused both outward and inward.

My vision for SSC is that it will successfully transition to the next generation of ownership and operation by our sons and their excellent advisory board. The divisions of the company are growing stronger and need to do so. The new marketing program of SSC is finally taking on a more complete form and process. My vision includes seeing this critical core to successful business operation become clearly understood and valued by all owners and the leadership of our company.

Marketing, marketing, marketing. I learned what it was to create a new brand to speak on our behalf now that our company has upcoming, younger successor-owners. It was hard, time consuming, costly and worth it all. We learned lots and have benefited greatly from the new branding, sales and marketing development, customer service program, web site, etc.

My management style is one of "develop and release." I am not a micro-manager and seek to hire individuals who are self-motivated and work independently. My organization is made up of strong, competent persons with various types of skills who are given the space to try out new ideas and test new territories within their area of responsibility. We are frequently asking individuals to find new methods to improve the way we do our work. I am very big on verbal cheering and praise when someone develops a new and better way to build the proverbial mousetrap in our company.

Our entire industry is reliant upon innovation.

Marcia Veidmark (continued)

Our entire industry is reliant upon innovation. Every job brings a new challenge and we have to create the new answer in order to complete the project in the field. Ours is definitely not a cookie cutter type of job where things are done in a routine, repetitive manner. We provide innovative solutions to every situation in the area of underground construction. Our services include placing steel casing under freeways, railroads and sidewalks. The casing can be as small as 2" PVC conduit and up to 10' diameter steel casing. We have placed steel casing as long as 900 linear feet.

We also locate utilities with a method called vacuum excavation using high-pressure air to simultaneously blow apart and suck up dirt from the ground thus exposing the buried utilities in the ground. This is sometimes referred to as "soft-dig." The newest division, Vacuum Excavation, is the focus of our development. Our goal is to add more trucks and crews in this division and gain multiple annual contracts with various cities within Arizona. We currently have a contract with the City of Tempe for this service.

Another goal is to build a new, state-of-the-art mechanic shop to service our equipment and vehicles as well as to be able to take in retail diesel repair work from a select group of customers. We have the new two-acre property on which to build this facility and the city has already approved the master plan for the development. We also have a one-acre parcel on which we plan to build another commercial warehouse-office facility to sublet to outside tenants as well as occupy one suite for our west-side offices. We are also looking for another facility in the Southeast Valley in which to develop a third construction storage facility from which to base our eastside work and crews.

Looking at all the existing and envisioned growth of capability for SSC, where are you on the most important asset – capable trainable people?

The year 2006 started with the same cry we hear all around us. So many work opportunities and so few workers. We truly cannot find the workers that we need. We are turning away work due to our schedule being full and so far out with contracts. With 35 percent too few workers in the trades industry compared to projects on the board, we are learning new and creative ways to search for workers.

We have added a marketing administrator who brings years of experience that we are tapping into as we look for workers. So today, our crisis is a different one from that in 2002 and 2003. Based on how we stepped forward to meet that crisis, I have confidence that we will find the answers for this need also.

My passion is to see SSC be hugely successful as the greatest place in the state to work in the construction industry...the best known company in the underground construction industry with a reputation that is stellar...a well-known community enterprise that does tons of good for many, many organizations and causes. I desire to see our sons Arvid and Aaron grow and be fantastic owners and leaders of SSC as their company in the future. I am so proud of the men they are. And, I desire to see our third son, Abe, grow and succeed in the sales industry while he is here with us at SSC and in all the future places he moves on to in his life with his young family. He is so entrepreneurial and curious that I think he will always be on the move. I am blessed beyond imagination to be able to work with our sons as adults in this manner and for this length of time.

I also see a vision of a future when I am moved beyond SSC. I see the company running well, the Advisory Board active, the strategic planning for future operation and growth is happening and it is all without me being there. They will be soaring!

And what about you personally, Marcia? What about the energetic, talented woman who has achieved so many successes? What about the person I see here and there giving of herself, whether it is working with the Afghan women who have come to Thunderbird seeking the knowledge necessary to change their society and rebuild their country or, enhancing her relationships with people in general?

Well, there is a future, although not yet totally seeable to me. I have some prideful achievements, specifically personally leading the company through years of

MARCIA AS PROUD GRANDPARENT ON ONE OF HER BUSINESS TRIPS TO HAWAII.

Marcia Veidmark (continued)

economic crisis and coming out with a new division that proved to be a great success. I am proud of the personal growth that occurred within me during this long period of tough times. I like myself better now because of those experiences. I have grown tremendously.

MARCIA FEELS FORTUNATE AS HER BOYS HAVE GROWN UP AND ADDED TO THE FAMILY WITH THEIR BRIDES.

The personal milestones that are missing in this record are the weddings of our sons which brought three amazing women into my life and the precious relationships I have with each of them. And lastly, the births of six miracles who are our grandchildren. Life is so much more and better since they have been added to it.

The Maui adventure has grown by one more property. Hopefully, this will be the last property for this small venture. My husband develops, oversees and manages the three properties. This has possibility for a nice future enhancement to our lives. When this day comes, I see my future in Maui as enjoying opportunities from the seeds that have been planted over the previous years. This will be an opportunity to spend time with my husband on a more regular basis and hopefully to entertain our grown family and longtime friends in this beautiful paradise. I see myself always being a part of the Phoenix area with so much of our family, friends and history here.

Marcia, your story will be an inspiration to others and give insights to the challenges and joys of being an entrepreneur. Would you like to add some advice to these potential pioneers?

Advice? Know the "business side" of running a business and not just the technical skill. The full scope of business ownership is very big, needs to be discussed and then clearly decided who will be responsible for each area. Once all the job duties and assignments have been made, it will show you who you need to hire. Seek out and ask outside professionals to help you with your business development from the beginning. These professionals can

"Seek out and ask outside professionals to help you with your business development from the beginning."

become your formal Advisory Board who will help you with a wealth of knowledge they have from years of experience in their fields of expertise.

Develop and call upon inner strength, personal confidence, drive and physical stamina. Focus on your goals, be willing to work hard, have persistence and patience. Throw in a good dose of humor because you have to learn to laugh or the load of entrepreneurship will certainly get you down.

Seek out outside specialists as your grasp of your industry or specialties becomes limited. You can begin to find this group of outside professional experts by joining such business groups as your local Chamber organizations, specific trade organizations and other leadership development groups in your area. You have to get out there and interact with other professionals in order to observe potential members for your advisory board. Be in some type of business group that holds you accountable for continued growth and improvement.

And finally, be very conservative with your money the first several years. Try to put away some of each sale in order to have a reserve cash account for the surprise that will ultimately come your way. Live frugally especially at the beginning of your company.

I will stop at this point, Shirley. I could go on and on but there has to be a point of stopping. As you can see, I have truly enjoyed being pushed to reflect on this part of my life. Thank you for this and for your friendship.

One last request, Marcia. If the reader of your story wants to know more, may they contact you?

Yes. They can start with our website and if that proves helpful, we are always open to further contact. Our web site is www.SSCBoring.com.

MYRTLE AND MANNIE BAUGHER - THE TWO PEOPLE WHO LOVED MARCIA UNCONDITIONALLY AND "INFORMALLY" ADOPTED HER AS THEIRS. THEIR ROLE PLAYED A GIANT PART OF SHAPING MARCIA AND HER VALUES AS SHE LIVED WITH THEM SO MUCH DURING HER FIRST 5 YEARS OF LIFE IN MISSOURI.

Geniuses in Fairyland

E ileen Joy Spitalny and David Kravetz refer to their extraordinary and successful business venture as "The Fairytale Journey." Both are motivated, creative entrepreneurs who could be successful independent of one another but choose to combine and intertwine their skills and talents forming and building an awesome business. Eileen is sales and market development, the outer world, and David is operational and strategic planning, the inner world of Fairytale Brownies.

"We wanted to be in business since high school"

I have known Eileen and David for about 15 years through their generous community work, ingenious promotions, and personal interactions – especially in assisting the work of the Center for the Advancement of Small Business (now renamed Spirit of Enterprise Center) I founded at Arizona State University in 1992. The center is devoted to assisting small, entrepreneurial businesses and students who are interested in starting their own businesses.

Eileen and David have simply the best interpersonal skills I have seen in my long career. Their friendship and compatibility go back to kindergarten. Their personalities are contrasting, dissimilar, yet their teamwork is symbiotic. Eileen is unassuming, tough minded yet gentle. She applies that combination in an exciting winsome manner. Her sales successes combine the word-of-mouth fame of Fairytale Brownies and her uncanny ability to convert this exposure into much wider national and international notoriety. For example, she got a call from Entertainment Tonight in July 2005 with a request to include the brownies in its gift bags at the Emmy after party hosted by People Magazine. Eileen said yes, customized a packet and Fairytale Brownies became an instant success with the stars.

a tale of sweet, sweet luxury

Her outgoing energetic manner makes her stand out in a crowd. She's quick to give credit to employees for their tireless efforts. Her title supports her point of view: Co-Founder, Marketing and Sales Team Leader. An excellent interviewee, she has captivated the press with significant features in The Wall Street Journal, The New York Times, Reader's Digest and other widely distributed publications, and is considered by the local press as one of the young business geniuses in Arizona. To be sure, this just wasn't luck. She is quick to see opportunity, persistent and tenacious in her communications. Just ask the people in the media such as the Food Network, USA Today and The Wine Spectator, to name a few.

"WE'VE BEEN FRIENDS SINCE KINDERGARTEN"

David Kravetz's title is Co-Founder, Strategic Planning Team Leader. David seems well-suited to stay out of the external promotional venues and sales activities. He is intensely serious, curious and involved in making sure everything in the company works as it should. He is precocious, analytical and interested in how every piece of equipment and system is designed, manufactured and assembled. He often takes things apart, examines them and then reassembles! Maybe, he's just short of being a technology geek. In his own words, "I love technology that is state of the art. I want the newest computer and the newest cell phone." He is always seeking more efficient ways to handle the business. At the time of this interview he was deeply involved in the design and construction of their new world headquarters in Phoenix, Arizona.

David and Eileen love what they have created together at Fairytale Brownies; their product is totally intertwined with their lives. As our conversation flowed it showed how this close-knit team strategized through their product developments.

As a team you have been successful in establishing and building your business. You are a respected national success story, with many forms of recognition and awards. I've known you all the years you have been building Fairytale Brownies. Over this 15-year period you have had many company-building adventures. Let's share those with the many people who will read your story. These adventures and misadventures could help other aspiring entrepreneurs. I am grateful for this opportunity and your candor. First, your product

Eileen Spitalny and David Kravetz (continued)

THE FAMOUS BROWNIE RECIPE COMES FROM DAVID'S MOM NANCY PICTURED HERE WITH HIS DAD ROBERT.

comes from David's mother's recipe. What caused you to select this as your product, Eileen, David?

We just sensed her brownies would be sensational if people tried them. We could not find a brownie product out there in the marketplace. Our problem was to find how to expand the basic family recipe, develop multiple flavors, and implement proper safety controls and the methods to market the product. We did a lot of experimenting in small shows and the like.

Eileen, tell us what you mean when you call your quest The Fairytale Journey?

Shirley, we set our course through three significant beliefs stated in our business plan and on the back of our business cards:

- OUR PURPOSE is to simplify gift-giving and spread joy through gourmet chocolate brownies.

- OUR CORE VALUES are product excellence, incomparable service, integrity, teamwork and leadership.

- OUR GOAL is to be the number one and best-tasting brand of brownies in the world!

From all indications you have achieved this and now must keep ahead of the imitators.

We do not take our success to date as an achievement. We look at where we are as just a milestone in the broad road ahead.

What do you most want a customer/client to remember about you and your business?

We want our customers to believe and remember that ours are the best tasting brownies ever, and to remember their total experience with our company.

Can you define that experience, please?

It starts with the joy of receiving our brownies as a gift, or from the customer experiencing the ease of ordering and the great service they receive.

In your industry how is that different from your competitors and how do you know that you're the best, David?

We know we are the best because we evaluate our competition constantly in a variety of ways. We offer superior packaging, product and service. Our brownies are made from the finest ingredients in small, hand-crafted batches. All our packaging is customized with the Fairytale design elements in our signature purple. Our branding is distinctive. We constantly monitor and put them to the taste test.

How do we know? Well, sometimes it is a trade show, sometimes a seminar, but we consider the trade show as the best. We always learn at least one big idea when we go to a trade show.

> "Our Fairytale Journey from the beginning says that our goal is to be the number one gift and best-tasting brownies in the world."

It seems people think of brownies as something Mom does. What made you think you could build a company on this kind of concept, David?

Right, it has been something moms do, but we want brownies to be considered the next really special cookie.

What's your take, Eileen, on this from a marketing point of view?

Well, our Fairytale Journey from the beginning says that our goal is to be the number one gift and best-tasting brownies in the world. One of the positions that we are working on is to elevate ourselves as a distinct brand, to put us more in the unique luxury category, communicating more that we are this high-end chocolate experience. You are paying a premium. I think some of that comes through and some of it doesn't. We just hired, for the first time, a PR firm in New York and we have worked with a local PR agency on some concepts. It is interesting that they both come with the same evaluation, that we have an awesome product but sometimes it does not communicate on its own how unique and high-end it is. And, I guess to us it is probably so obvious. Some of their ideas are very simple to implement and some of them are very big, so long-term, I see that as something we should consider incorporating.

Aren't you are already doing some things that would indicate your uniqueness?

EILEEN AND DAVID ARE GENEROUS AND SUPPORT MANY PROGRAMS INCLUDING DONATING BROWNIES TO OUR TROOPS.

Eileen Spitalny and David Kravetz (continued)

RIGHT: IN THE EARLY YEARS THE BROWNIES WERE CUT BY HAND.

BELOW: DAVID AT 3 YEARS OLD DESTINED TO BRING BROWNIES TO THE WORLD

To a certain extent, yes. But we want to be the best gift-giving business in the country and we're not there yet. With future technology, perhaps someday by tapping into our website you will be able to smell the flavors. We have to stay on the cutting-edge of technology because today you are paying $32 for a dozen premium brownies. In enhancing the buying experience, technology may cause you to pay $34 and perhaps more as we romance our product.

Do you worry about pricing?

Well, yeah. But we must keep an eye on quality and the other factors that make us the best. And quality does cost.

As far as the Fairytale side of things, is there a long-term vision for Fairytale? It is brownies right now and you seem to be focused on mail order, but is there something more in the offing, Eileen?

Brownies for now. We have much more opportunity and the market continues to expand as more and more people discover us.

Is your Fairytale Journey going to extend its vision, David?

As Eileen said, we are going to stick with brownies for now. So we configure ways to change appearance on sizes, like brownie sprites and the magic morsels, the small sizes, sugar-free flavors, and the like.

But you already have add-ons like special coffee and cocoa and ...

Yes, we also have cashews and chocolate-covered coffee beans called wish beans and jelly beans.

And, Eileen, you were saying?

We also have sugar-free and chocolate-dipped. We have talked about double baking, like brownie biscotti, and crumbling them up or making them into ice cream sandwiches. We are always in the think tank mode.

All this is a single product with multiple configurations. You are re-inventing your brownie but it is still

one product. Are you considering having an enhanced dessert menu with brownies as the central player and all the other things the customer might want to have with their brownies, Eileen?

We've talked about chocolate sauce. We have talked about making our own caramels because we have a caramel brownie. Yes, we have the coffee but that is not the thing that brings more profit or revenue. So for now it is about figuring out what is the right thing to focus on to bring us more business and maybe changing the messaging. We are currently trying to work on sampling in a more targeted, national sense, because sampling is what made us grow in the beginning. It was doing all those trade shows and farmers' markets. So now how do we do that so that we can reach business people in New York and L. A. and Chicago? We have tried some trade shows and we are doing chocolate shows, too.

David, from a strategy point what else?

One thing we learned, too, is to listen to what the customers want us to do. For many years, we just brainstormed new products and some of them were total tanks, just failures, because we just thought, hey, that would be really cool, let's do a tin. You know, we spent all this time and energy to do a tin which seemed really cool to us, but we still have tins.

Eileen, your comment?

It was cool, but those dang tins are still around! Got a lot of them!

So, David, what's best?

What we have that is really great is our business reply card, which is in every gift we send, on which the customers rate the quality of the product. If they give us a fair or poor rating, we send them free brownies. There is a space for comments and new product suggestions. We started tallying those about a year ago and it is amazing - there is some really good feedback.

Eileen, what kind of feedback?

What we realized was they are voting for their top flavor. What they say is the flavor they want is often not the flavor we would pick if we did it on our own without asking.

David?

Eileen Spitalny and David Kravetz (continued)

Sugar-free came to the top clearly, so we did that, and now blondie will probably be our new product for 2007. It is the Toll House cookie, so it's back to the cookie thing. It is a Toll House cookie made into a brownie.

Eileen, please elaborate.

Right, it is a cookie bar. So would a blondie to you have chocolate chips in it? Maybe, because that is the big thing with blondies. I vote chocolate chips, but some people may want non-chocolate, but David has an opinion here.

Maybe we will have two, with chocolate and without. The big thing we learned is to listen to what customers want to buy.

FAIRYTALE CONTINUES TO BE SELECTED FOR BUSINESS RECOGNITION AND EXCELLENCE.

I'm a loyal customer, and I keep trying to come up with different things for some people who are on my list each year. I've done the coffee, the beans, so I am running out of changes. I gave a lot of morsels last year.

Shirley, we will continue to listen to customers and evaluate our progress. We believe changes will be needed. It is a sense of timing and presently we are pursuing product reconfiguration.

Fair enough, so let's go in a different direction. I want to pursue more about the two of you. Would you describe for the reader the type of person you believe you are? Who wants to start first?

David does!

Okay. On my college entrance exam I had to describe myself with one adjective and I chose the word curious. That was because my childhood hero was Curious George and I have always been very curious. I am more of an engineering type. I think very logically. I have an appreciation for good design and bad design and, in addition to engineering, studied design in school. Bad design really upsets me and good design really pleases me, so with simple, everyday products I am really interested in how they are designed. That plays over into how we design our packaging and products. I think I am nice to a fault sometimes in business. I guess Eileen might have the same problem. We have been told we are too generous in giving away brownies, too generous in avoiding confrontation with clients and suppliers. Sometimes we're kind when maybe we should be a little more disciplinary to employees who aren't doing what we expect them to do.

I enjoy golf. I just took it up. I have never been much into sports, but I really like golf and it is my new hobby.

Eileen, your turn.

I would say I am laid back and easy-going. A little kooky is how I would describe myself. Pretty outgoing being in marketing. I would describe myself as very interested in what's new and the arts and kind of leading-edge types of things whether they're in food or arts or education. As far as my personality, I'm pretty easy to get along with. My husband and I actually have a relationship where we let each other develop our strengths and interests.

Then as far as business, both David and I are probably permissive to a fault. We try to encourage our employees to stand on their own and come up with ideas that help the business, do their own thinking, show independence and imagination. As a businessperson, I want them to work with me. I don't like standing and looking over the shoulders of people on our company team. I think I'm a good listener and patient. I expect a lot, so sometimes I get annoyed when things are not done well.

What Eileen is saying is that we both also consider ourselves perfectionists. We have appreciation for high quality and zero tolerance for low quality. And yeah, I still like to dissemble things, gadgets, systems. I have been trying to fix our water softener for about three months. I finally threw in the towel and called the service guy.

Eileen, please continue.

That is why our product is in the category that it is in. The thing that I would say about David, that he didn't say, is that he is very sensitive and I think he is very sensitive in a good way. We are both independent thinkers and have been from a very early age. We have known one another since kindergarten and have been good friends since third grade. David did independent animation projects on which I helped. Innovative and creative things have been happening in both our lives all these years.

Have you both always been the way you are describing today or did all of this evolve?

ABOVE: David's new hobby is golf. He's been known to manage not only growing business concerns but also was good at solving puzzles like the Rubik's cube.

FAR LEFT AND BELOW: Eileen's whimsical creativity was sparked by Smurfs and music as she grew up.

Eileen Spitalny and David Kravetz (continued)

It's my perception we have probably always been driven to succeed. We've become better, especially in taking care of problems. Eileen and I have definitely learned from our mistakes, but the core persons we are today are very much the same from when we were in high school.

Are you both natives?

Yes, we were both born and raised here in Phoenix. In fact, we grew up less than a mile from each other. And we are both left-handed and right-brained.

Would you each describe some of the highly personal principles that you have followed? You first, Eileen.

I would say honesty, open communications, self confidence. I'm trustworthy and believe in confidentiality.

David, how about you?

I would say I have high expectations for myself and a strong desire to achieve and be successful in business. I have strong expectations for my family and our employees as well.

What do you believe are your greatest strengths Eileen?

Okay, I would say my easy-going personality. People tell me I'm approachable and make them feel at ease. Adaptable, I guess. Whether I'm with the president of a company, a world-famous entertainer or a five-year-old kid, I adjust. I know I think outside the box and can come up with creative solutions and ideas.

Your turn, David.

I would say, probably, my ability to multi-task. Eileen is very good with that, too. We are just constantly being bombarded with so many different aspects of business and personal life and having to make decisions and trying to keep it all straight in our heads - all these different little mini-projects that are going on that we oversee. So I think we both have a great ability to be able to keep track of all these different things and keep them clear in our heads. I would say we both have a good sense of design, understanding what makes good design and bad design. It could be the design of a product or a package or the design of a system or a process that we use internally. We are good at figuring ways to make things easier and faster and more user-friendly. User-friendly is really important to me in all aspects of the business and my personal life. My project, when I was a senior in college, was a toilet paper dispenser for my class in general engineering/product design.

And he won best design for it.

Thanks, Eileen. The curriculum was basically like a mechanical engineering degree but they took out all the thermo science track and replaced it with human factors, design, ergonomics, and it really gave me an appreciation for user-friendliness. It was an awesome program at Stanford. It really took off and resulted in a school of design. I firmly believe user-friendliness should be universal and go across all products and systems. That is why I love Apple Computer. I am an Apple evangelist! They take really complex technology and make it easy for everyone. In fact, I worked for the Macintosh line at Comp USA when we were experimenting at night with my mom's brownie recipe.

I'm going to take you back to when you were kids. We touched on this a little bit, but your history together is unique and people need to know more about the two of you as kids. What was your greatest interest, David, when you were young?

Since, I liked to take things apart and try to put them back together, sometimes I got into trouble. I took apart our phone system at home and couldn't get it working again. I'm always curious about how everything works. I used to take my bicycle apart in my bedroom and have little pieces all over. My mom never stifled that. So, I'm an engineer from a very early age, pretty much into technology.

Eileen, what's your biggest interest?

My biggest interest (call it hobby) was dance. I took dance starting at about age four at the Phoenix School of Ballet. I pursued it all the way through college. I performed in college and when I returned to Phoenix, I joined a group called "Open Dance." The other interest was traveling. My mother worked for American Airlines so we were able to travel a lot. My interest was people's culture, food and art. We traveled all over the world taking advantage of Mom's flight benefits. In 8th grade we went to Japan, Hades, Samoa and England. I studied Spanish in college and spent one summer living in Mexico and one summer living in Spain. I think my true love is probably Latin culture just from growing up in Arizona.

As for dance, the Scottsdale Center for the Arts gets lots of our family money. We have donated for a long time and we go to lots of shows. My husband is now into modern dance as well. In grade school and high school we had a lot of fun and David and I had a lot of mutual friendships. We have stayed connected with many of these friends all these years.

ABOVE: EILEEN IN THE SHAKESPEARE AT SCHOOL PROGRAM IN EIGHTH GRADE.

BELOW: EILEEN PARTICIPATES IN A DANCE PERFORMANCE.

Eileen Spitalny and David Kravetz (continued)

CHILDHOOD FRIENDS EILEEN AND DAVID WENT TO CENTRAL HIGH SCHOOL SENIOR PROM IN 1984. DAVID'S GIRLFRIEND ATTENDED A DIFFERENT HIGH SCHOOL AND DIDN'T WANT TO GO TO CENTRAL'S PROM.

So, starting with you, Eileen, when you play today, what do you like to do?

I guess with the occasional day off, I would go to yoga class, play with my very young daughter, go to the spa and have a really good dinner.

Do you have other hobbies or sports?

Not really. If I had the time it would probably be a lot more yoga and dance.

Your turn, David.

Well, as I said, I took up golf three years ago and just love it. I'm getting my son involved, too. I find it totally consuming and challenging. As to that occasional day away from work, I like to be just a homebody - sitting on the couch watching TV is perfect. Or doing something on the computer I've been putting off - some project, working on a building project around the house or working with my kids.

Tell me more about your life-long friendship that is so intriguing.

We'd wanted to be business partners since high school. We always worked well together as kids and we both had a desire to own a business. David was a paper boy in grade school and started a small button-making business as well. He always had a project working and he always counted on me to work with him. We just seemed to influence one another in positive ways.

Sounds to me like a one in a million relationship. But there was the pause for education and you went your separate ways in that pursuit.

Well, there was no question we would be going to college. No question, no options. Our families raised us with that expectation and we both went to college and graduated. After college we both pursued careers, each in a separate sector of industry for about five years. David was pursuing his career at Proctor & Gamble in Cincinnati. He was due to go on an overseas assignment for two years and the assignment got cancelled at the last minute. David decided it was time to move on and start a business and he called me.

Yes, I called Eileen, then contacted Mandy whom I was dating and proposed. Changed my life in one fell swoop!

I had been working at the USC Entrepreneur Program and saw first-hand how an idea could become an exciting business. Besides, I had become frustrated with the office politics at my job so, when David called, I was eager and ready to move on.

Yeah, I was ready to move on and as it turned out so was Eileen. My grandfather was an entrepreneur, a butcher, and his first effort was a milk delivery business. And then he owned a small grocery in Jersey City. He was always involved in starting and building businesses. He was his own boss for his whole life, so I always aspired to follow in his footsteps. He was my early mentor and hero.

Eileen, you mentioned your mother, your respect for her and her independence. Do you consider her a mentor?

Yeah, in a way she taught me some special lessons. My parents are divorced. They waited to get divorced until I finished high school. I was enrolled to go to USC and I felt I should not leave my mom at this critical time. It was like, Dad and I were going to leave her at the same time. Mom said, "You don't know what you are talking about. You are not leaving me, you are going where you are supposed to go." I realized how tough and determined she was. She started a significant career after the divorce, achieving her own success. She made me realize the importance of standing on your own. She is special. I am proud of her. So yeah, she is my heroine.

Eileen, you and David founded Fairytale Brownies in 1992. You had a little money and each contributed about $7000. Not nearly enough, right?

We were 26 and the bank wasn't very impressed. We asked for $40,000 and our parents had to co-sign for us to get that loan. Pretty deflating!

It was hard from the beginning. We didn't pay ourselves for three years. So, right from the beginning, there were many signals and challenges that would make people who knew us just say, "why don't you chuck this?" We just kept thinking that we were learning. One more year. It was coming. We just were persistent. We had a picture of success in our minds. Things did get better every year, but the money from the sales increases had to go back into the business. We believed in investing in it for the long term. In the beginning, maybe we thought it was going to be a short-term success and we were going to make money, but once you start a business reality sets in and you know it will take time. Fact is, it took us five years to get back to the salaries we were making when we quit our jobs.

EILEEN (ABOVE) WITH HER DAD LAWRENCE AND (BELOW) WITH MOM SHARON.

Eileen Spitalny and David Kravetz (continued)

AN EARLY RETAIL SPACE OF 2,000 SQUARE FEET.

David, your comments?

Eileen and I got a lot of moral support from our families. Financial, too, at times to get us through the lean times. I remember one experience very early on when we started our bakery. We had this meager $40,000 bank loan and we bought our first oven sight unseen. It was rusted so bad you could see out the back of it. We were so inexperienced. My father offered to talk to the vendors. We accepted. We set up a meeting and my dad talked with the vendors without our being there. He was tough and told the vendors they had no right to treat us that way. We were green at that time and didn't know what to do. It was hard for us but we learned a lesson. I believe this was the only time either of our parents really intervened. That was our first year.

David didn't say no to his dad about the help. It was hard for David and me to concede - we made this mistake. It was our first year and we were so trusting. We looked at one another and said, like, Oh my God, we got this thing! We were smart enough not to hide the mistake, even though we were tempted to hide it and to live with the mistake. We also made other vendor mistakes that first year. Sometimes we got taken advantage of but we listened, we learned from the mistakes. We also learned to practice open communications, however painful. Sometimes I got demeaned and taken advantage of because I was female. Basically, we were young and inexperienced but we learned who to trust and who not to trust. We also learned there were honorable people we could do business with.

David you mentioned some other painful experiences that nearly sank your budding business.

It was our second year and our landlord at that time forced us to move. We thought our lease protected us, but it didn't! It was November of 1994. We were only in business a year. We were displaced right when we needed to be baking for the holiday season. It was at Thanksgiving and we ran out of brownies. It was the Thanksgiving weekend and the place was a mess. We managed to get up and running and got through somehow! We really had two bad years. In 1995 things really exploded. We ran out of brownies about two weeks before Christmas which was even worse than the previous year. Mike and I had to take care of everything because Kim and Eileen had all the shows scheduled like street fairs and other kinds of sales commitments. We were all tired. That was the year a special customer made Eileen cry. We had run out and we couldn't give her her order. She was a special friend of my mom, and she would not take no for an answer.

David and I had tried to solve the dilemma by establishing a limit on orders. We had a great season going for our third year and it became obvious we were going to run out. We actually had mail order sales we had to fill, so it was very touchy. We had to put up a sign. I think each person was allowed up to six.

Seemed that would be a great strategy. Brownie rations. Did it work out that way?

Well, not really. It was a painful experience. But looking back over the years, it does seem funny today.

David, let's go back to the "oven" trauma. Did both yours and Eileen's parents press for further involvement?

Eileen's mom has been 100 percent supportive, never gives advice. Happy as can be to let us do whatever we believe is necessary and want it. My parents have been more opinionated and do tell us what they think we ought to do when they don't agree. We have listened to their advice and then weighed it against our knowledge of the industry.

Eileen, your take on this?

Both our moms have helped us work here as we grew in the early years, but not in the last five years. They were here mostly in the first five to seven years during the brisk holiday activities. We always keep in mind Fairytale Brownies were evolved from David's mother's recipe. David's mom, Nancy, was our gift basket maker and my mom answered the phone and handled Vincent's Farmers Market every Saturday.

Are there other people that you would call mentors or people influential in your lives or business, David?

Yes, our advisory board now. They are a big help.

In the beginning, we relied on Alan Bank, Bill Crookston and Ken Royer. Bill is still on our advisory board.

Alan Bank is from Tupelo, Mississippi, and a family friend of David's. He owned a mattress spring manufacturing company and he taught us from day one to think about ourselves as a big company. He said we were just like GM. Same concepts in business apply to us all - we listened to that and we have always tried to be one step ahead and operate and market ourselves as if we were a $100 million dollar company when we were still trying to reach our first million.

Bill Crookston was a professor of mine at the University of Southern California. Bill really coached David and me

THIS IS THE FIRST DAY THAT FAIRYTALE BROWNIES WERE SOLD TO THE PUBLIC.

Eileen Spitalny and David Kravetz (continued)

Eileen and David were awarded Arizona Retail Entrepreneurs of the Year by Ernst & Young in 2002.

that being entrepreneurs and business owners is really about becoming leaders and visionaries for our employees. Also, he taught us to be a unified front when "in front of the troops," as he would say. Employees do not want to see their employers deciding/discussing in front of them. He taught us how to listen, nurture and let our employees do their thing and grow. As we mentioned earlier, don't stand over shoulders or micromanage. We want our people to learn on their own and to feel empowered.

Another wonderful advisor is Ken Royer. Originally from Sheboygan, Wisconsin, he owned a very large gouda manufacturing plant and then a dry mix plant. He really helped us get our food safety programs in order as well as the quality and consistency expectations of our brownie. We created brownie standards for each flavor (visual and taste) and vendor requirements for everything from temperature of egg and butter deliveries to pallet standards.

And there was Lou Gibman. He was my dad's CPA. He would only meet us in his backyard on his porch. Anyway, he gave us great advice after we got our bank loan.

We had found a little A-frame and were going to move into it and convert it. He got us to abort at the last minute with his famous line, "Do you want to be in the construction business or do you want to be in the brownie business?" That stopped us from a really big mistake. That A-frame would have been a disaster. We found instead an old restaurant that needed nothing.

It is good of both of you to remember these very special people. I believe in giving credit where it is due. There are people in our lives and business without whom we would not enjoy the success and position we have today.

What size is your advisory board, David?

We have four members plus our consultant, Dr. Richard Gooding. Our board was at one time composed of up to eight people. It was just too big to serve our needs. For ten years we had a volunteer advisory board and a number of consultants before arriving at what we have now. Some were helpful, some were not. The good advisors we have now have helped us to make some really tough decisions. This board and its advice does influence our philosophy.

Could you elaborate a little on the areas of bad advice from those very early advisors whose recommendations were not helpful?

Yeah. We realized early on that we could not prosper on street fairs and the like. The conclusion we reached was that direct mail would get us a broader market. What we experienced, as we morphed into a pure mail order company, was that the mailing list kept growing and growing and we just kept mailing our catalog to the whole list all the time. There was never any filtering. After a while, we knew that direct mail was a science and we needed help.

It got so big we were wasting money with people who would never buy. So we tried to do it ourselves for a while where we just kind of chose what we thought should be the right list. That's fine to a certain point, but you are just spending a lot of money in printing and postage. So we hired our first consultant, Jim Pageant. He helped us by suggesting we mail more at the holidays and less at other times. He called it shooting fish when they are in the barrel. So he helped us a little bit. Then we kind of outgrew his advice and went to another consultant who helped us get more into prospecting and hitting our true buyers. But we soon overextended ourselves. Applying his broad template was too general for our business. We should have been digging deeper into where the opportunities were, narrowing our focus, not broadening it at that point.

You're talking about selectivity, Eileen.

Yeah. We had some opportunity as far as prospecting to do it, say with our gift recipients and inquiries versus buying more and more lists that weren't performing. We had gotten to the point where the more we mailed, the more we lost. When the return drops below your break-even point, there is no profit. We did an analysis after the 2001-2002 season and found we could have mailed 400,000 fewer catalogs and made $200,000 more in profit. Some of our advisory board members at that time just didn't get it, either. So we looked for board members who understood the direct mail side of marketing in the gift foods business.

> *Do your homework and pick the right people.*

So your advice to others is what?

You have to do your homework and pick the right people. That goes for consultants as well as the board. Some consultants had cited Omaha Steaks as a template. They seem to have mailed and talked to every single person in the U.S. We just knew their methods would not help us. We are different and have figured out the right methods for our unusual product.

How have you compensated your board members, David?

Eileen Spitalny and David Kravetz (continued)

Originally, we just gave them free brownies! Then after a few years we paid them. But none of them are doing it just for the money. They are serving as advisors because they care about us and our success.

You've had these problems associated with the building of your business. How about some great milestones that excited you, Eileen.

When we hit a million in sales. Everyone sat around and watched the computer switch to a million. What a thrill! And then having the food writer at the New York Times publish a super review and yes, being on the Food Network on national TV.

David, what milestone was your turn-on?

I would have to say the $40,000 order from Double Click in the 2004 holiday season. It really got us pumped up! Double Click is an on-line advertising company and they ordered for 500 client gift recipients. What a wonderful thrill!

Let's talk about another key element to the growth and success of your business, your employees. You mentioned earlier that staffing was one of the difficulties you had initially. David?

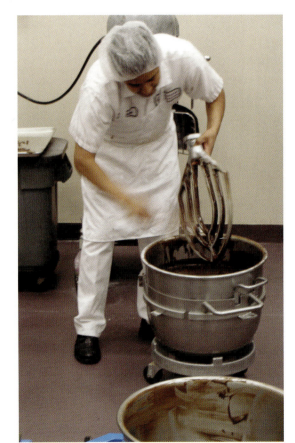

Hiring and training people was something we were not very experienced in. It is hard when your company cannot function without special people and it's complicated when you are inventing a business and know you have to build the business with people and it all has to happen at once or everything can come to a halt. We hired people. We trained the best we knew how. We are all human, and I'm sure we had some people too long; we just thought they will learn this business as time goes on or at least get better. Some did but most didn't. We had to learn right along with them. We know now that you can't rehab people from a personality standpoint. Frankly, we couldn't afford to pay the people we really needed. Somehow, we got through. Now we are able to hire people to start with who have the experience we need. And now we know what we need to teach them. I guess we have also learned you can't find people with all the skills, but they must be willing to learn and change if need be.

What kinds of training do you require? And, is it in-house or external? Eileen?

Our in-house training includes shadow training with different teams and more extensive special training by members of their own team. We offer tuition reimbursement to encourage team members to take outside classes, as well.

Sometimes it is a trade show. Good trade shows are quite educational. You meet a lot of people and can get experience talking with them. There are always great ideas exchanged at trade shows. At least one great idea comes out of each show.

David, what kinds of seminars do you encourage?

Negotiations seminars are good, where all team members are involved. Some we schedule in November. Our comptroller has to do continuing education so that she can get her CPA renewed every year. In her field it's been food safety. Our team leaders all go to specialized seminars. The baking team and the shipping leaders are going to Las Vegas this time to a packaging and food equipment show with seminars. It's these types of outside programs we send them to.

What other kinds of education do you encourage?

Well, all ongoing education relates to the job here. It could be an Excel class or online marketing or operations.

I'm pleased with your comment. In my experience you hire good people with a can-do attitude. Then you teach them to do your work, your way. Avoid at all cost those who come with "baggage" from a previous job. How many people do you have on staff?

Roughly around 35 year-round and it grows to about 80 seasonally.

What special ways do you involve your employees in growing the business? Do you have special incentives, Eileen?

We actively seek suggestions and serious input from team members. We have weekly team meetings, monthly team leader meetings and monthly all-staff meetings. We also conduct an annual strategic planning retreat after the big holiday season in February. We offer an incentive to team members who refer another new hire. We have an open-door management style.

Do you encourage your teams to be entrepreneurial?

THE NEW RETAIL CENTER IS SO ATTRACTIVE AND SHOWS THE DEPTH OF BRANDED OFFERINGS.

EILEEN SPITALNY AND DAVID KRAVETZ (CONTINUED)

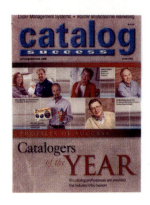

Yes. We offer an annual cash bonus plan based on the company's operating profit. This makes them think more like business owners.

You have an extraordinary ability to get great press, media and special recognition. Eileen, give us some insights on how you do this.

GOOD BROWNIES!

More than that, I open the newspapers from local to national and the Wall Street Journal and there you are. Do you have a purposeful plan? Do you seek out special opportunities?

Yes, we do, purposely. We first got publicity in '95 by sending a box of brownies to a food editor with a press release that talked about the story of David and me. I was in sales before and learned a lot of it by volunteering. I was on the PR committee for the very first Sunday on Central in Phoenix and so I learned a lot about writing press releases. And David had a family member who gave us a little advice, too. She said you always call and get a special name to contact. And so it took some time, but it was all done purposefully. We know we are very seasonal, so now we do PR more heavily at the time leading up to holidays, because this is the time of year that people tend to be looking in magazines and papers for a gift ideas. It is relationship building.

Your comments, David. Eileen is really an extrovert and she likes to constantly meet people and it's always the big joke that Eileen knows everybody in town. And she has an incredible memory for names and faces.

And David knows, the brownies help out. We are just lucky we have a great product and our packaging is eye-catching. So to get in the New York Times, it wasn't me that was there. The brownies could stand on their own and did.

I remember many instances of people close to us criticizing Eileen's ideas about PR. They were concepts that didn't come to fruition for maybe six

or nine months or a year later. At the time, it did seem to some like a waste of money or energy to be doing whatever she was doing, and then all of a sudden one day it pays off. So many people are, you know, short-sighted.

Eileen, you know it takes time and smart, hard work. Give us some of your insights.

Well, you have to have credibility. People don't want to write or talk about something they are not sure about, either. They are going to lend their names to our product only when they sample our brownies. Then they're hooked. The food network is pervasive and it has helped. Then you hit the Internet. People have gotten to know us through our website. Our quality. We are a small intellectually-honorable company with a great message that resonates with the marketplace.

You are talking about word-of-mouth advertising – the best – and a technique that worked for me throughout my career.

You bet. We love word-of-mouth, especially since it has morphed into other forms of PR and free advertising. Every recipient of our brownies is a potential spokesperson. I guess it's been called guerrilla marketing. We do have some new challenges since 9/11. You can't send food to food editors. Many don't eat what they get anymore. But still we do get our product out.

David said in the very beginning that we were going to have to give away a lot of brownies to be successful. And so we have!

You have to get brownies into peoples' hands and into mouths, right?

Exactly. It's all about sampling and we do it in a more sophisticated way. It costs more money and product because we have to do more personal involvements.

But it is an investment, not a cost, Eileen. You do a lot of more expensive in-kind, right?

Now that we are bigger we can do these product investments, like the 2005 Emmys which cost $5,000 in special product and packaging and my personal attendance. Ten years ago they would not have called us. This is a very select audience and it

Eileen Spitalny and David Kravetz (continued)

was like a dream come true. We really were able to reach the stars!

You were able to really do a lot at that venue?

Right. They let us include our catalogs with a note that said, "If you enjoy these brownies call me personally and I will send you a box for your birthday, the holidays and Valentines Day." It is signed by me and it has our phone number. A little kooky, maybe, but it could start a valuable relationship, get us more exposure.

Isn't that a kind of "Pandora's Box" for you?

Exactly, but it is what we believed could open the celebrity market phase big time. Who knows? We'll see.

We now include our catalog in all gift packets sent by our clients. We are now getting increasing numbers of orders from people who have received brownies as a gift.

I am aware of that, Eileen. My sister-in-law, a successful real estate broker in California, is using your brownies as client gifts. Aside from your present word-of-mouth, do you plan other types of advertising or promotions?

Not at present. We have wonderful feedback and results from the programs already in motion. But we are always seeking ideas to help us in the future.

FAIRYTALE HELPS KABOOM IN THEIR MISSION OF PROVIDING SAFE AND HEALTHY SPACE FOR KIDS TO PLAY AND SOCIALIZE.

Eileen, let's look at another of the relationships you and David hold special. These would be your community involvement and other special charitable activities.

When we started in business we began to be approached by many organizations. We donated here and there and realized we couldn't say yes to every one. To administer a broad program just wasn't possible. Locally we chose Waste Not and St. Vincent De Paul. We researched and chose a national organization because our customers were all over the U.S. The organization is KABOOM. It is creative and innovative, so we liked what they do. KABOOM is a non-profit whose goal is for every child in America to have a safe and healthy space to play and socialize within walking distance of where they live. We give them money and product. We've been involved since 2002. It is all about playgrounds. You know that David and I met originally on the playground. Many playgrounds have become unsafe in some areas and schools have cut recess in many places. KABOOM works to create safe playgrounds and skate parks. Children must have safe places to play and socialize.

Many schools are being built without playgrounds. KABOOM is dedicated to filling that gap.

They have an office in Washington, D.C. and Atlanta. Home Depot is its major funding sponsor. Home Depot's founder grew up in an orphanage. Some of our employees also have participated with us in helping to build a playground for the Foundation For Blind Children.

We donate thousands of pounds of brownie edges to local food banks. We donate finished product to various groups and charities, including The Spirit of Enterprise Center at ASU. We have responded to the Katrina disaster and other disasters, as well as local needs.

We give of our time by speaking to classes at local schools, colleges and events that focus on starting a business. We also meet with prospective business owners who contact us, one-on-one, to help them with problems and issues. We also donate to our former grade school.

David and I also support and belong to some significant business organizations dedicated to the support of entrepreneurship and small business. For me it is EO, the Executive Entrepreneur Organization. David is a member of the Advisory Board for the National Conference on Operations and Fulfillment, the largest conference dedicated to mail order operations.

I am also involved with Les Dames D'E Coffier, a national non-profit group of women business owners in the food industry. I also volunteer my time with Free Arts teaching homeless children basic nutrition and cooking skills. Many of our employees are involved in their local schools, churches or synagogues.

Would you share some selected advice and counsel for all who are reading your story and contemplating a business of their own, Eileen?

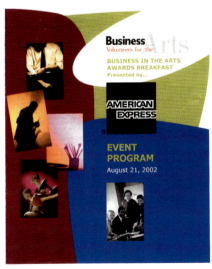

When you create a company, be sure to consider that you may start as a doer, a worker, but for success you will have to transition from worker to leader. David always makes the point that you leap from doer to leader and must understand you do both. Also, you may love what you do and your business, but as a leader you won't end up doing what you love every day. You are really a leader of people, functions and processes. Know how and when to switch.

David, your special advice?

Well, be careful who you pick to advise you. Do your homework and don't choose only friends, because you need objectivity. Also, don't plan on getting rich quick. One of the most compelling reasons people start a business is to make money or ensure they have work. Be aware it takes time, often five or more years. Plan on how you will make it. Have some source of personal resources to tide you over.

Eileen Spitalny and David Kravetz (continued)

Ask a lot of questions of people who are knowledgeable. There is so much free advice from naysayers as well as self-styled experts. On the other hand, don't set yourself up as a know-it-all. Accept you don't know everything, even if you are well-versed in the business as a worker. Listen and learn from others with experience.

Eileen, what else?

You must write a business plan. The time is gone when you can fly by your wits, personality and seat of the pants. Seek legal advice. You have to protect yourself. You need structure that is legal. Research protection of trademarks. Research your name. You will need to own it as you grow. You have to be in a position to protect your intellectual property.

Would you be agreeable to extending an invitation for people interested and wanting to ask questions to make contact with you?

Without a doubt we love helping others. They should take a look at our web site and then e-mail us with any questions they have. It could be helpful to us, too. When we talk to people who are new, they bring up questions we might never have thought of.

Let's talk about family. You both have kids. Eileen?

I have a little girl four years old.

David?

I've two children. A boy 10 years old and a girl 12 years old. My daughter wants to be a graphic designer. She is an artist. My son is much like me.

Phoenix Mayor Gordon and other city council officials attended the grand opening.

Let's talk about legacy. If one of you should disappear, the other could prevail, right?

Of course!

If something happened to both of you at once, do you have provisions for the continuity of your business?

If both of us died, our spouses would own the business. Neither one wants to manage it. They would have to turn to employees, and I think there are some key people who could rise to the challenge. Day to day they would be fine, but eventually someone with vision and leadership would have to be hired or rise from the ranks to ensure a future. We have initiated measures to ensure we seldom travel together.

Does that extend to your teams?

Sometimes in the past we have had them together on an airplane. Scheduling is a nightmare, but more recently we have tried not to schedule groups of employees to travel together. We are aware of some companies that have been literally wiped out when all their executive staffs died in crashes.

You have talked about landlord problems over the years. Were these incidents what triggered the idea of owning your own building, Eileen?

No.

David?

It is a natural progression. We got some good advice and some negative reactions. But all along in our thinking was to have our own building, customized to our needs.

Eileen?

We have had ongoing discussions together and with the board. It became a necessity to have more space and at that juncture we decided to own rather than lease. What we have is a personal investment, not a corporate one. It is a separate company. It is Demm Holdings, short for David, Eileen, Mike, my husband, and Mandy, David's wife. We are going to have a tenant until we need the extra space. The building is 36,000 square feet. We have 25,000 and the tenant has 11,000.

Do you consider your business a family business?

Yes, we do. We've been such close friends our entire lives and consider each of our families "family." We would be thrilled to have our children take over the business one day.

ON SATURDAY, MARCH 3, 2007, THE GROUNDS WERE BUZZING WITH PEOPLE OF ALL AGES TO CELEBRATE THE OPENING OF THE NEW FACILITY. FESTIVITIES INCLUDED A ROCK CLIMBING WALL, JEWELRY BOOTH, ICE CREAM STAND WITH SPECIAL FAIRYTALE BROWNIE FLAVORS MADE BY COLD STONE CREAMERY AND ENOUGH FOOD TO FEED EVERYONE.

ELECTRIC - eclectic

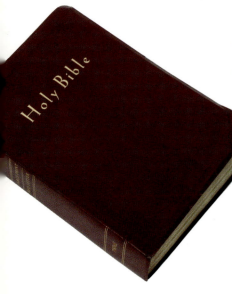

These words describe this immigrant citizen from Nigeria. His electric charisma lights up a room, captivating those present as he speaks of his businesses, philosophy, family, life goals and wide-ranging interests. His zest for life and regard for people genuinely sweep his listener along exuberantly. As our interview moved along, his manner was genuine, warm and open. He had dancing eyes, an infectious smile and an easy, receptive approach to often probing questions.

My prior research left no question that Ogbonna Abarikwu (pronounced O-bun-ah A-bear-e-coo) belonged in my select list of intriguing successful small business leaders. My experience during our interview was much more gratifying than I expected. It was full of lessons that can help readers who may be eager to create their own businesses, yet hesitant and fearsome of the risks they might encounter.

Ogbonna, a man of small physical stature, with a commanding poised, presence and a giant appetite for life and his work, presented me with a great range of contradictions.

He is eclectic with wide-ranging interests in skiing, golf, antique cars, theater, the arts and music and enterprises and businesses totally unrelated to each other on the surface. Some already operating and growing. A secondary group of businesses in the planning stage and others on his future wish list.

Also attractively religious, he spoke eloquently of his faith as taught and practiced by his parents. He had a solid, self-reliant manner; he was sure of his skills and knowledge. Ogbonna is a decision-maker without fear of risk - very much an engineer who sweated out all the details before tackling each challenging job opportunity.

Ogbonna involves his staff in all the processes with obvious respect for them, that is returned in kind. And, he is proud of his family with extensive plans for their education.

His is a story of striving to live the life that immigrants come to America to obtain. The difference with Ogbonna is he is determined to give to get, to share his fortunes with his employee family, his community, his family back in Nigeria and with the younger people whose education he wishes to contribute to. He strives to earn the rights he has struggled to obtain. Ogbonna is a unique type of entrepreneur who believes it is his obligation to help build his adopted country's future and protect its vital environment.

Much of Ogbonna's story you will read are in his own words. He will share his thoughts on family, faith, childhood, work, play, country and future.

Before getting to know today's Ogbonna through his work ethic, accomplishments, personal philosophy and his community activities I explored his early formative years.

I led into the past by asking Ogbonna to describe the person he believes he is today.

Okay, I believe I am, well truthfully the first thing that comes to my mind is humble. I think I was raised that way. My dad was an extremely humble individual and I think in watching him and in growing up around him, I just couldn't help but inherit that. I am an extremely hard-working person. I don't want to use the word workaholic because it has a negative connotation to it sometimes, but I am a doer. Words are wonderful, I like words, but prefer actions. When I do, I completely believe that I like to give it my all, I don't like to settle for less. That attitude has served me very well. But when I was going to school and when I graduated and first went into a professional job position here in America, the combination of determination to give the best at every opportunity significantly resulted in some of the opportunities that I was given. So I do believe and I hope I am seen as a humble person and one who really works hard. I want to always provide a solution of problems. I don't dwell on results once I get there. It may frustrate some people because while they want to pop the champagne and celebrate, I am ready to go to the next task. I love my family so very dearly. I really believe

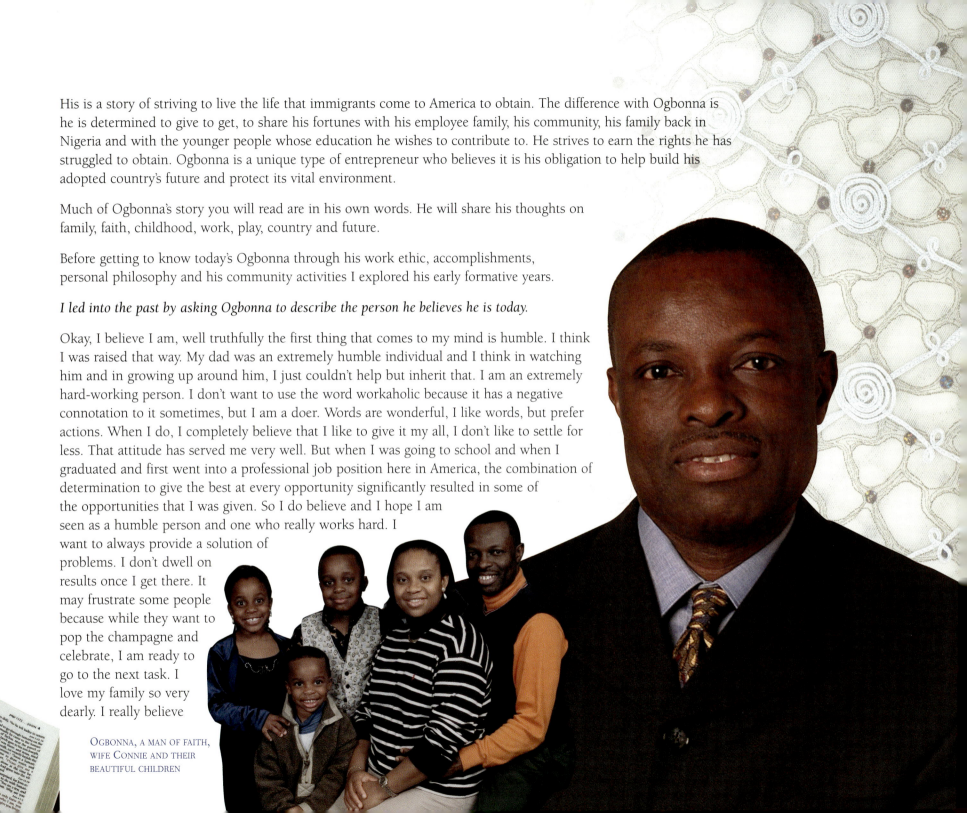

OGBONNA, A MAN OF FAITH, WIFE CONNIE AND THEIR BEAUTIFUL CHILDREN

Ogbonna Abarikwu (continued)

BELIEVING A MAN IS MEASURED BY THE EVIDENCE PRODUCED BY HIS CHILDREN, OGBONNA ADMITS HIS DELIGHT AND AMAZEMENT IN RECEIVING THE FATHER OF THE YEAR AWARD IN 2005. FAMILY IS IMPORTANT AND CONTINUES TO MAKE HIS HEART SMILE.

that when it is all said and done that is where I really will decide for myself if I have succeeded or failed. It is not maybe succeeding as a business person and making money or having buildings all over the place or having a fast food restaurant. Those things are icing on the cake. I think my true judgment of me will come when my kids are 20, 22, 26, and I see how they fold into society. What is their relationship? What have I taught them to give the greater society? What is my relationship with them? What have

A decision maker without fear of risk, he possesses a strong sense of balance.

they learned from me? And I say that because that's why I believe my dad was a great man. I can look back at the kids that he raised. You know, it is not the money, but it's the caliber of people that they have turned out to be. I don't know that there is one direct answer. And maybe, I hope I am not rambling, but these are some of the ways that I would like to qualify who I am.

In the interest of getting a better assessment of Ogbonna, I asked, Have you always been that kind of person? Or, did that person evolve? How did he evolve? Was it a process of your interaction with people you respected? Your father? Mother? Other family members?

I think without a doubt, the person I am evolved. When I was a teenager and going through high school, my life was not what I have become. And, I hope that 10 to 20 years from now, I continue to evolve for the better. I have been shaped by so many different events and people. Certainly I do believe that the core individual was established back when I was a kid under the guidance of my parents. I was watching them and the way they did things and the way they interacted with people and their allegiance to the work that was before them. The faith they had. But truthfully, my faith was and still is really my anchor. As a teenager, I really didn't appreciate or recognize these values. When I grew older and started confronting some of the things that adults confront, I reached back into that bag and began to grab some of those lessons I was not aware I had learned. In fact, I am amazed that when I talk to my children today, I hear my father talking and I just think, oh my, did I just say that? So yes, the straight answer to the question is that the person I am evolved. Some of that evolution came with the experiences with my family. Obviously, as you move up in your profession and are given more responsibility, there is greater expectation. You have to rise to the occasion. When you marry, that is a different thing. And then when you have kids, well, you have to adjust to that.

As an individual and with my company, we are always reaching out to make things better. I was born in Nigeria and came to the United States in 1980. My family did not emigrate. I came here for my university education. All I had was my family values, my faith and the confidence I could build a better life and take the lessons learned here back to Nigeria to build a better country there. I was 19 and an idealist.

When I arrived at Ogbonna's business location, I was early. That gave me the opportunity to look around the site before going in. I was greeted by a highly professional woman and taken to his office. Everything about the external and internal environment indicated a perfectionist touch. Great attention to detail and a rich flair for color, balance, decoration and content. He obviously pays attention to a visitor's first impressions. With this all in mind I pursued further with Ogbonna to learn more about the life and conditions that shaped this man, more about his parents, family and childhood in Nigeria. In his words:

My parents were wonderful people who taught me respect for others, love of the Bible and God. The Bible guides my principles as it did theirs. Well, the truth is that it has guided my whole life as well. It (the Bible) keeps me on the ethical path in all I do. There is absolutely no circumstance that I have confronted in my adult life, that I couldn't relate back to the Bible and it's very specific to me how to deal with whatever that situation might be. Now, do I always obey? No. By no stretch of the imagination. But I know enough to admit that the times that I haven't, there have been repercussions. I know exactly why things went wrong and it is my fault and not to point the finger somewhere else. So I think that the first thing is to be said about how human beings to a great extent need to custom their lives, it should be couched around the word of God.

My parents? Well, I lost my Mom when I was a small child. I lost my Dad in 2001.

There are two key "beings" in my life. Christ is the most important. While I know there are some people who don't like to mix religion with anything, I think it's key. I have studied the Bible and the way He lived his life. I am trying to model my life

ABOVE: IN NIGERIA HE WAS GIVEN THE TITLE "UGONWANNE" MEANING THE PRIDE OF HIS PEOPLE.

LEFT: PICTURED WITH HIS SIBLINGS TWO YEARS AFTER HIS MOTHER DIED. FROM LEFT TO RIGHT - OGBONNA, ULOMA, ODY THE OLDEST SISTER AND NANNY, NANCY, AND CHUKS.

INNOVATORS - CHANGEMAKERS PAGE 133

Ogbonna Abarikwu (continued)

after him. Then, my daddy, I refer to him a lot. He was incredible. He did some incredible things. I always knew he was a great man, but nothing made me realize it as much as I did while attending his funeral and seeing all of the people. He was loved and admired by so many for his fairness, honesty, respectfulness for all things, and most of all, he was humble. He passed these lessons on to my siblings and me. He was the one that led us to Christ. Yes, after God, I hold my father next.

Ogbonna, you talk with such reverance about your early teaching and the importance of your father in your life. Does this reflect on your relationship with your children?

I look at my littlest child and I see a lot of me when I was a kid. He loves to play. I loved to play. I am fairly blessed. Perhaps there were two of me. One endowed to learn quickly and one who just wanted to play. I could read very quickly and digest it. That gave me a lot more time to play. So I did. I still love to play. Then when I entered high school many things changed. I became involved in a wide spectrum of activities outside my studies. The arts, debating. I was the lead debater for my high school team, the first kid in my high school admitted into the Drama Society - indeed the youngest ever. A lot of my family back in Nigeria still think I should have been an attorney. In all these special activities my greatest interest was in the management part. In the drama group I preferred being a stage manager. All these interests are still with me.

ABOVE: HE WAS A MEMBER OF THE SCHOOL DRAMATIC SOCIETY AT THE SECONDARY BOARDING SCHOOL, METHODIST COLLEGE. OGBONNA IS SECOND FROM THE RIGHT.

RIGHT: OGBONNA'S GRADUATION FROM THE UNIVERSITY OF COLORADO.

Ogbonna, you arrived here in 1980. Why did you pick the United States to attend college?

I came here to attend university in Colorado because my oldest brother was in school at Colorado State and would be near me. I actually came to go to medical school. That was really my admission coming to this country. But when I got here, after two years, I very quickly realized I could not do it for two reasons. One was that it took too much time. Medical school in my country was a six-year program and you were done. Over here it is like nine years or something like that, twelve years in some instances. So when they broke all that down for me, I just didn't think I had the time. But truthfully that wasn't the key thing. The key reason was being afraid of cadavers. For some reason I never knew or it never dawned on me that you have to deal with the dead. The University of Colorado has a really neat program where the pre-med students, once they get into a second year are matched with students who are ahead in med school. They take you on tours. So we had to go on a tour to the morgue. When they explained all that, that was the day I knew medicine was not for me. I didn't take the tour. And to make the transition from med school to engineering was just automatic. We have a lot of engineers in the family so that was a natural digression.

It is obvious that Ogbonna's early upbringing in a dynamic family structure prepared him for stepping into the life of America. He brought with him family values of faith and honor. Couple this with his insatiable drive to learn and excel, confidence in self, abundance of ideas and you have the making of an entrepreneur.

My first experience with Ogbonna was in October of 2004. The occasion was at the Spirit of Enterprise Awards sponsored by the Center for the Advancement of Small Business at the W. P. Carey School of Business, Arizona State University. He received the Emerging Entrepreneur Award. His company is CK Engineering, which he founded January 1, 1995. I thought his presentation of thanks was genuine and winsome. His story was unique and special in the true sense of an immigrant pioneer successfully over coming all the usual problems of starting and building a business. Tough for anyone, but more so for a small minority business in the highly competitive civil engineering arena.

"I believe that every client deserves nothing but the best professional and technical commitment possible on any project awarded."

Ogbonna, your success is a testment to your personal attitude, philosophy and driving work ethic. What do you want others to remember about your company?

What I want a client to most remember upon hearing the name CK Engineering is they are responsible, quality and creative. When people remember me, I want them to be able to say, "integrity." I believe that what makes us different from our competitors is our fortitude, to "think outside the box" and our insistence on staying at the cutting-edge of technology. We use only the most up-to-date software, tools and equipment so that we can produce the highest quality product for a fair price. CK Engineering also strives to empower the whole team and that in turn produces a "go get it" attitude. I find this combination brings added value to each and every project. We are also a fun place to work!

I started CK Engineering not just because I love engineering, but because I believe that every client deserves nothing but the best professional and technical commitment possible on any project awarded. I feel the desire to make profit should never interfere with the desire to produce the highest quality product. I also wanted to give something of value and quality to the community. Through CK I can leave my mark on the community with pride and dignity.

Ogbonna Abarikwu (continued)

I don't think any one person influenced my decision. I believe that my strong passion for doing exceptional engineering, the desire to give to the community and society in general, and to leave a legacy for my children inspired me. I also recognized that with a stalwart working environment, built on integrity, the people who I hired to work in my office would grow, and as they succeeded the business would succeed realizing my vision and become an inspiration to others.

We faced - and still do - many challenges. Our biggest and most difficult challenge was to be taken seriously as a small minority business. We worked through and overcame this challenge by making sure that only top quality work left the office that it was above reproach and reliable. Our customers could always count on us. The second major challenge we faced was convincing my staff that I could do anything I set my mind on, that my vision was real and that if we worked together we could all realize a life's dream. People in general don't have patience, but through example and perseverance I proved good things can come to those who wait. My staff now believes and we all work together building the vision brick by brick. Major challenge number three was winning a "prime" project. We've done it now, but it was a long slow process. Along the way it became evident that a name doesn't mean a thing, however the people in the process do. Cultivating relationships through diligence, responsiveness, responsibility and quality, while remaining humble, makes the difference. It's all about the people.

"I might have stood still for a while, but have never had a failure."

What failures or setbacks taught you the most?

I have no answer for your question. I feel that I haven't had a failure or major setback. I might have stood still for a while, but have never had a failure.

That reply best reflects the indomitable spirit, optimism and attitude that has sustained Ogbonna and inspired his staff. Why did you come to Colorado to pursue your college education and why didn't you return to Nigeria?

At the time I came I knew my siblings came here, studied and got educations and would go home to Nigeria to live and work. I came and studied and then decided I didn't want to return to Nigeria. I guess I wanted to go back to Nigeria, but not immediately because again, I was looking at what was going on in Nigeria with engineers and the work they did and I was trying to reconcile the difference in what engineers did here and what engineers did there. And for some reason I said to myself, well, maybe the reason things are not working so well is because it was

Ogbonna shown in a ceremonial robe that represents a titled person in Ibo Land, Nigeria.

more the blind leading the blind. People get an engineering degree but that doesn't necessarily make you an engineer. So they go home and they are put in a position of authority to make decisions that they don't understand. There is no mentor or training on the job in Nigeria to really learn the art of engineering. I didn't want to practice that kind of engineering. I wanted to graduate and get a job as an engineer, train from the ground up, really understand the rudiments of engineering and become a top-quality engineer and then go back to teach others. Well, it is 25 years later and I am here to stay and the United States is my country.

I then took our discussion back to more recent possible influences on his life and career. Are there others who now have impact on our life?

Well, yes, a couple of individuals that mean so much to me. Mahatma Gandhi is one whose philosophy and life influences me. I want to be like him in some ways, even though we are different individuals. Looking back he initially practiced law in South Africa. He seemed to me to be one of those types of people who had a sense of who he wanted to be and he wasn't going to be denied. And he went after it with everything he had, even when a lot of people probably didn't quite understand where he was going. He tried real hard to explain it. And whether others understood it or not, it wasn't going to stop him from trying anyway. He was a selfless person. He gave in the most phenomenal way. He could have lived a life of privilege but chose to live a humble common life that was dedicated to the people. His wife chose to live that vision with him. So I draw from him humility. I draw from him a great sense of determination to accomplish and not be denied.

The other person is The Gipper, Ronald Reagan. Five years after my arrival here, I realized I wanted to stay and learn about this society. I paid attention to everything that was happening, including politics. I focused on Ronald Reagan. For starters, he came from very humble beginnings and made a lot of sense to me. I wanted to live in the

ABOVE: OGBONNA'S FATHER, HERBERT, SHOWN HERE WITH HIS GRANDMOTHER (CENTER) CATHERINE AND HIS DAD'S BEST FRIEND.

Ogbonna Abarikwu (continued)

Ogbonna married Connie in June 1990. Connie graduated from medical school at University of Colorado in 1991.

kind of country where a person like Mr. Reagan could rise from humble beginnings to become its President. There were people who did not give him the credit for the special way he helped our nation, just because he had been an actor in Hollywood - a cowboy. He was a man who was a victim of their prejudice. He had courage. I appreciated that. The first time he ran for President, he was defeated. He was no quitter. He was determined and sure of his own value. He believed in the American people and won the nomination and the presidency the second time he tried. Like other Americans I admired his persistence and honest set of values. He gave me a sense of stability and I took comfort in the fact that he was our President.

I sensed there was more to Ogbonna's life changing decision to stay here in the United States while most of those dear to him were in Nigeria so I asked him. Tell me the one most defining moment in your personal life?

Hmm. Well, I don't think I need to think too hard to answer that one because I am forever cognizant of what that has been for me. And that is the day that I was invited to a birthday party. This was in Denver, Colorado. And I had a girlfriend with me to attend this party. This party was in the basement of a friend's home. We happened to come a little late and as we were walking down the stairs to the basement, I saw immediately in standing by one of the walls, two gentleman and a girl. I very quickly recognized all three of them including the girl. And I don't know what it was in me that just said to me, that is the girl you are going to marry. Even though I had a girlfriend with me. I walked straight up to her and I said you've been a bad girl. Where have you been? I haven't seen you in a long time. And she said, "Oh, I have been in school and I came back. I just finished school and I just came back." I said, "Really. Why have you stayed out of touch?" Laying a kind of a guilt trip on this person. And she tried to defend herself and I said, "Well, let's not worry about what your reasons are. The fact is, I am glad I just saw you and guess what, you will be married to me." And she just about flipped out and I told the girl that was with me that I brought to this party, you know, I am sorry, I am going to follow this girl the rest of the night. And anyway, to make the long story short, she ended up being my wife and I think she has been the one single turning point in my entire life. I think that for any man to really, really succeed, and I think it cuts both ways... for any woman to truly succeed, you have to have a spouse that just absolutely believes in you. Not in an unrealistic way, but somebody who can reason with you and say you are right on the money, go get it, or say you know, maybe we should wait or why don't we try to do it this other way. Here is a different idea. And she has been all that I knew she could be. I can say this with a bullhorn to a million people that I look forward to going home at the end of the day. There are people who can't say that. They have to stop somewhere and while away some time. A lot of my time is taken here because I have to be here. It is a small business, not really having a lot of staff to really free me up to be home at 5 p.m. or whatever. But if it is 11 p.m. that I am going home, I know that she is waiting for me, not to fight me for being late, but with great understanding that there is a good reason why I stayed late. She has given me three beautiful kids – nice combination – boy, girl, boy. Couldn't ask for better. And these kids, we call them low maintenance kids. We have been just so tremendously blessed, you know. If the kids were sickly kids, we couldn't do what we do. If these kids were difficult we couldn't do what we do. We send them off in the morning to school. We don't have to worry about how they will act. So in every way she supports me. Meeting and marrying her has to be the one most defining part of my life. Indeed she daily supports me in every way, including influencing my philosophy. She is always there to discuss my problems or share my successes.

Ogbonna let's go on to your business and outline for us a few of your professional projects you are especially proud of.

THE NEWLY MARRIED COUPLE CELEBRATE ON THEIR HONEYMOON IN VANCOUVER.

The first is being involved with the light rail that is in the news and on everybody's mind. As a sub-consultant to do one of the line segments and to do a meaningful piece of that huge project, I think is a great achievement and accomplishment for a little minority firm. So certainly the light rail project, working on line segment number one and being responsible for the drainage analysis for that project and all the drainage design associated with that project and some of the traffic engineering components of that project is significant. Something we are very proud of. That is one. The second one is really not one project, it is a culmination of things because it is a contract that we were awarded by ADOT, Arizona Department of Transportation, what they call an on-call consultant. ADOT puts out the solicitation and consultants respond to these solicitations for on-call services. They sift through these different responses and they select. In this particular instance, they needed to select five companies in the Valley to put on their on-call list. Then projects come up, they assign these projects to these on-call consultants. And some on-call consultants do more work, more projects than others. It is a function of your responsiveness, the quality of work you do, your relationship with staff. All of those things dictate how much you end up with of the total pot of money that is set aside for the on-call. This is a very, very difficult thing for a small business and a minority business to be in the on-call list. We were just blessed tremendously after about five years of working under other consultants as a sub-consultant to get to the point where the state decided they had seen

"When I look back at where I came from, my accent, my immigrant status I can't help but to just say, thank God. We may just be doing something right, here."

Ogbonna Abarikwu (continued)

CERTIFICATE DESIGNATING HIM AS A FELLOW OF THE INSTITUTE OF ENGINEERS

enough of our performance to award us prime status on the list. They awarded us last year close to $600,000 of work. Actually we are now on the top tier. I don't believe there is another – maybe one more company – that did that much volume of work. There are firms that are doing $60,000 and we did $600,000. Now that is a great achievement that we are extremely proud of.

The most recent exciting project is one that is actually ongoing. We just started this project with the Maricopa County Department of Transportation. MCDOT, with this particular solicitation set aside four projects. They put them together in one solicitation. Those responding were ranked and the highest four firms were selected. Of these four, the top firm got to take the project of their choice. These projects vary in complication, in their scope and they vary in the money. So we were one of the 32 firms that responded to this solicitation and the county narrowed the list down to six firms out of 32 of which we were one of the six. Out of the six firms, they asked us to turn in a technical proposal. Now here is what is really most exciting about these six. The other five firms are in the top 50 engineering firms in the nation. CK is the only one of the six that is not only a small business, but also a minority firm. So as you can well imagine, nobody gave us a chance. Some of the other firms that were not selected for further evaluation told us we were there just to be a token and would be dropped. But we didn't think so. We worked harder than we've ever worked. We walked the job and talked to any and everybody that needed to be talked with. We put together a technical proposal from specifications the county wanted. In addition to the technical proposal, we covered the method of doing the work. We just came at it from a totally different angle. We submitted the proposal along with the other six firms. MCDOT looked at all six. They ranked the six by the submittals they received, then requested a face-to-face interview. The review panel said use no power point, no presentation materials. We will give you a board that shows the project corridor and that's all you are going to present with. So we did. And, we were the first company on that day to interview. Our interview was at 8:00 a.m. We loved being the first to present because we were going to set the pace. They were going to have to compare everybody else against our performance.

We realized at the interview in talking about our processes, that our approach was not what they expected. Within a week we got the phone call. Not only were we one of the four, CK Engineering was the

top firm. We beat out five other highly ranked top 50 engineering consultant firms in this nation to take the key prize, Patton Road, a 23 mile corridor. The county liked it enough that based on our presentation, they added part of the remaining projects to our project. And while they were at it, they came up with an entirely new project for the Hassayampa River, what they call a candidate assessment report. We ended up with not just one project. We have three projects rolled into one. And a huge fee to go with it. I'm so very, very proud of that. So I think in terms of projects and have tried to rank them. As the years have gone by, there have been some very interesting things that we have done. The City of Goodyear last year put out a solicitation to do Van Buren Street. It is a two mile corridor. Twenty six firms submitted. Two firms were selected. Each was awarded one mile corridors. We were one of the two. The other firm was AMEC. It is a top ranked multi-national firm. We are doing the first mile and they are doing the second mile. The interesting thing about this project is that as it evolved, MCDOT has now asked us to do a drainage report for the entire area. They didn't give it to AMEC. They gave it to us to do. And while we are at it, we just received a change order. They now want to do a storm drain under the street. They gave it to us, not to AMEC. So these are some of the highlights, some of the projects. When I look back at where I came from, my accent, my immigrant status, I can't help but to just say, "Thank God. We may just be doing something right, here."

Watching and listening to Ogbonna I could feel his excitement and energy. I told him that, that kind of progress and responsibility was exciting. That he had obviously led his team well. I continued by asking if he had someone else who could provide continuing leadership if he was temporarily not able to do so or when he was away for some other purpose. He promptly said that he did. That he had set up what he called a consensus team within the office. The team consists of three people. Judy his office manager, whom I met when I arrived, and two senior engineers one of whom turned out to be his cousin Mohammed. I did not meet the engineers who were out on jobs. Judy, however, impressed me as a competent, attractive, well-spoken individual. I had dealt with her on the phone during the process of arranging to meet with Ogbonna. She did not have problems with making decisions necessary to facilitate my meeting with Ogbonna. While I did not meet the engineers, Ogbonna went on to say:

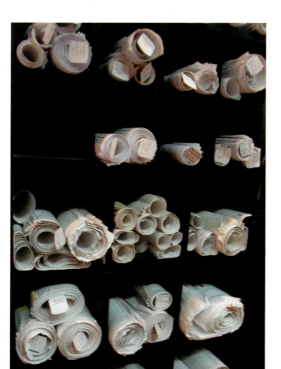

Ogbonna Abarikwu (continued)

I have trained them from day one. They have a sense of how I think. They are their own individuals and I encourage them to bring that flavor to the mix, but I think on certain critical issues, more than likely they would think or perform or do something the way that they know I would want to see it done. So these three people typically are the ones that I leave in charge of things. I do go to Nigeria once in a while and I am gone for two or three weeks. They are the ones who have the authority to do things and they do it as a group. Naturally, there are certain things that an individual must do, but if it's anything of great significance, they meet as a group to discuss the actions to take, and who will handle each phase of the job. We have worked to support one another, to develop depth of leadership. I have no fear that CK Engineering would slip in its professionalism when I am not available. I enjoy the role of teaching and take pride in the success of each one of my employees and the many others we contract to work with us when the jobs are sizable and require outside professionals.

> *So, don't settle, and don't give up. Stay focused.*

That led into my next area of discussion. I said, "You are a determined teacher. Do you do all your training in house or do you provide resources for your employees to seek outside training?" Ogbonna was eager to talk about these programs.

We do have an in-house training program that consists of mentorships and empowerment. We hire bright young EITs and they are assigned to work directly under a licensed professional engineer. They are coached and trained through hands-on experience up until the time when they apply and take their professional engineer's exam. During this time, we also get them as involved as possible in dealing with clients and customers, answering client questions and figuring out "red lines." We will send them out periodically for special training to broaden their sights and help diversify our office, all at our cost.

I asked, "Are you mentoring any outside students at present?"

Not outside of this office, although we have a commitment to be involved with the School of Engineering at ASU. I am very happy to do this. It is critical. The art of engineering in and of itself is a great art. And certainly we will need to continue to teach that because we want to continue to build reputable structures to support our way of life. But I think that there is that other second element to engineering which is not really getting the kind of attention that I believe it certainly deserves and that is the human side, the community side. Engineers have a tendency to be people who have pencils in their shirt pockets with their slide rules and many want to be off in a corner and away from the public. So I think while we are going to be teaching the whole business and the technical side of the profession, we need to begin to teach the public relations side of it as well - we need both to survive as a profession. We try to teach this here in our office with the young engineers we have on our staff and we work very, very hard to do that.

This discussion led naturally to the subject of employee incentivizing and I asked Ogbonna: What special ways do you involve your employees in growing the business? Do you have special incentives?

I believe in the principle of empowerment. A few examples of the way I empower my employees is by encouraging open dialogue and exchange of ideas, joining of professional groups and providing a budget for employees to socialize with clients. CK also provides a first-rate salary and benefit package, 401k plan and bonus, and I am currently working on the possibility of some form of stock plan to share the results of our success.

Are there special ways you encourage your staff to be creative?

The ways I encourage my staff to be creative and entrepreneurial can be said in one word - empowerment. I can't say it enough. I think I am unique in that I encourage my staff to look for ways, even outside of CK, to better themselves. I have at times advised and encouraged members of my staff about outside exploits.

Following on these comments I asked Ogbonna: From your experience what special traits or beliefs makes a successful entrepreneur?

What I feel is a special trait or belief - "Win Baby, Win!" To succeed, you can't settle for "it can't be done." It can always be done. So, don't settle, and don't give up. Stay focused. I find that no matter what the odds, it just makes me fight harder. You must be fair-minded and you must be humble. Combine winning with these traits and you will succeed.

I continued on this all important facet of entrepreneuring by asking, "Ogbonna, tell us some of the ways you keep your personal enthusiasm high?" He laughed and said:

Ogbonna Abarikwu (continued)

IT'S IMPORTANT TO BALANCE LIFE AND HAVE FUN.

I am a busy bee. I like to find new projects in the heart of the old. I'll tell you a secret. I don't dwell on past successes. I keep my sight on the future. The fun for me in looking for new adventures and developing them is the "ride." When I'm on that ride is when I am having the most fun. There are times however, when times get tough and then I draw from past history and my deep belief that to be successful you must always think of success as just a matter of time and effort. I say it again, I might stand still for awhile, but I will not allow failure to dominate my life.

I continued by asking Ogbonna this. If you had to start your business all over again would you change any of your actions you took initially?

No. Everything we have done has helped us to learn. To improve our productivity. To learn new techniques. To experience from the trial and error which is always a part of the engineer's life. I would start the same. The difference would be I would have come to more alternate solutions. Engineering is always changing - improving. Always demanding.

Ogbonna we've discussed your youth and your love of play. Do you still play? If so, what do you like to do?

Yes, I do still like to play. It helps to refresh me and since I love to be with people, my fun time involves people. Lots of learning types of activities and ventures, very diversified.

I love to go to amusement parks, like Six Flags. I get an incredible thrill out of roller coaster rides. The more daring, the better. And I love to golf. Unfortunately, I just haven't gotten to the point where I am able to tell myself that it is okay to take a day off every week or every other week to golf. I am hoping someday in the future we will get these. I really love to golf. And, I truly love doing kid stuff. A lot of times when I take my kids to Ringling Brothers Barnum and Bailey Circus, it is more for me than it is for them. I get a kick out of that. If one of the Disney shows comes to town, I love to get into stuff like that. Play. I love basketball. I love to go to the arena to watch a game. I love theater. If my wife was heavily into that we would probably be doing a lot of that, you know, going to see shows. I love Broadway shows. There are many things that fascinate me about these shows. The way the stage is put together, the amount of work that goes into perfecting what they do, the music. Incredible stuff.

I love to go skiing. But what I really enjoy about skiing is when the lift takes you up to the highest point. The serenity is just breathtaking. The serenity is just incredible. It is

just as perfect as God made it. You are just up there and you can hear the whispering of the wind and it is inspiring especially if it is early in the morning after the night snow.

What about hobbies Ogbonna?

I love jigsaw puzzles. I love to put things together. That would be it. You know, someday when I grow up, I would love to own a vintage car. I go to the Barrett-Jackson shows and look at those cars and I bite my fingers and I think, someday. I have seen cars that people said they put together. They take old, beat up, rusted cars and they just transform it. I'd like that too. And, I like to cook. When we have guests, I enjoy cooking and presenting food with all the trimmings that go along with it.

When asked what the most satisfying accomplishment he had achieved, Ogbonna turned very thoughtful and pensive. His answer seemed to me to best describe the deep beliefs he had shared with me during our personal and often invasive conversation.

The most satisfying accomplishment for me is finding the balance between work and home and making it all come together. It may seem like a small thing, but I've seen one or the other go down the drain. I attribute my success at home to the unselfish, supporting role my wife takes. Simply stated, she believes in me. At work I have surrounded myself with core people who I trust, that see and believe in my vision and want that vision to become a reality almost as much as I do. In turn I am constantly challenged to pay attention to the needs of my wife, our children and my employee family. We all make it work.

That opened the door to my asking, "Ogbonna, please share your vision for the future and also tell us if that vision differs from your original vision."

My vision today is slightly modified from my original. I want to have a full-service engineering and construction company that provides civil and engineering consulting services as well as performs construction of select engineering projects for the core company. A dream of mine is to develop realistic holdings as well as branch out into the food and beverage industry.

I said that the vision seemed to be more than one vision for the future and would he please clear up this disparity.

While CK's consulting services originally offered and still include grading and drainage project analysis and design for site development, roadway, sewer, storm and water lines, geotechnical,

Ogbonna Abarikwu (continued)

JOHN LYONS SHOWN HERE IN THE GEOTECHNICAL LABORATORY. THIS IS UNCOMMON FOR A DESIGN ENGINEERING FIRM BUT IT'S WHAT SETS APART CK.

environmental and traffic engineering projects for public works, we now offer general contracting services emphasizing project management, project administration and inspection services, material testing, analysis and design for concrete, asphalt and soils, and general engineering project construction. CK also offers geotechnical and environmental analysis, soil and environmental analysis, and design. To expand on the latter services, we have constructed our own geotechnical and environmental lab. Construction was completed November 2005. We continue to survey future needs and develop in a timely manner what our clients may need. We will stay ahead of the competition. For example, we are on the lookout for businesses we might acquire. If not available, we will develop. One such opportunity is to secure an engineering surveying company. Additionally, we want an engineering construction traffic and roadway lighting firm.

You mentioned a term I'm not familiar with Ogbonna. What does a geotechnical and environmental lab do? Is it an additional business or division of CK Engineering?

It is actually in process across from this building in that other building. It is being done as we speak. Geotech is basically the science and engineering of soils, pavement, asphalt, concrete and such. It relates more to construction of roads, construction of building foundations and that type of stuff. And the environmental side is more environmental issues associated with the implementation of transportation infrastructure. It deals with construction's impact on people and their environment and health. Before we do any building or make a proposal we ask ourselves how this can help, not hurt, people. Without people concerns there is absolutely nothing we should do to harm, only help.

Ogbonna, is CK and its divisions you've mentioned the only business you have started?

No, CK is not the only business I have started. I started ObiOne, LLC, which is a land development company, and Oasis Medical, a facility specializing in internal medicine for my spouse. In progress is a joint venture with another entity to provide construction services to the federal government.

This is a strange combination for an engineering business. Are they part of CK or separate companies?

They are individual companies. Stand-alones, but there is a method and a reasonable explanation. I describe the situation in two ways. One way is that some is actually borne by necessity. The second way is very consistent with who I am. I have a tendency to like diversity. I am not typical for just being boxed into doing one thing. I like the challenges that you face when there is a multiplicity of things that are divergent in ways; And so I think it is kind of consistent with my true personality to want to have a land development type business and have a medical office type thing, set it up and then have an engineering business that I am now trying to stretch to have a construction component to it. So, now the reason why I said that there is a necessity to it is that my wife happens to be an M.D. She is a medical doctor by profession and I have watched her struggle working for somebody else. We have three young ones and there was a need for her to be in better control of her time. So I thought what could be better than if she started her own medical practice. She could take as many patients as she could accommodate at any given time to still allow her to be the mom that she very much wanted to be and the great spouse that she is and needed to be. So out of the necessity, we established Oasis Medical Center. Another necessity is OBiOne. In 1999, after I had grown to five or six people in the company, we were housed in a small office of approximately 750 square feet. There was a need to move to a bigger building. Instead of looking around, I really wanted to stay in this area because my home is about seven minutes away from here. I didn't want to have to go to downtown. We started looking for a place to expand into. In 1999, believe it or not, we didn't have opportunities around here for an engineering office. So I said to myself, what if I build one for myself? What if we started one? And that is how the OB1 component came into being. Actually this building is one of our projects that we have done. Shortly thereafter, when my wife needed to move and have her own medical office space, I built the one across the street for her. So, these were logical business decisions.

But why the food franchises you hope to own. How can they fit?

You know, there are certain things that I believe that catch people's attention. For me, it is the fast food industry. I come from a third world country. People are very impoverished. Food is not as bountiful. That is especially true in Nigeria where I was born. When I first came to the U.S., fast food was the place you could go to get a job. As a student in Colorado I needed to work so I got a job working at McDonald's. Always in the back of my mind I thought what a great way for me to serve the greater society. What a great way for kids to get work experience. It doesn't pay much but it is a great way for kids to earn and learn. Always in the back of my mind has been to own some fast food franchises. It wouldn't be McDonald's or Burger King. I like Wendy's or In and Out Burger. So owning a restaurant is actually not far-fetched from who I am as a person and also the idea of providing an additional place of employment. If I can't hire a high school kid in an engineering office, well maybe I can give that opportunity in a fast-food environment. I'd like it to be a brand new concept. One that would have food that is good for you and yet easy to get for people on the go.

Ogbonna Abarikwu (continued)

SPIRIT OF ENTERPRISE AWARD AND BUSINESS JOURNAL EXCERPT.

Then you are building a family business based on the talents and education of both you and your wife.

Yes, I do consider this a first generation family business. I believe very strongly in the bonds of family and hope to leave my business as a legacy to my family. As a matter of fact, my nephew works with me now as a professional engineer. My wife is involved with her practice and the clinic.

You first caught my attention Ogbonna when you received the Spirit of Enterprise Award in October 2004. I was really impressed when you brought your wife and children on stage with you to receive your award. Let's talk about your children - your family. I know you would like your children to follow into your business so that the legacy you are creating has young legs to move forward. Do you involve them in any way right now?

They are still kind of young. Nonetheless, I bring them in on the weekend. They help shred papers. They help me make copies if I am working on something. But there is definitely the hope that as they get a little bit older, we can begin to bring them in to do parttime stuff and learn. I have actually even in some of these cases taken the oldest one and the second one to meetings; I put them in a chair on the side to sit there and watch and listen. Their young brains are impressionable and it is our obligation to teach our children good behavior and the value of work. I believe these opportunities can provide lessons.

Another important lesson for my children is one I learned when I came to the United States. That this is one nation under God. A God of many faiths. And that the first immigrants to this country actually came because of religious persecution. Also, many people were poor and persecuted and imprisoned because they could not pay their bills. They came for opportunity, just as I did. They made a nation and I have an obligation to continue to uphold those rights. I study the Bill of Rights and the Constitution and I make sure my children understand all of this as well.

Sounds like you are deeply involved in community life. What special contributions do you make to the community? We are talking about community in the broad sense, Ogbonna.

Well, a couple of areas. Obviously, the family is a component of the greater society and I have this belief that charity should begin at home. Begin at home with me and I think if we take care of the home well, the greater society benefits. They are the ones who I go to bed with and I wake up with, technically, I touch their lives the most. Whether it is in watching the way I conduct myself or in providing for them. Then the next group would probably be the people here on the job. Again, I think we spend a lot of hours together here. And, so again, an opportunity for me. I don't know if role model might be the appropriate word, but I guess they give me the most opportunity to live my life and they observe it. If there is anything good in it, maybe they can use my behavior to make their own lives better. I believe that the reason why I am a business person or I have different businesses is really not completely to make money for myself. I think that first and foremost, the whole essence of being a business owner is providing opportunity, community service, whether community service is with the way I treat the people that work side-by-side with me on a daily basis. Being fair in creating opportunities for these people and compensating them for their performance, I see that as a community outreach. Being open and willing to listen to their personal issues when I can and being honest in offering help in any which way that help might be found for those people to make their lives better. I think that is community service. And then, you know we can then begin to look at other things such as the affiliations we have with different associations. Servicing some committees to help the greater society – maybe create policy or implement policy. Give to charity. Volunteer for things that help other people. I think, at the broader scale, it begins for me at the level I am today. I think it gets kind of watered down because I am not able to do things more significantly the way I would like to feel that I am actually making an impact. But I see that more within my smaller circle of influence with what we are doing with the folks here at work. I don't know if that attempts to address the question the way you intended.

OGBONNA WITH HIS FIRST SON AT HIS BAPTISM

It begins to address the question. You are not making separations. You are building from the ground floor up in your relationships with your family and extended family. Are there special ways you help your extended family - your employees?

We provide a 401k plan and a generous pay scale and give opportunity for promotion. We look to provide other benefits as we grow.

I also believe we help the communities in other special ways. I've mentioned before that we are careful when we bid or do projects to keep the people in mind and their health and welfare. There needs to be balance between so called progress and protecting the community. Engineers have a great obligation here. We absolutely try to strike a balance. God actually calls on us to be responsible with His earth and people. He created the earth and its beauty, so the Bible tells us.

Ogbonna Abarikwu (continued)

I understand the need to use natural resources to sustain humanity. I am also extremely aware of the fact we have to be careful in the way these resources are utilized. So, I favor any science or any approach that tries to balance the need for humanity to survive and the need to sustain nature. So, between the geo-technical and environmental lab you can get both. The environmental lab addresses some of these issues. For instance, when we collect storm water from our streets we have to dispose of it at some ultimate location. We have to do it carefully. A lot of times those locations are washes, rivers and things like that. Also our sewer, our sanitary sewer. What do we do with it? Do we treat the water? What do we do with that effluent? The environmental side tends to address all of that. We don't get into things that have to do with cutting down forests and things like that. We are pretty much limited to the transportation related environmental issues that we have to deal with. Say there is a new roadway corridor or transportation corridor that we need to build. Well, we have to be sensitive to where we put that alignment. We make sure that there are certain sensitive animals or things that habituate that corridor, that it is mitigated. I counsel my team constantly to look for the best protective ways.

So, don't settle, and don't give up. Stay focused.

In our earlier discussions, you made reference to special community activities you are personally involved in. I'd like you to elaborate on special programs, organizations, causes, schools, etc.

Yes, I support special programs. Aside from the support I give to the ADA, I have also contributed to under privileged youth, the National Day of Prayer, the new Human Services Campus for homeless, the ASU Foundation, and the American Cancer Society. I am also involved with professional organizations such as National Society of Professional Engineers, American Consulting Engineers Council, American Society of Civil Engineers, and Society of American Military Engineers where I serve as a board member.

Besides working with my church and donating to the local police and fire departments, I work with Habitat for Humanity. During my "Father of the Year" nomination, where I raised several thousand dollars for the American Diabetes Association, I became involved with the ADA and am now on its board of advisors.

Would you like to elaborate more on these involvements? Let's start with the American Diabetes Association, Ogbonna.

My involvement with them actually started right after the Spirit of Enterprise. They happened to be in the audience at that event and coincidentally, they had the board of directors meeting the very next week to begin to identify individuals that they were going to honor as part of the year of 2005. So there were a few of them that were in the audience including the chair of that committee. And apparently when they left that event, they met and it was my understanding that my name came up immediately and they got the idea from seeing my family on stage. And unanimously said, this is definitely a guy we want to get involved. The Father of the Year Council of Phoenix supports the ADA as their charity so if you are nominated, or if you are going to be recognized, one of the things you are supposed to do is help the ADA raise money to help people with diabetes and their relatives. After some discussions, I said ok and we were invited to a reception where they basically gave us a quick education on diabetes and what it has done to people, including kids and what some of the struggle has been. It was just mind boggling to me. My mother-in-law is diabetic and she has been for some time. My brother-in-law who is my older sisters' husband is also a diabetic. And so, you know, I had some motivation on the personal side. But beyond that it was just looking at the terrible statistics.

I was tickled pink when the Father of the Year Council and the American Diabetes Association actually said we will honor you as a Father of the Year. I resisted it initially because again, in my mind, there are millions of dads in the Valley. But eventually I kind of rationalized it this way. I said, you know, you have always talked about an opportunity to be of help on a larger scale, now here is that opportunity. To go out in the name of the ADA and work hard to help raise money that could be used to help people who absolutely have this need. We have been involved with the breast cancer society through the town of Paradise Valley. My part in all of that looks small to me. I look forward to the day I can do it at a much bigger scale. What gives me absolute satisfaction is being able to help somebody and see that smile on their face. I think that is just not something money can replace.

What about your employees? Are your employees or members of your staff involved in special community support activities?

During my campaign for Father of the Year, my administrator Judy was my campaign

Ogbonna Abarikwu (continued)

manager. Judy was also moved by the work that the ADA was doing and volunteered to work at the children's ADA camp in Prescott. She is also involved in the local chapter of the National Audubon Society. One of our principal engineer', Amara, volunteers his time at the food bank, and Tony, a junior engineer mentors troubled kids and works with local outreach programs. Arica, our management associate works with her church youth group and serves as a coordinator for various community outreach programs.

I'd say my company as a whole is very community minded.

You have received a number of awards. How did you use them to enhance your business? Did these awards help motivate your employees and your clients/customers?

In 2004 and 2005, I received three awards. The Spirit of Enterprise, sponsored by the ASU W. P. Carey School of Business; Father of the Year, sponsored by the Father's Day Council in association with the American Diabetes Association; and the DBE Firm of the year sponsored by COMTO. Winning these awards has definitely broadened the exposure of CK Engineering, Inc. through the media. People tell me that they have seen clips of the awards on TV, in the newspaper and heard them on the radio. It definitely gets the business name out there and it validates us as a business. I've had clients tell me that they didn't realize how well we were doing until they heard about us through the media because of an award. That is not why we do our good deeds. It is just a wonderful result.

What special dream or desire do you have that is yet unfulfilled, Ogbonna?

Well, there is one on the personal side and I think there is one on the business side. We have touched on both, actually. The personal side for me continues to be raising my children. I think again, for me, that is purely how I would want to be measured in the end, is how well have these children turned out. So, it continues to be my desire. It is not fulfilled yet. We see traces of promising things but they are not adults yet. And until they get there, my fingers remain crossed. More on the business side, we already talked about this strong desire to someday have a fast-food franchise. I think that is something that we will continue to work on. I certainly will welcome any opportunity for me to give some of me back. I never refuse to do that. I hope that because I have met some people who have said to me, "Oh we saw you and boy, your story is so intriguing, it is helping us." So maybe there is some value here for others who read my story. I would also invite a reader of my story to contact me if they have questions or comments or want some help.

What special advice would you give others starting a business?

I think the best advice I could give someone just starting a business is: don't believe the lie that you are going to be your own boss - be prepared to have many bosses and to be subservient to double the number of people you have had to be in the past. You will have to work twice as hard but if you know your stuff and stay humble, good things will happen.

As I look back to where I came from, the wonderful Dad I had, I know all is possible. And to young people, if you want success badly enough it is absolutely possible to get it. Go back to Genesis "for everything there is a time." The Bible will tell you that we are created in the image of God. God created us in his own image. And when I look at this incredibly breathtaking thing that we call the earth, this thing that God made, it wows me every time because you know, we are talking about being made in the image of the being that made this stuff. If this isn't engineering at its finest, I don't know what it is. So, if we are made in His image and He is able to do all this, it means that we are endowed with the same power to create these things and actually we have! I am an engineer, but every time I go into an airplane and it takes off, I go wow, how did they do that? The cell phone, the camera space vehicle, etc. Human beings made these things. The only way I rationalize it in my mind is we are capable of doing these things that blow people's minds because we are created in God's image. How badly do you want it? If you want it badly enough, it is all possible.

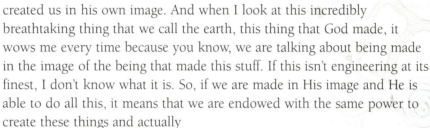

"If you want success badly enough it is absolutely possible to get it."

LEFT AND BACKGROUND PHOTO: FORMAL ROBES WERE WORN IN PLACE OF TRADITIONAL FORMAL WEAR AT MAJOR EVENING EVENTS.

Two make a

"KRISTIN INFLUENCES MY PHILOSOPHY - KEEPS ME GROUNDED. I COULD NOT DO THIS BUSINESS WITHOUT HER."

Mother and daughter innovators, whose strengths compliment and supplement to form a pre-eminent team of change makers. A first and second generation with unique generational differences. Put 'em together and positive sparks create a fire of energy resulting in a successful enterprise. Their story ranges from Carol's hard years and individual success, to agonizing, mutually shared tragedy of the death of daughter Ann and healing, to success as a team. It is a mother's towering drive and desire, creativity and vision. It is a daughter's special management skills, organized approach and acceptance of the generational and personal differences coupled with a desire to work with her mother. Together they are a meshing of first and second generations. They daily make their differences work successfully.

I often reflect on the fortuitous circumstances that led to meeting this special entrepreneurial team. After a 50-year, highly successful career as an entrepreneur, I came to my alma mater, Arizona State University with the intention of setting up a program to help entrepreneurial students and small businesses. This was the early 1990s. After many discussions, I financed and founded a program which was named The Center for the Advancement of Small Business. It was quite unique for a university College of Business in that era, in that we set it up like a business with a vision, mission and operational statement. It was based on a full business plan that planned for and involved local small business owners in concert with academic professors.

Midway in the '90s we began to seek out support from selected successful entrepreneurs to build special programs for students and small businesses. One of those programs was for family businesses. That's

POWERFUL ONE

when I first met Carol Den Herder. Carol immediately understood the purpose and need and subsequently Carol and Kristin Rezler, her daughter, agreed to support the efforts of the center. This meeting began an association which I have increasingly valued through the years.

When I decided to write about selected everyday pioneers whose efforts have largely gone unnoticed, selecting the Carol and Kristin team was a no-brainer.

I interviewed Carol and Kristin separately with the thought of sharing with the readers their special relationship. We will get to those interviews as they tell their stories but first I'd like to share my assessment of each.

Carol is very creative and energetic. She is a sensitive person with ideas which she generates into reality. She is quick to assess people and situations, as well as being inquisitive and empathetic. Carol is a perfectionist who will not settle for less than the best. The company Carol and Kristin have created, Identity Marketing, provides more than a million products and special services customized for their clients. Their facilities and equipment are state-of-the-art and beyond. Whatever a company, non-profit agency or individual needs to promote, Identity Marketing can and will provide.

I've a word to say about Carol Den Herder's unique, honest, captivating "what-you-see-is-what-you-get" style of delivery. It is spontaneous and often emotional as she races through her productive, adventuresome life. She often jumps ahead and then returns to past events as they cast relevance on her present and future success or failures. As with all of our stories, we have tried to capture the essence of Carol's personality, drive and philosophy. You will find her delivery dynamic an top-of-mind. I trust she will intrigue you as she has me.

Carol is a serial entrepreneur, having personally started more than 10 companies and has actively assisted others in their start-up adventures. She and Kristin are giving people and regularly provide resources for individuals and community groups.

Kristin is a strong, stable individual. She is well-organized, yet adventuresome, willing and able to take chances on people and willing to take business risks. She is a decision maker who has carefully honed her skills in organization and implementation. Kristin encourages her staff to take social responsibility and

"MY MOTHER HAS ALWAYS ENCOURAGED ME TO MAKE MY OWN DECISIONS. SHE SUPPORTS ME BOTH PERSONALLY AND PROFESSIONALLY."

Carol Den Herder and Kristin Rezler (continued)

Carol shown here in the Sioux City Journal at 12 years old. She even beat her older brothers to win Best Beef Showman.

supports their efforts. She is the president of Identity Marketing and responsible for all aspects of the business. She makes it possible for Carol to do the outside work and sales as well as take care of their other varied interests in the Midwest. Kristin's ideas and special skills enable the company to perform and assure stability of staff and client relations. While Carol is charismatic and always seeking new challenges, Kristin makes it all work effectively. The team functions because each wills it to be successful and backs that up by performing as one seamless entity in the critical areas.

CAROL A. DEN HERDER

Carol, you were born in 1945 in Sioux Center, Iowa raised on a farm and attended Iowa State University. You started your first business in Iowa. What was your chosen focus in college and when did you graduate?

Actually, I didn't get to choose. As was the tradition in that era and midwestern locale, my father chose home economics for me. My focus and desire was to study business, architecture and design. And I didn't graduate. I had Kristin and dropped out so that my husband could finish. That was the old tradition there.

When was the first business you started, Carol, and what was it?

I started it in 1969 and it was called Young American Shop. It was clothing for infants through ladies sizes and infants through size six in boys. I saw a need. My entire line was high-quality clothing. There wasn't a shop for quality clothes in our area. People had to go to a major center like Sioux Falls or Sioux City. I have always believed quality doesn't cost, it pays.

We were very successful so I decided we should start a men's clothing store for my husband to run. We had the building, sources for garments and then I discovered my husband was having an affair and the decision was made for him to pack and leave. By this time I had two babies, Kristin and Ann. I was so devastated I sold out.

Kristin was about to start kindergarten, so I went to Sioux Falls to shop for her. I walked into Michaels and Burkes Clothing Store. They thought I was shopping the competition, I told them I had sold my store. They offered me a job, I accepted. That was Tuesday. Wednesday, I found a place to live, Saturday my brother moved us in his feed truck. There I was, two babies, a new town. Monday, Kristin started kindergarten and I started my new job.

I have to tell this story. Being a single parent, a very young single parent left with two babies ages two and four years old, I decided very early on that part of our success as a family was going to be that I would teach my children to make decisions for themselves. That was something I was not allowed to do when I grew up.

Carol, you put action to your ideas. You implement them and then you drive them until they are successful. That is a unique quality of your entrepreneurial tendencies. I want you to get back to your early years and the businesses you started then.

In 1969, when I started The Young American Shop, it was my first and I needed some money. So I went to the bank. That banker is still living today, by the way. And I said to him, "Vern, I need to borrow $8,000." And he said to me, "Well, we don't lend money to women and women don't own businesses in this community." I said, "Really?" I had not a clue. And he said, "But you know if your father comes in and ..." I stopped him and quickly said, "No! My father isn't starting this business, I am." And as I started to get up and leave the office with the girls, Ann was three weeks old and Kristin was 19 months old, he followed me to the front door and said, "Well, by the way, what kind of business were you going to start?" I said, "I am going to start a clothing store." He said, "Well, have you ever done this before." I said, "No." He said, "How do you know you can do it?" I said, "Because I want to."

I left there pretty down but not so down that I stopped wanting to do it. But I did make a stop at my mom and dad's. My mom happened to be home and I quietly told her the story. I would share things with my mother that I couldn't share with anyone else. She put her arm around me and said, "You know what? When I was your age, I couldn't vote. Look how far we've come." I will never forget that. And then sometimes I play on it. I did start the business and it was a success. And this leads to my gas station story.

Carol worked at the Iowa Capitol as a page. She's shown here with her father, Elmer Den Herder, who introduced Carol to community involvement.

Carol Den Herder and Kristin Rezler (continued)

CAROL, HERE 10 AND 11 YEARS OLD, SHOWED AN EARLY INTEREST IN BUSINESS AND EXCELLED IN 4H.

At one point, I needed some short-term cash. By this time, I had been depositing a significant amount of cash each year. But I am a woman in business and I am divorced. Now I have four marks on my forehead. And I needed $50,000 for ten days. And one of the things I have always done is keep my credit score high; my credit is unbelievable. I have never not paid a bill in my life. And I am at the gas station filling up my car. My emotions are written all over my body. Dave, who owns the gas station says, "So, having a good day are we?" I say, "No, not!" Then I just spew it out. I am just livid about the banking system. He said, "Well, how much do you need?" I said, "All I need is $50,000 for ten days." And he goes, "Well why wouldn't they do that?" I said, "I am a woman. I am divorced and the rest is history. Just don't even go there."

One of my Herefords Taken on our farmyard

Taken at home

My other Hereford Taken in the showring at the Fair.

He comes to me as I am finishing up my car, hands me a cloth bag. I said, "What is this?" He said, "This is for you, for ten days." I open it up and it is full of cash. So I went to the bank and I laid the cloth sack on the counter in front of the banker who had turned me down. I said, "Don't even ask where it came from because I am not telling you. Put it in my account." I turned and left the bank.

Ten days later, I went back with a brown sack, filled it up, put a little interest in there, and took it to the filling station owner. Out of curiosity I said, "Dave, how do you get all this cash." He looks at me and says, "Air and water." He owns seven stations and as was the custom back then, he sold air and water to customers. That gave me an idea. The next company I had, I put in vending machines. They make money!

Carol, you have told me in the past that you have been instrumental in starting ten plus companies. Let's talk about some others in the midwest.

Shirley, in those early years I was a restless entrepreneur. The Michaels and Burke's that I went to work for in Sioux Falls came after I had made the snap judgment, sold my business and moved to Sioux Falls very quickly. I didn't last there very long, maybe six to eight months. And I walked into Mike's office one day and put my keys on the desk and said, "I quit." He said, "You can't quit." I said,"Yes I can because I don't like how you treat your staff." He said, "Well, I have never done anything to you." I said, "I didn't say me, I said your staff." I didn't have to explain that. He was not a very kind person in business. That was the only time I have been scared (financially) in my life. I thought, what are you doing? You have these two children. But, I answered an ad in the newspaper for a job at a western place. They wanted to put in a western store in Sioux Falls. Long story short, I did. I set it up for them and it was called Dakota Westerner. Then I got remarried and Dick and I moved to Green Bay, Wisconsin and I went to work for a gal by the name of Mary Morgan. One of Mary's biggest challenges was finding employees for her company. She owned a printing and mailing company. Printing mostly but she also did mailing. And so I started an employment agency for her so not only could she staff herself, but others.

Then I came back to Sioux Center – Dick and I actually had our marriage annulled. He had four children and I had two. His ex wouldn't let him see his children because he had remarried. I told him that I couldn't survive if someone said I couldn't see my children. To date, he and I are both still single. I dedicated my life to my children after that, as did he. I moved back to Sioux Center and I started a business called D Bar H Country Western Store. I thought this is a business that would do well in Sioux Center.

Always thinking of something, aren't I Shirley? I had that when my dad was very ill and I did the nursing thing. Moved to Sioux Center then back to Sioux Falls. I suffered encephalitis in between there so I had 16 months when I couldn't really work and my mother rehabilitated me. And I am living. I don't know why. Historically, less that 5 percent survive that and the ones who do are usually vegetative. Have you ever seen the movie Awakening? That is kind of... well here I am, awake. I lost some hearing. My mother kept me doing handiwork and rehabilitating me. So I really give her credit for that.

CAROL WITH DAUGHTERS ANN AND KRISTIN AT THEIR LAST FAMILY VACATION IN ORLANDO, FL IN 1993.

I helped start so many companies it would be hard to list them all, but here are a few. I helped start a division inside of an organization that monitored pacemaker patients. From there I moved to Arizona, and went to work for Medtronic. Dr. O'Brien picked my brain to start the heart care clinic in Sioux Center. He wanted to have the main branch in Sioux Falls. I set it all up for him and then he wanted me to move back and be a part of it. It is the old story that money talks. Reluctantly, I left Arizona and returned to South Dakota and started Heartcare. I stayed three years, returned to Arizona and started my medical business consulting company. From that grew Carantin and the printing and mailing business. Kristin will have a lot to say about the Arizona activity as she was very involved here. And, we sold that and started Identity Marketing, then started Okoboji Concierge and Horizon.

Carol, we'll get back to details on all this entrepreneurial activity later. You have mentioned your family, your father and others somewhat positively and somewhat negatively. What influence did they have on your directions then and as you see where you are today?

Carol Den Herder and Kristin Rezler (continued)

CAROL'S PAGE CLASS AT THE IOWA STATE LEGISLATURE.

I was so interested in how my grandpa came to America and homesteaded. I loved to just drive down the road with him and hear the stories. And then how my parents impacted the community where I grew up. I am the youngest of six and my dad was a farmer and I would see him giving his money at the community to invest in the future. I watched him pioneer and start a hospital and be president there until he died. And that hospital still exists today. And through him, I got thrown in the political arena when I was very young because he became a politician and my mother, you know, right at his side. I was almost, raised by my siblings. But I kept clinging to what I saw the generations do before me. I don't remember too much about my childhood. I was always scared. I don't have many good memories. The things I remember were what impacted me through family stories. So I just take those values and those lessons from the past and apply them over and over again.

I think maybe if you have to have a single word, I would have to say integrity. If you have to have a statement, I would say that I was very fortunate to sort out all of the good values and lessons learned from my family and take them forward and use them and leave the bad behind. And I think I do that every day of my life.

I still recall stories from my grandparents. And I recall values from my parents who have both been gone for years, too. An older brother who died very young was kind of like my dad and he influenced me. He brought the humor out in me. Then sometimes hurt changes the way you process the information and move you forward. So I have made a lot of decisions based on hurt. If you make a decision and you move with that decision, it is okay because not everything is perfect. But if you decide to make it right or if it isn't right or if you have made a mistake that you would fess up to and learn from, that's been pretty decisive in my life.

I wouldn't change a thing. In fact, I have lost jobs over my integrity. I have lost positions over my integrity and honesty because I can't change that, nor do I want to. So yeah, my kids were born and raised around it and had to make decisions. I thought Kristin and Ann were nuts when they wanted to come and work with me and yet that was the biggest compliment I was ever given in my life. I went to college so that I could get off the farm and stop milking cows. That was my only reason for going. I never thought so far as my daughters wanting to be educated. And the formal education part of what I have had in my life is important. My dad's death wish was that I become a nurse, so I did. In my late 30s I traveled 45 miles one way. I owned the western store at that time. Two kids. Single parent. And I did it! I graduated with honors. Right away I realized cardiology was where the money was at that time and was the most aggressive part of medicine. Strange how I base some of my decisions. All of my past affects my future. See, one of our largest customers today is Banner Health. I understand healthcare. I understand the realities of how they make their money and I understand how to market to them, so that is one of our accounts that results from my medical training.

Carol, we will get back to Iowa and your new division there, but I'd like to have you tell us the full story of how you got to Arizona the first time.

As I mentioned, I began early to teach my girls the art of making a decision. So when Kristin was a senior in high school and pursuing where she wanted to go to college, she looked at some options and then chose Arizona State. She applied and was accepted. I said to her, "We'd better go look." So we got on a plane. It was fun. Ann, Kristin, myself and a friend of theirs flew to Arizona and rented a convertible. It was Easter. The friend who came along, her friends owned a home in east Mesa. At the time I didn't have a clue where east Mesa was. I-60 ended at Alma School in 1985. The weather was beautiful - riding in a convertible, what's not to love. Kristin decided to go to Arizona State and we found her accommodations in an apartment versus a dorm room for a couple of reasons. One of which was financial. It was more cost effective for her. She could share the expenses with a roommate. I delivered her here that August in a motor home pulling her car and bicycle. That was my first drive here.

KRISTIN'S FIRST YEAR AT ASU IN 1985.

I had prior, maybe even six months prior, made application to a company called Medtronic because I wanted to work for them. I had now accomplished cardiology clinical status, specializing in pacing, working in the heart business. Medtronic was our pacemaker provider and Gary Younger with Medtronic is the one whose daughter had gone to Arizona State and recommended it to Kristin. So I pursued employment with Medtronic thinking I could make more money and I would love to sell because I really understood the technology. I will never forget, Bill Erickson with whom I interviewed, looked at me and said, "You know, Carol, women don't have sales positions inside of our company." That was the fourth time I ran into that brick wall. Now it is 1987. I said, "Really?" He said, "But you could become a technical support rep." "Okay," I said. So I made application. Wouldn't you know there was a position open in Arizona? So I made

Carol Den Herder and Kristin Rezler (continued)

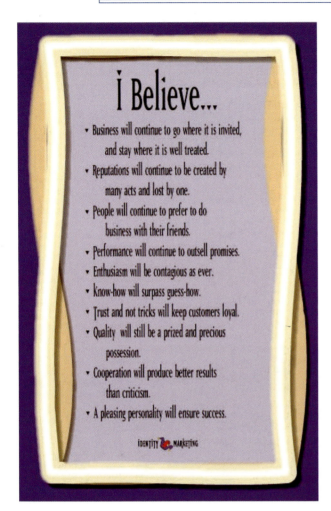

Their business purpose authored by Carol in 1969.

application to Arizona. Eighty some people applied; they narrowed it down to five and I was still in the running. Kristin was now delivered to Arizona State. But since Ann was just starting her junior year in high school in Sioux Falls, I took my name out of the running for the position. About a week into school, Ann came home and said, "Mom, did you ever hear about that job in Arizona?" I said, "Well, I would not do that to you. I would not move you in the middle of the school year." She set me straight saying, "Are you crazy? I can adjust. I have been adjusting all my life. You taught me well. What's most important – if you are happy; we are happy. Call him up and see if the position is still open." It was. I got it. I took it October 2 that very same year; we moved to Arizona - lock, stock and barrel. So that is how we originally got to Arizona.

Well, what next, Carol? You were working for Medtronic in Arizona, Kristin was at ASU and Ann was in high school.

Ann graduated and went off to New York and entered New York University on a scholarship. After Ann went off to college I returned to Sioux Falls to start up the Heartcare clinic I mentioned earlier. I set it up, managed it and promised to stay two years but actually stayed three years. Then I came back to Arizona to take some time to evaluate what I wanted to do next. This is when I decided to become a medical consultant.

So, Carol, describe what a medical consultant would do?

To begin, I started going back to my old network of people I knew and explained what I had in mind if they had any project, to let me know. When asked what kind of projects I told them, if they need anything done, just let me know. Seaman, Pace, Sutter out of California hired me to write their marketing materials on a brand new device, a chamber of an external pacemaker that they wanted to launch and get out in the marketplace before Medtronic. So I rewrote their sales program. I took the job, worked out of my home. Didn't even know how to run a computer at the time. When I took that job, the State of California needed to have a name for my company. I couldn't just say Carol Den Herder, the medical business consultant. So I was filling out this form for California and Ann was home on break from NYU. I said to Ann, "I need to name my company. What should I name it?" Just like that she said, "Carantin." "What?" I asked. She said, "Carantin." I said, "How do I spell it?" She said, "C-a-r-a-n-t-i-n." "What is it?" I questioned. She said, "Carol, Ann and Kristin." This was before we had our mailing company. I wrote down Carantin and it became the name of my consulting company. I registered it and Ann went back to school and I became a consultant.

With this job, after everything was said and done, the president said to me, "Okay, take care of distribution as well." And I came up with the idea that it would take way too long. They knew that 287,000 individuals in organizations around the world needed to receive this package of information. If we went through the sales organization from corporate to regional to district to sales to all the physicians, hospitals, clinicians and everyone that needed to receive this worldwide, it would take too long. I said, "How about we put it in the mail." He said, "Okay, put it in the mail." I went to the post office, weighed it - $2.90 postage. For this company, that's peanuts. I said to the postal clerk, "Is there a business that does mail?" She said, "Sure." She gave me the names of all the businesses in Phoenix that do mailing. So I started at the top to find out who was the best. I intended to visit five. I only went to three and stopped. I went back to California and said to Dave that I had found a way to mail the packet, but did not recommend any of the companies because they were sweatshops. There was mail laying all over the floor. They were dirty. I am thinking one of these packages could potentially be a million dollar plus sale. So he said, "What do you suggest?" I said, "We should just do it from inside your shop. You have the mailing list. We can process it and put it all together and mail it at $2.90." We got all done with it and I am curious. There has to be something better than this for doing mail. I called the United States Postal Service in Washington, D.C. When I finally got to the right department, I said, "I am a medical consultant in Arizona and am wondering, could you tell me what is being planned for future mass mailing in the United States of America?" She said, "We are going to barcode and automate the mail." I said, "Does anyone in Phoenix do that?" She said, "No." "Does anyone anywhere do it?" I asked. She said, "No, but Phoenix could be designated a Beta site." I said, "Oh really." She gave me the name of the person to contact. I researched automation compatible bar-coded mail. I then called my contact in the Phoenix post office and asked her to lunch. I threw a package in front of her and said, "If this were automation compatible and we had a delivery point barcode on it, what would the postage be?" She about fell out of the booth because I had introduced myself as a medical business consultant not a mailer. She said she didn't know but we could sure find out and asked why I wanted to know. I said, "Because I visited the sweatshops that were around and I was thinking if there is a future in mail, maybe I could get into it because I see some potential." She got back to me and said by automating the piece the postage would be 13 cents.

CARANTIN BUSINESS WAS FEATURED IN THE USPS MAGAZINE.

Carol Den Herder and Kristin Rezler (continued)

Ann's graduation

I went to Pennsylvania and bought a printer that would print barcode and put it on my kitchen counter. At that time, that company was the only one in the United States that manufactured a unit that would print barcode. So we are the first company in Arizona and one of three in the whole United States to barcode the mail. Now I had something to sell because I could go to a business and say, "If I barcode this, the three things that you have to pay for in doing mail are the print piece, how you process it and the postage. And I could save you money if I process it for you." So we started with a newcomers welcome service package. Eventually, we did our first mailing for Basha's upscale market AJ's. Basha's called again and said, "We have some money to spend from a company and we can do a mailing to wine enthusiasts." I thought, is that ironic? "So anyway, can you find them?" I said sure, because we were now into the data work. We found the list and processed 27,000 pieces. I left for a trip on Friday and when I returned on Sunday, Ann, her boyfriend and Kristin were stuffing envelopes, wetting them with a sponge and running them through our printer so now we could charge for the processing and still save the client money on postage. We acquired more printers, more automation, more inserters, everything which when we sold the company to Central Newspapers we had 35,000 square feet with 50 some employees and the premiere mailing service in Phoenix. You could eat off the floor because we maintained a clean, state-of-the-art mailing house, and had happy employees, no lost mail pieces and all of the advantages that drove me into the business originally.

Carol, let's go back a step before all this. How did Kristin and Ann get into this project or business? When we left them, Kristin was at ASU and Ann at NYU.

Well, Kristin graduated and shortly after, Ann graduated from NYU. They both got super positions. Ann was working for Chase Manhattan out of New York City traveling all over the world and Kristin was in upper-level management at the Gap. They both gave up their positions and came to Arizona, lived with me, ate mac and cheese and didn't get paid. And why? Because they wanted to experience what I was doing. They wanted to work with their mother.

I need to tell this part of the story. Kristin came first then Ann came. Ann said she wanted to be in sales. Remember we were in this rented house as we were a home-based business. Kristin was in one of the front bedrooms and Ann was in one of the back bedrooms. I noticed she spent a lot of time back there. So, one day I went in and she was crying. I said, "You can't be back here in tears. We need to talk!" That started a flood of more tears and she stammered, "I want to be like you." I said, "Well, that is a huge compliment but darling, you cannot be like me, but we can work together. Would you like that - be a team? Instead of going out and cold calling to open business doors like me, why don't we complement each other with you facilitating my sales activities?" She agreed. I removed the door of that bedroom and cut a big hole in the wall, put a desk right in between Kristin and I, so now all three of us sat together in the living room. All of this in a rented house! I think that was the first time my children realized that we really were a team and that we each brought talent and ideas to the table. This was our first business together. What a privilege for me to work with my children and to realize what they gave up to work and experience with me.

And that was Carantin, Carol?

Yes, Carantin. We had a lot of bumps and problems - too many to cover but steadily Carantin became a huge success. We eventually sold out and that left me with a five-year non-compete agreement. After a period of time, I got bored and made the decision to start a new business. I called Kristin and said, "I am going to start a new company, do you want to be part of it? I have registered the name Identity Marketing." She said, "What are we going to do?" I said, "We are going to do specialty garments for businesses."

Carol, for a change of pace, I have some special personal questions to ask you. These have to do with the emotional, softer side of Carol Den Herder and her philosophy. You game?

Sure.

Do you think it is difficult for Kristin to be in the shadow of you, her dynamic mother?

I am sure it is. Maybe as difficult as it was for me to be in my parents' shadows.

Could she, if she made up her mind to do so, follow in your entrepreneurial footsteps?

Good question, Shirley. I believe she could do anything she wants. It's hard for me to make that assessment. Kristin is and always has been her own person. She can move to new

heights. Together we are more powerful as a team than as individuals. I would not be able to do all we do without her. Nor, would I want to.

CAROL'S LOVE OF PHOTOGRAPHY

Carol, let's go back to your youth. You have mentioned some provocative things about your early family years. I'd like you to talk about grade school, high school, young adult. What interests meant most to you in that time period?

Grade school. Hum. I don't know if I had anything special. It was a farm life. I worked, ate, slept went to school, came home, worked, etc. I remember going to the hospital with my dad and the meetings that he had. I loved it when he would ask me to go along with him. Even if it was just to close the storm windows to save energy.

I remember politicians at our table and many of which, like Dick Nixon, I could imitate. And it just really disturbed mom since she really liked Nixon. He especially loved mom's fried chicken. I remember being taken to a Broadway show, South Pacific. I still love Broadway. I remember funerals. I remember how things weren't, how I had to figure out myself why people were emotional. I still try to get into the emotions of people.

High school. I have always loved music. I had some talents. I had vocal, instrumental, acting. You know we did plays and musicals and I had some roles in them. I think it was because I wanted to, not just as a way to get out of farming. I took piano lessons for seven years and hated every minute of it. I think it was the attitude of my instructor. She was not inspirational. Today I want to play piano. So high school ... I was always good at it. In our family there were four boys and two girls. My sister is older. I am the youngest of six. She is just two years older than I am. It was important for her to be a cheerleader. For me, it wasn't important to be a cheerleader because I have never been about being in front of a parade waving a flag. When we had the President's physical fitness challenge, I won the biggest award for physical fitness. Both my parents were from very large families - 11 and 8 siblings. And of course they wanted boys for farming. Then when my sister came along, she was the princess. And when I came along, I was just another kid.

Carol, when you play, what do you do?

I play golf. I just took it up a few years ago and I love it but I don't keep score. I still enjoy entertainment of all sorts like Broadway shows and things like that. I love to go to casinos. I love to have someone call and say, "Hey, let's go to Minneapolis for the weekend." A friend in Iowa called yesterday and said, "We are thinking about a trip to Florida this winter, would you be interested?" I said, "Sure."

So when I play, I go out or go somewhere with friends or take trips. I love the outdoors. I think that is why I have loved living in Iowa and Arizona because I love to be outside. So a lot of my playing is outside. My work is play to me. My work is fun.

How about hobbies, Carol?

A friend said to me awhile back, "Carol you need a quest – not a business one, but a personal quest, that you could really enjoy." I told him that I had a couple of them. One is wine. I've wanted to pursue this for years because we used to have vines on the farm that grew wonderful grapes. When Ann was alive, she stoked my interest in wine making and we started to learn together. I stopped after we lost Ann. I recently found a new friend and he took me to an individual to buy something for our new Iowa business. He likes wines and I asked him about his interest and mentioned I was thinking about regenerating my interest, and he said, "Follow me." So we went down into the basement of his store to a lovely old wine cellar. Old table and chairs there and everything. So now I am introduced to two or three people who own companies, one is very unique, family-owned Okoboji Wines. So I mentioned this to Norm who is our financial advisor and he said, "I have been into wine for years and it is one of my personal quests. We could share our wine interests."

MORE OF CAROL'S LOVE OF PHOTOGRAPHY

My other quest is photography. I have always wished I could really capture what I see because, I think I may see things differently than other people. Instead of seeing a tree or a bush, I am looking more at the details of a leaf or of something that is on that tree or bush. Then I think, how could I capture that? So that is another possible quest. You need personal things in your life so you are not so captivated always by work. Well, that is what I'm going to do. Revisit wines and revisit photography. Get better equipment and get started.

Carol, what are your greatest strengths?

My greatest strength is that I am not afraid to take a risk. My beliefs are my strengths. I would have to say my integrity. My creativity is huge. I can just think outside the box and come up with ideas. I don't know where they come from but I love to be creative - come up with ideas and suggestions. You know, all of life is about marketing. So, my strength is in my talking too. Communications.

CAROL DEN HERDER AND KRISTIN REZLER (CONTINUED)

Carol, Tom and Kristin

That leads me to another very personal question. Would you describe the type of person you believe you are?

I believe I am a good person. I believe that I don't have to stand on the mountaintop and profess myself or my beliefs but I need to live them every day. I believe that I am tough and that I am strong. And at the same time I am weak. I have a lot of underlying emotions. I am driven. I start business after business after business. I teach it, sleep it, eat it. I love helping people start and grow in business. I am enthusiastic so there are always some people in the process of learning from me. I have moods and disappointments and I'm not always happy. When I'm having a bad day I tell Kristin so she knows right up front and can respond accordingly.

Have you always been the person you just described or did you evolve into that?

I think we keep changing every day. I think the older we get, we are more aware of what we have done in the past and what our potential is for the future.

I know you are always a dreamer, dreaming and implementing. That is what makes you different. A lot of people dream, but few can pull dreams into reality. You can and have, Carol. Do you ever think about retiring or seeking to slow down a few paces?

No, to retiring, but I know I'm not going to live forever. I've just plowed through life without thinking about my own fatality, because there is always an exciting challenge around every corner. I'll just keep perfecting our business as I can and starting other businesses that seem to be of benefit.

Would you consider acquiring a business?

Never acquire! We believe it is better to start, rather than to solve problems, retrain a staff and deal with strange, deep-seated business cultures that are so different from our philosophies.

You have two locations, Arizona and Iowa. Are they separate?

No, the Okoboji region is a division of Identity. Our Tempe, Arizona headquarters is home base. Like all our businesses, we saw an unfulfilled opportunity with extraordinary possibilities. The Okoboji Lakes Region is a premiere destination for individuals seeking recreational property. There are five lakes in the region. Almost seven years ago, I bought a home there. I was treated badly. They sold me the property and walked away. I wanted to remodel and could find no one to help. People started and never finished. In frustration, I formed Okoboji Concierge. All the people buying property there needed goods and services that were tough to find. This division is being developed to bring a whole new level of service to the real estate industry above and beyond what is available. We are doing this with a network of other businesses. The client can get whatever they need through our office and showroom cost effectively. We understand how to do this. Identity offers over a million products and services to our customers. We are the experts, so who better to offer a comprehensive concierge. We are just taking the business we know to the next level. We succeed where others fail because we believe in and teach our people to utilize their skills and our sources. We base our business on creativity, vision, drive, passion and energy. To back up what we promise we have created some very special sales pieces and usable materials that are portable.

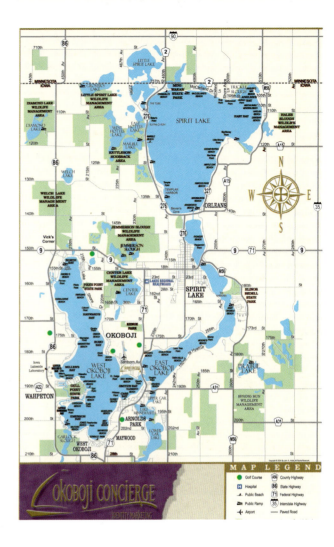

Your time, Carol, is divided 50/50 Arizona and Iowa. Are you mentoring someone back there to handle affairs?

Yes. She will invest time in both locales so she becomes steeped in the Identity culture. Her name is Karen and she is 42. She is bright and determined. Together we are structuring an awesome array of services.

Carol, if you were asked by someone considering a business of their own, and just beginning to think about starting, do you have some advice you think is baseline?

You bet! Go for it! But be sure you have the passion and courage needed to sustain you through all the situations and challenges. Prepare to face a wide array of opportunities by making a workable plan to guide you.

CAROL DEN HERDER AND KRISTIN REZLER (CONTINUED)

KRISTIN AND TOM'S ENGAGEMENT PHOTO TAKEN AT OKOBOJI IN 2000.

KRISTIN M. REZLER

Kristin, you have been in business with your mother most of your adult life. I know you were born in Iowa, April 1967, attended ASU and graduated December 1989. Your focus in college was general business with major emphasis on marketing and management. As I recall, you made the decision to come to Arizona and your family followed a little later. From your perspective, how did that come about?

I was working in a cardiology clinic through high school in South Dakota. One of the pharmaceutical device reps, Gary Younger, asked me where I was going to college. I was going to stay locally and he said, "You need to check out Arizona State University. My daughter went there and the business college has a good ranking." I respected his advice, applied and got the acceptance letter in mid-February of 1987 when there was four feet of snow on the ground. I decided I wanted to go, told my mother who said, "Let's go and check it out." We did over the Easter weekend. I loved it, signed a lease for an apartment, moved in and I've been here in Arizona more than 20 years. Met my husband Tom here. This is home.

Kristin, let's go back in time. Tell me about your interests, activities, the formation of who you were then?

Well, I guess the first thing that comes to mind was sports growing up, because that was just something I naturally did well. I had a very strong passion for music and singing, actually toured around the country with a group when I was in high school and was offered a place with a national organization called Up With People when I was a senior in high school.

That was the group you toured with?

No, the group I toured with was a youth group I was in in Sioux Falls, South Dakota. There were about 100 high school individuals, and every summer we toured around the country and various places in the Midwest and of course did a lot of shows locally. When I was a senior in high school we hosted many individuals from the Up With People organization who were visiting our home town and did a performance for them and I was offered a position with them. At that particular point of my life I was getting ready to go away to college and passed it up and maybe, as an afterthought would love to have continued to pursue that. Golf and reading were my passion and still are. I can definitely tell the difference when I'm not reading and when I am because I find a different level of relaxation - even if it's a chapter a night before I turn in. It helps me shift the gears of my brain into another mode. There's definitely a difference between what Carol would call my required reading for the industry and all of that, versus personal enjoyment reading. The kind of reading depends on my mood. I think I can personally see a difference in myself. Golfing I don't do nearly as much as I would like to.

What do you believe are your two or three greatest strengths?

My patience, my kindness and my integrity.

Well spoken. This is a loaded question, okay? It's a very important question everybody needs to address. If you were to disappear today from your business, would your business survive? Don't use your mother as part of your playcard because your mom would pick up or you would pick up if your mom were to disappear. Do you have backup for you? You're the president of the company and Carol says it in her comments, that she is the marketing person but you do carry the company.

KRISTIN'S BROWNIE PLAQUE MADE IN SECOND GRADE IN 1975.

To date, I don't have a backup in one person or even a completed team yet. We are growing in that direction. I have someone who is under me right now who shows promise to be to me as I am to Carol when it comes from her marketing and sales end being the behind-the-scenes person who can take the information, process it and do the production and the implementation. I believe we have found that individual and anticipate she will join us in the near future.

I do know from what both of you have said, that you do all your training in here so you are telling me that you have people you are going to train and mentor. Do they have any idea who they are?

Yes, absolutely. Both the current employee and the future employee are very aware of it. To finish the question, the individual who is currently here, originally was brought on to train to take over as the general manager as I either transfer or divide my work load. With the growth we have now achieved and the direction this individual's life is taking personally, we've re-grouped those directions and realized that really it's going to take two individuals.

Kristin, you and your mother are like a unit when it comes to handling issues of a serious nature. It takes that to carry the load. You do it admirably and the two of you play well together. And there are more than two functions in your present situation. Obviously operations, implementation and production. These are different. You just happen to be able to do them all. Which does not necessarily mean there is another individual with such multiple skills readily available, right?

Right, and we understand that conundrum.

Carol Den Herder and Kristin Rezler (continued)

Kristin, you have often said that you are the behind-the-scenes person. I have seen that role, but from your comments it would seem you picture other roles you want or need to be ready for that are more visible? Is there something where you're going to be more outspoken and be more noticed in the community?

As the company grows, not only is the need there for it but as we talk about transition plans for the company, Carol, I'm sure, will tell you that she's not young anymore. She's going to look at retiring, which like I said, I don't see happening soon. But, with her really being the face for the company, I guess is the way to put it because she's the one who's really out in the community and making the sales calls and looking to slow down, someone needs to take on some of that role. That's why I feel like I need to be that person. I know that I have the ability to do it. Do I feel it's my strongest point? No. Is it a strong point? I've been told I do very well at it. So I think it's my position to take that on. So in doing that, I'm now grooming someone to take some of my activities on the inside. I can do what I do right now very comfortably, but I don't know that I could take on that additional responsibility and still be able to do all of it to the degree to which it deserves to be done.

You can transition. I have faith in you. You're a learner. You have the attributes to be the face, should you choose.

Well, I've learned from the best. There's no doubt about it. I learn every day listening to Carol and teaming with her. My grandfather once said, "The day I don't learn something new is the day I die." Even in our day-to-day interactions, now a lot of it's by phone and email from a distance when she's in Iowa. I don't think a day goes by that I don't learn a new phrase, a new tool, a new direction, a new approach to any variety of areas for our business. And it's not just the marketing and the sales end, because she is really my total mentor. I call and bounce stuff off of her all the time. I am the president of the company, and she always says, "Yeah, the buck stops with you but it drops off with me." That's what makes our relationship good because we can bounce ideas and decisions off of each other. I'm trying to become more active in that respect and will become more active in our organizations and in the community as well as the sales and marketing end of it.

Kristin, let's go back to the company prior to Identity Marketing, Carantin. Carol has given quite a lengthy story of its founding and how it got its name. And that you and Ann gave up exceptional positions to join her. Can you tell me about your role in that company?

Identity Marketing drives business excellence in all areas. Shown here is the Advertising Specialty Institute 2004 - Spirit Award and the Tempe Chamber of Commerce's Business Excellence Award in 2003.

I was involved very actively in the company. Ann and I joined Carol after the company was formed. We all had ownership initially. Ann and I talked about it and finally said to Carol, "We don't deserve this, we want to earn ownership." We turned back the ownership to Carol after our first year. When we sold to Central Newspapers, Carol was the owner, I was the vice president of the company, really responsible for all of the management, the staff, human resources and customer service. I think I did a little bit of everything. And Carol was really our only sales rep, as she is primarily now with Identity Marketing.

And Carantin was founded shortly after you arrived here?

Carol actually arrived about two months after I started at ASU. She went to work for Medtronic and was with them for two to three years. About a month after Ann graduated from Marcos de Niza, because she did her last two high school years here, Carol moved back to Sioux Falls to set up a cardiology clinic and had committed two years, stayed three, and returned to Arizona in 1990. We started Newcomers Welcome Service in 1991. We were independent contractors for a group out of the Midwest that wanted to do something similar to what they were doing in Lincoln, Nebraska. They said, "Do you think this will work in Mesa?" And Carol said, "No." So they said, "Well what would you do?" We came up with the publication that we did for about four years. One of the clients at that time approached us about another bulk mailing, because we were in direct mail and marketing, and Carol tells the story that she was headed out of town and we were going to do a mailing for this client and it was 30,000 pieces. Ann and I along with Adam, Ann's friend who also worked for the company said, "Oh, we'll get this done this weekend." Carol came back on Sunday and we were still stuffing and sealing envelopes and preparing this mailing. And that was really the start of Carantin. That was when we realized that there was an opportunity, outside of just the welcome service, for direct mail and that's when Carantin really took off. It was sold in September 1998. We stayed on as active management for about a year after the sale which was part of the deal.

November of '99 they put us into more of a consulting role for them, and we, in essence, as Carol would say, took about a year off. She got bored, I loved life because we were under an employment contract while I was preparing for my wedding. Two weeks after the wedding, we had just gotten back from our honeymoon, we flew to Iowa and met with Carol. Prior to that, right before the wedding, she had said, "You know what? I want to start a new

KRISTIN AND CAROL RECEIVE THE TEMPE CHAMBER BUSINESS EXCELLENCE AWARD.

Carol Den Herder and Kristin Rezler (continued)

IN 1985, KRISTIN TRAVELED THE COUNTRY SINGING.

company." I asked, "Okay, what are you going to do?" She said, "I think I'm going to do garments." Obviously, being in a no-compete, we were not going to do the promotional products. She asked, "Are you interested?" I said, "Yeah, I think I am." So we met on October 1, 2000 in Okoboji, Iowa and decided at that point we would partner. About six months after we started it, the newspaper closed their promotional products division and that's when we added the "tchotchky." We think of promotional items as carrying billboards, walking billboards, but the garments were and still are our first focus for the company.

There are some personal questions I would like to ask, some of which are introspective. I would like, if you would, to describe the type of person you believe you are?

That's funny, because someone asked me this morning about the interview, and I said I have never really thought of myself as an entrepreneur, but more an implementer because I've always been a bit reserved. I think I have many talents, I just don't take them into the spotlight as much as most people do. I'm a very patient person, which is important in the role I play, especially in the company and the growth of the company because as we grow and staffing changes, you see a lot of needs. I think I'm a very kind and caring person, I enjoy giving back. It's the one thing Carol taught us from day one, that it's important to give back to your community.

I guess I've always felt like I was the "behind-the-scenes" person. The best recollection of that is the day we were at Ann's funeral, we had a lot of very high-powered individuals from the business community who attended. I had spoken to many of them on the phone but never met them over the years of managing the company. I think that is a very strong point for me. Can I do the community contacts? Absolutely, and that's something I'm growing into right now. I'm a very sensitive and emotional person. I always have to think of the business needs when it comes to dealing with the personal side of my staff, and yet being able to draw that line because they're still our family. We have 18 employees right now and I feel like every one of them is a family member.

I have known you and Carol at least ten years, and know you both to be caring people. Your generosity to your staff, as well as to the community is legend. My own efforts at the university have been the beneficiary of your caring and generosity. You are on one hand thoughtful and caring and on the other hand you are also an adventurer, Kristin. You take chances and put your capability at risk. There is a lot of the entrepreneur in you whether you admit to it or not.

But what is most obvious is your propensity to take care of people. Were you always like this, even when you were growing up?

According to my mother, yes. She tells the story that when she would give us our allowance, my sister Ann would put hers in the bank, and then look to me to go buy her a candy bar or whatever. Of course being "the little mother" I was, that's what she called me, I would do it. I would buy her whatever she wanted. I made sure to take care of her. I dressed her, and you know, Carol says it started from the day she tried to pick up a spoon in her right hand and I told her she did it wrong and put it in her left hand. Ann ended up being ambidextrous because I was left-handed, she needed to do it the right way. She tells that story all the time and I think it goes all the way back because I think being the three of us, it was just Carol, Ann and me, we became more than just a family. We were just a solid unit. So when the three of us worked together at Carantin, and now I have the pleasure of doing it here with Carol, there were a lot of times that we knew what the other person was thinking. We didn't have to ask the question and Carol will tell you I finish a lot of her sentences when questions are asked because I know what her thoughts are and I tend to be a lot of her memory. I guess, to answer that, yes I have always been that way. I have always felt like I needed to take care of someone.

Kristin won first place at her 8th grade track event.

This question overlaps to a certain extent, the one I asked you before. What are the highly personal principles you followed that have made a difference in your personal life? Not your corporate principles, your personal life.

You know, I think it always just comes down to treating people the way I want to be treated. If one of my friends hurts, I hurt for them, sometimes more so. I have been kind of the psychologist or the advisor or the shoulder that someone can always lean on. I hope that by being that person for them, they've become that person for me. I think just to appreciate everything you have. There were times we didn't have a lot and I was never aware of it. I always felt like we had the moon. That we had everything and more than we ever needed just because we were so close. So not to take things for granted, because you never know when you're going to lose something that's so valuable.

If you were starting today, all over again, which is something that you had an opportunity to do from your first company, Carantin and I'm sure a lot of the lessons you learned there washed over into Identity Marketing. But if you were starting today, would you change some of the actions you took initially? And if so, what would those changes be?

Knowing what we know today we would not change how we operate. A big portion of what makes us so exceptional and different from others in our type business, is the quality that we bring to our workmanship. Having total control

Carol Den Herder and Kristin Rezler (continued)

CAROL AND KRISTIN AT IDENTITY MARKETING.

over the products we provide wins us clients who have had bad experiences with what is called in the industry, brokering. Even at that we have vendors who don't meet our expectations. We really considered the system we had used at Carantin two years ago when we questioned whether we would invest in equipment and production. We thought it would have allowed us a little more freedom to broker. We then would have had a core staff of sales and customer service only.

Kristin, would you tell us what you mean by brokering, vs. the system you have here at Identity?

Yes, we would not have the equipment and production and the actual hands on from raw product to completion. As is my mother's philosophy – nothing but the best – state-of-the-art equipment. We would, under the system we considered and rejected, have gone out of house for graphics, digitizing which is creating sewing files for embroidery. You buy your garments from one company, send them to somebody else to be screen-printed and embroidered. And, when it comes to promotional products there is a whole other group of vendors. What we do separates us from most of the others in our business.

Your quality and methodology, Kristin, have always impressed me. In all my years buying promotional merchandise, I've never seen quality control like yours, combined with customer concern and integrity. You exceed expectations.

What has been the most defining moment in your life, Kristin?

The untimely death of my sister, Ann, who died in a scuba diving accident on October 2, 1994.

It turned you and your mother in directions that are not only admirable, but absolutely unique. We'll discuss these a little later. Do you have special people that you turn to for support or that keep your life in balance?

Well, obviously first and foremost, my mom. Beyond my mom, Carol, certainly my husband, Tom. He is very much a part of my personal life as well as my business life. He is actively involved in the company with us. It took a while for the three of us to find the right mix, the right role for each other and make it work to take us to where we are now. And though Ann is gone, her influence is ever present. Over the years and the times I just wanted to say NO, I don't want to do that - she was always the one that was like a stick in my back that said - you have to do this! Always supportive, always the first one to jump in. The three - Carol, Tom and Ann, are the biggest influences in my life.

Kristin, has there ever been a time when you thought or said to yourself, "I think I'm going to move on and do something else?"

That's a loaded question! There are bad days where I feel like - is it really worth continuing? With a family business, there are all kinds of pressures. Is it a high number of days? No. The days of excitement and growth far out number the trying days, and this industry is fun. This industry is ever changing, growing and exciting. There are new products, new inventions, new ideas - that can be overwhelming but fun. And there's never going to be a perfect, mistake-free business. Doesn't matter whether you're a service or a manufacturer, there's going to be errors, there's going to be mistakes because we're still human. We rely on a lot of technology. I have a computer in Iowa that's down. It's going to happen. Now, can I learn from what happened there to make certain it doesn't happen again and put a backup plan in place for the future? Absolutely. But if I don't, then that's my mistake because I need to look at every error/process/mistake as a challenge and make certain we learn from it. And that's what we encourage our staff to do.

That's good advice for anybody in life but also in business, Kristin. I know you have the office in Iowa and your mother does invest a lot of time there. Are there any other areas besides here and Iowa that you plan to have a base?

Headquarters will always remain here in Arizona. I don't foresee in the near future that we would add an additional base other than the area where Carol works from. A lot of what this company allows us to do is the opportunity that if we found a candidate that candidate really could work remotely from wherever they're at. We wouldn't need to have a physical base really anywhere else.

This is a question you may or may not want to answer. I try to avoid questions that might give competitors opportunity. How much of your business is local versus national?

That's a good question. Because a large quantity of our clients have a national presence. I would have to say over 50% are located in Arizona, yet have national reach. We can operate our business from this one base. As to Iowa, Carol originally worked out of her home there, but when she found the individual interested in the business, it became a convenience to have a small office and it gave us an opportunity to have a small showroom. Considering the new divisions Carol is developing for Identity, would it be necessary for what we do there? I don't think so. It's just a convenience. All the support is done through here.

What is the most important advice you would like to share with the readers of your story who may themselves be

Carol Den Herder and Kristin Rezler (continued)

interested in the kind of innovative career you've had?

I think it's just to find something they are passionate about. I enjoyed everything I did with Carantin. I loved what we did with the company and saw myself finishing my business career with Carantin even after we sold it. I never expected that I would be anywhere else. In hindsight, was I as passionate? I think I gave 150 percent to it because I do with everything I do, whether it's working through college, in retail, to Carantin, to where I am today. I think I gave everything I could give but I didn't feel the love and the passion that I do for this company, because this company excites me more. They can achieve anything as long as they keep that passion and their focus.

Do you have any special dream that you have that you sometime want to work to fulfill?

I think I'm doing it now! From the time I was little, Carol owned a retail store. My early memories are of that store. Even through grade school, she then had a different store, but had a retail presence. I remember being very little and telling people that someday I was going to own a business with my mother. I finally achieved that. I have the other standard goals, but working with my talented and brilliant mother was and is my special dream.

Do you have a special message that you would like to convey to the readers of your story?

You know it ties back to if they're passionate about what they do. Too often you see individuals in jobs just because there is a paycheck. It's not something they enjoy. They have learned to tolerate. I believe you have to love the person you are but you have to love what you do. Not everyone is entrepreneurial but everyone has be to a contributor. I have a message on my wall. It was given to me and it touched a cord in my life. It says, "My work is something I do, not what I am. What I am is far greater than anything I can do." Everyone has a puzzle in their life. They have personal, community and worklife issues that contribute to whether they enjoy their lives.

Kristin, please share your vision for the future.

My personal vision is to continue to foster a company that doesn't forget the human element. For as long as I'm involved, no matter how large we get, there will be a human who answers the phone!! Carol and I have talked about the turn-off that mechanical messages are. It gives the client the impression of a company that is just an order taker. What we feel we do every day is customer service. Answer the questions if you can answer them when you are on the phone.

If you don't know the answer, find someone who does. It's that human element. We talk about it frequently in our customer service and our sales meetings, that it's not just about sending an email with a quote, and then following up to say, "Do you need anything else?" It's about calling the individual, and making the personal effort and sending a note of thanks and doing those types of things that are really important. As technology allows us to do more electronically, the tendency is to over rely on it. I insist that we all use technology in a balanced fashion. Control it rather than it controlling us. I've occasionally taken our network down so that we go back to manually looking up a vendor/supplier's information and having to pick up the phone to make a call instead of placing the order on line. We need to use both options so that we don't forget that we still need to communicate on a personal level with individuals.

So, my vision for the future of Identity is to keep it a human-to-human business and to reflect that in my life. I write personal notes along with using email.

Kristin, thank you for reminding our readers of the power of person-to-person communications and sharing your strong company philosophy that is definitely worth emulating.

GUARDIAN SCULPTURE

POST SCRIPT

As I interviewed Carol and Kristin and especially as I brought each of their stories together, I was struck by their differences, accommodations and how they came together as a team and family. It seemed to be especially beneficial for readers to cover three special programs with unique qualities for family business. Their philosophy, performance, intense dedication and creativity is special and different than other family businesses I have researched. These areas are community giving and support, family and business separation and employee involvement and training. While their comments on these issues were voiced in separate, personal interviews, they are remarkably cohesive when viewed together.

COMMUNITY GIVING AND SUPPORT

What special community support do the two of you personally provide or are involved in?

Over the years we have given of time, products and money directly to a wide variety of organizations as well as to major organizations that support multiple charities. In addition we are involved in four chambers of commerce.

Can you give us some specifics?

We give two percent of all our sales to probably more than 50 different organizations. The give ranges from monetary to donations of product, special discounts along with relief needs resulting from catastrophes, local, national and

Carol Den Herder and Kristin Rezler (continued)

international. We give our special talents supporting and participating in several health walks. All of these receive great participation from our employees as well. The variety is wide ranging. We support about 99 percent of children's programs that come to our attention from little league teams, children's hospitals, special child campaigns, March of Dimes, polio, YMCAs, Salvation Army, Red Cross, just to identify a few.

We did a huge campaign for Katrina hurricane relief. It started with our immediately gathering and shipping six boxes of clothes, hats, jackets, T-shirts, all new merchandise. About an hour after we shipped, one of our employees said she knew there was a need for personal items she provided and could we gather and ship these. "You bet, absolutely," we said. Our staff, 15 individuals, came up with 20 cases of materials. We were going to ship and happened to get a call from Robin Sewell, a well-known, talented T.V. personality who was working with the Salvation Army. They came by and picked up these cases along with 50 tote bags, all for the evacuees that were being housed here.

We get asked to help a lot. We just have to sort out the best ways and causes that benefit our community. We are also generous in our support of educational needs of our communities. Our employees make us proud with their generosity and personal time. They participate in related events such as the Heart Walk, Breast Cancer walks, food banks, just to name a few.

Both of you cited as the one most defining moment in your lives as the untimely death of Ann, your daughter, Carol - your sister, Kristin. It turned you both to foster and support a unique program, your Guardian Foundation to benefit the Banner Heart Hospital in East Mesa. Would you tell us about the Guardian program that you both created in memory of Ann?

Kristin: Absolutely. Ann was very committed to women's and children's programs and those which had a tie-in to the start of her work career. When Ann went off to college she was the recipient of a Medtronic scholarship.

Carol interjected: In 2002 we got a call from the CEO of Banner Heart Hospital, Kathy Bollinger, for Kristin and I to come to lunch as she wanted to discuss a project with us. Kristin and I were intrigued so we joined Ms. Bollinger at the hospital who related this story to us. Dr. Pearlstein, the medical director, has a patient, a sculptor, who had suffered a stroke and during rehabilitation had pretty much given up. Dr. Pearlstein had said to him, "Jim, sculpting is in your mind and not in your hand and I challenge you to sculpt something for me." He did. The Geronimo sculpture is in Dr. Pearlstein's office. He did it with his non-dominant hand and from his mind and heart. It is an amazing piece. They have a fountain at the hospital and if they could find a donor, that patient would do a special sculpture for them.

Kristin continued, "When she explained what they wanted, Carol and I thought it was a natural fit for us. We agreed to participate. When the statue was completed it eerily looked a lot like my sister, Ann, yet the sculptor had never seen her picture. The sculpture is a six foot bronze of a nurse holding a heart. It's so symbolic of the work of the hospital and it's dedicated nurses, who hold the hearts of their patients and patients' families in their hands everyday.

Carol and I pondered over a name that would be symbolic of our Ann. It was logical to call the statue "The Guardian" because we believe that Ann is our guardian and watches over us every day. Each year we award one or more staff members who represent the five characteristics of Ann's life - wisdom, warmth, strength, integrity and gentleness. The program has continued to grow and has really created a community within the heart hospital and an environment that is so different then anything we have ever seen. Each year the celebration dinner and award ceremony is held in the hospital parking garage and is attended by hundreds of employees, their families and the community. Each year attendees receive a special memento and Kristin and I have the honor of presenting these special awards to the selected staff recipients.

We both believe the Guardian program is our most significant contribution to community and the future. We have never been the kind of people to toot our horn about what we contribute but we hope this will encourage others to find it in their hearts to consider something like the Guardian.

FAMILY AND BUSINESS SEPARATION

Kristin, I noted that you refer to your mother as Carol not as "my mom." And, you do it in a natural, matter-of-fact way.

It seemed to us both as the most important way to handle our roles in the company and keep our employees comfortable with business relationships. We are a family - Carol, my husband Tom and me. It took us a while, but it is natural for me to call her Carol. It was like the gel set and we knew what we were doing and we are all natural about the business being separate from family. Carol taught me a very good lesson and I share it with our employees, that there are three important areas in your life. First comes you, second comes those who you deem significant others and third comes work. Those priorities need to be kept in that order. However, if any one of the three is out of sync, it affects the other two. We share that with our employees all the time, and ourselves, because there's a lot of times that it's easy to make number three, work, more important than number one or number two. We absolutely keep family out of the work relationship.

Dr. Pearlstein, Carol, Kristin and artist Jim Lee.

Carol Den Herder and Kristin Rezler (continued)

It is important to all three of us that we keep business business, but we have to maintain family and our personal down to small things, like having a date night. It's so easy to get wrapped up during dinner and talking about what happened at work that day or what needed to be done that we didn't have the time to talk about - the dogs, or the house or the you know, whatever, just us. So we've really made that even more of a priority because it was too easy for us to become the 6 a.m. to the neverland.

Carol, are there special ways that you and Kristin have worked out that keep your relations running smoothly. You are both very different, yet compatible and very dedicated to one another. You have to have some things that you do that someone reading what we write could profit from. Please share.

I believe number one is respect. And that goes both ways with us. Respect for each one's point of view, each one's innovations. Respect for each one's responsibilities. Differences are sorted out privately, never in front of employees. Trust is the second most important. And when you can walk away and trust, it becomes a huge complement. Not just to both of us, but to all our staff. I have always practiced these special relations. For example, I never set hours for my children. They set their own. Never set destinations, they set their own. Supported them emotionally and physically as much as I could. Thus, they learned to manage themselves.

The happy family - Kristin, Bentley, Cooper and Tom. Their new dog, Austin, had not yet been added to the family.

The other thing is that we maintain family unity outside of the work place. That is another thing I have always told my kids. My kids have always known I consider it a privilege to work with them. We work hard to keep family, family. Not to bring work issues to the family gatherings. We do things as a family as well. I consider it a privilege to work with them. I think that is so important. You have to keep that balance. Balance is another key word in my life that needs to be there.

The other thing you need to note is when we have an issue, we don't let it burn. We just bring it up, cough it up, discuss it. Try to get over it. Sometimes there are tears. Sometimes there are hugs and laughter. Sometimes it takes the three days where you need to just wait the three days before you make a decision. Try not to do anything or say anything that hurts the other individual. Because when that happens, we all break down. And there are a lot of emotions in having a family business. It is not all a pretty picture. But trust enters into the equation and along with that goes our integrity. I try to always do business with the highest integrity. If you always tell the truth, you don't have to remember what you said. Keeping our family time is a priority. It is all too easy to assume that since we see each other at work we do not need to spend time together. We make a priority of scheduling family time outside the work environment.

EMPLOYEE SELECTION, INVOLVEMENT AND TRAINING

Kristin, can you tell us about selecting, training and keeping good employees?

We find and get our employees through friends, business colleagues and our present employees. When we have a position to fill we ask for recommendations. If the recommendee stays six months we pay a referral bonus. That gives our employees a true involvement in the future of the company, since they participate in recruiting and are encouraged to make suggestions on how to do a better job as a team. We also have an employee recognition program which allows them to recognize one another's special talents and contributions. We encourage them to seek additional education and have an education reimbursement program. All of our training is done in-house and everyone is involved. We call our training program See One - Do One - Teach One. We plan for the unexpected through this process by having a backup trained for each position.

We have a great team in our production area and when we have clients in, they are invited to watch the team do their jobs. One of the women who does beautiful finishing work and finaling work was a referral from another employee. She was doing such quality, we gave her a raise. She said, "No, I don't deserve a raise, I don't know how to run the computer on the embroider equipment." We said, "But you do deserve a raise because of everything you have learned and accomplished." One of our men took his notes, showed her how and now she's teaching it to someone else. It was so overwhelming. She literally said, "I am not deserving of a raise." Now to watch her train others is most rewarding.

Carol and Kristin do you have a message you would like to give the readers of your story?

Well, I guess what I would like to say most is what I wrote back in 1969 which was my business purpose because I live that every day. And I think that truly the principles that I lived and worked by, they just work for me. I believe in asking for business. I believe in what I am doing. I believe that you shouldn't use any trickery in life. I think that you, your preferences need to be based on outcomes and I think a pleasing personality. I think about all the things that I have made statements on and have made statements on all my life. That would be my statement I would want to leave with people to say that if you really and truly set down your values when you start any business in life and stay committed to those values, you will be successful. I don't know. I want to say that I love the challenge of doing my own business. I know it is not for everyone and I am really thankful for people who just want to come to work every day, and give their best.

Kristin, do you have a piece of advice that you think is baseline?

Sure. Helping others has always been our policy.

TOP DOG In Flight

Any day, somewhere in action on radio, TV, in a newspaper, a magazine, a seminar, or non-profit event you will meet Eileen Proctor. Eileen is a talented, exciting, rebellious, daring and often quixotic serial entrepreneur who founded IT'S A RUFF LIFE, a unique cage-free doggie day care center in October 2000. She is an avid dog lover who turned her love of dogs into a business that pampers, respects and cares for your dog during the day while you work or can't be home to see to your canine family member's needs. She left a successful corporate executive career to build her own business.

I first met Eileen in 2003 when she won The Spirit of Enterprise Emerging Entrepreneur Award given by the center I founded at ASU in 1992. When she talks about her love of dogs, and her future plans, the ideas, dreams, projects, helping entrepreneurs succeed and the like, words tumble out in a romantic persuasive stream. When her ideas become a framed process with an inventive unique name already to present, she springs into action.

When I decided to write this book, Eileen seemed to me the obvious example of the category of serial entrepreneur. To capture her in flight took two formal interviews and one informal off the record interview session. She has not flinched at telling her story fraught with problems, missteps, successes and failures. You will feel in her story energy, musing, wisdom, excitement, altruism worth the listening to. I've pulled a fair amount of nuggets you can take to the bank if you listen. Each of my questions was answered without hesitation.

Eileen, I can hardly pick up a paper, turn on the TV or radio without seeing you or hearing you. You seem to capture the interest of the media. Behind the public persona, how would you describe yourself?

I am a proactive person. I don't sit around waiting for someone to ask me to do things. I like to contribute where I see opportunity to make a difference. I'm a compassionate person who tries to see other sides of an issue before making a judgment. In some ways I'm kind of rebellious. If someone tells me I can't do something it's the surest way to encourage me to do it. I'm adventuresome and like challenge. Solving problems is fun. And, yes I'm curious and inquisitive and always want to know the why so I can improve whatever needs improvement. That leads to setting good examples. In my work with business people and clients being a role model is essential. Setting an example for employees is a part of the process of teaching them. From an emotional sense I'm a spiritual person as well.

HERE AT 6, EILEEN FLANKED BY HER BROTHER PHILL AND SISTER WENDY, SHOWS HER AFFECTION FOR THE FAMILY'S FIRST PET, TINY TIM.

When did you discover these facets of your personality or were you like this as a child?

That's hard to explain. I was the middle child always trying to get free. I guess the answer would be they were a part of me influenced by having to deal with an older sibling and manage the needs of and relations with a younger sibling. I just came to feel these traits were always a part of me and I honed them through my challenges as I got older and interacted with a wide variety of personalities.

You have an extraordinary ability to get press and media recognition. Is there a purpose to your actions in seeking notoriety? Is it for business or personal vindication?

Eileen Proctor (continued)

EILEEN WAS UNDISPUTEDLY FUEL-INJECTED AT CONCEPTION WITH HER FATHER JAY'S ENTREPRENEURIAL "NOTHING IS IMPOSSIBLE; NEVER SAY DIE" ATTITUDE.

Vindication sounds negative. It is both for business and personal satisfaction. I'll explain, because I want other businesses listening to see that they can do it too. I have very little to spend on marketing, so I have to invent ways to get the attention of the public that don't cost me a lot of money. I have to be creative. I tend to be a bit off kilter so they get recognized, like my annual BOWL-A-RAMA for Animal Rescue. It's to raise funds to help homeless animals and reduce euthanasia. We've done this for 4 years. Or, our DIM SUM FOR DOGS. It's a kick-off of Chinese New Year which I've orchestrated and it was catered by a dog business called Just Dogs Gourmet. I found out early that if you are unique in such programs you give people a reason to talk about you in a good way. The things I do make people smile and capture the interest of press, TV, radio and the like, who are always looking for community activities. It's a valid way to get your message out. You do enough of these and you become a media magnet. You even begin to get calls from media contacts when they're looking for another community interest item. Get one and it is easier to get a second and even easier to get a third. Whatever your business you soon become recognized as an expert. I get calls from friends and other business people asking how do you get all this attention? I tell them to put together some interesting idea that helps the public and is unique to your business. Then send out a press release inviting the public and follow it with a call to the person you sent the release to. There are a lot of other ways, just have the business owner call me.

Another way I use is to pursue and apply for various business awards. I've won some recognition in this way as well.

I've learned over the years, if you don't risk and at times change direction if something isn't working, you are soon going backward. I believe all these special activities and programs I've invented help all the communities I work in. You see, I was born into an entrepreneurial family. My dad was an entrepreneur, his brothers were entrepreneurs and I was the first female entrepreneur in my family. It is in my genes. My business career started with the good old lemonade stand in Canarsie, Brooklyn at age five. During college I had a part time business called Resume Writers. And, I supported myself for seven years as owner/operator of home-based Untypical Graphics/Graphic AdVentures - a marketing, graphic arts and print brokerage company specializing in the needs of small to medium sized businesses. When I moved to Arizona, I was overwhelmed by the huge amount of art and cactus tchotchkes so I started Squaw Peak Trading Company and The Cactus Connection. They never took off due to lack of lack of capital. So, to pay the bills I went to work for a major corporation.

Eileen, in your answers to my first set of interview questions sent prior to this interview, you seemed disdainful of the corporate world, their attitudes and requirements. What caused your disenchantment and when did it begin?

I consistently pushed my inborn entrepreneurial inclinations and fervors aside to pursue a path in corporate marketing because it paid the bills, but my zest for life and positive attitude diminished on a daily basis. I dislike the structure and conformity that corporate life invariably required, along with constantly changing paradigms and increased expectations with decreasing resources. In one instance, I got 90% done on a supposedly critical project that required 24/7 attention for months only to find that the new CEO had a different agenda and all the work went into the proverbial round file. The pressure to achieve a bottom line that kept moving up along with a bending of ethical practices and behavior, as well as decisions that hurt employees and customers. At that time I got higher in the organization, probably about a foot and a half away from a vice presidency, but it was getting harder and harder to get up in the morning and face the day. About then, I knew in my heart and soul that I'd rather kiss a dog on the mouth than a boss on the butt.

That all changed in 2000 when the company I was working for as Director of Business Development was sold. I was faced with an equally undesirable decision of relocating to the new corporate offices in Seattle or looking for a new job in my beloved, adopted home state of ten years, Arizona. I actually looked to the heavens and declared, "God there has to be a better way!" And sure enough there was!

Is that were doggie day care evolved for you?

Yes, almost immediately. I had heard about daycare for dogs going on in California. Dogs had always been my big love. They had been my furry kids. I visited over 25 different day care centers in California where it started in the late 1990's. Fueled by my belief that I had found my calling, October 2000, I pioneered dog daycare in the Valley of the Sun.

Let's pursue a little of the process in creating It's A Ruff Life, Eileen. Go back to that start up.

Ruff Life responds to the evolving needs of society - one that embraces pets as beloved members of a family. We were the first such business here, although the model existed to varying degrees in many other major cities in the U. S. Recognizing there's never a second chance to be first, I made the decision to let my life go to the dogs! It took a solid year of explaining what we don't do such as overnight,

Eileen Proctor (continued)

Eileen found a way to feed her fur-vent love of four-leggeds, pioneering the Valley of the Sun's first dog daycare in October 2000. Here she is surrounded by loving canine clients.

training, etc. and the benefits of what we do, such as socializing, a channel for excess energy, a solution to leaving your dog at home all day when you are at work, no cages, supervised and cared for like a part of the family. Lots of open space indoor and outdoor, play areas with toys, lots of water and all of this with loving supervision of people who love dogs. We had to overcome great difficulties in a market unaware of such options. I met a lot of resistance. The industry didn't exist and the city did not know what doggie day care was. All they knew was kennels and there is very limited zoning for kennels. I went to the City of Phoenix and stated that I was opening a doggie day care facility. They stated that I could not do it. I asked, "What do you mean, I can't." They said, that there was not more zoning available for kennels. To make a long story short, I persisted and insisted we did not want a kennel and after explaining in detail our business plan, giving them proof of day care in major cities across the United States, they agreed to a zoning for doggie daycare, at which time I set out to find a suitable location they would approve. What is interesting about this location is the building was a day care center for children originally which meant we did not have to perform too many modifications. Here we are, six years later and having a doggone awesome business.

What other challenges did you have Eileen?

Staffing is difficult as we must insist on a high level of experience working with dogs in a professional capacity, not just dog lovers, although that is a plus. Training people to have a positive attitude about their position and its importance and yes retaining good people. Of course, achieving a balance like properly managing my business and simultaneously paying attention to my home and social life. I'm still trying to figure that one out!

Eileen, you talked about the essential importance of employees. Please tell me more about this aspect.

Our employees are critical to our success. They put my promises into practice serve as Ruff Life's ambassadors on a daily basis. I am constantly looking for ways to show my appreciation for their efforts. We have monthly celebrations in the form of treats like a snow cone machine during the sweltering dog days of summer, excursions to a Diamondback's game for team building, dinner celebrations whenever a major award or recognition is bestowed on our business. When we won the BBB Ethics Award, I promoted everyone on the team to the title of CEO – that's Canine Enjoyment Officer – gifting them with a special t-shirt and set of business cards so they can display their status to all they meet. These small but important validations of their esteemed place in our business success have been a reason that our turnover has decreased and morale stays high. All members of the staff are encouraged to take advantage of my open door policy for questions and suggestions and our monthly staff meetings provide a forum to share with the entire team. We all take pride in the ten awards and trophies we earned in the first five years in business. We proudly and prominently display the trophies in our reception areas as a consistent reminder to employees, customers, prospects and vendors. We just don't talk about good business, we practice it and incorporate all in our marketing campaigns and on our website. But most importantly, we continually strive not just to meet, but exceed the criteria that won us awards in the unending quest to better ourselves both personally and professionally.

All of that is internal, what about the clients whose furry kids visit your day care? What kinds of ways do you get them through your door and keep them?

Our community activities bring us people and their dogs, word-of-mouth advertising by happy owners, media people and a little inexpensive advertising has brought us a steady stream of clients, many of whom have turned into regulars. When we get a first time client we not only interview them but we interview the dog as well. We truly want to know just how sociable the dog is. We maintain clean and inviting premises from the entry to the fun rooms and the outdoor spaces which are humidified and covered. All of these areas have employees who watch, care for and play with the dogs. There is always a responsible person at the front desk and I personally work that desk periodically to experience the relationship with our clients. There is nothing like a hug, a smile and a thanks for being here for our two-legged customers and a sloppy kiss and a whipping tail from our four-legged customers to remind us of why we put forth our efforts. Our human customers can tour any time to view what is going on. The inside rooms all have windows to view through and contain couches, dog beds, fresh bottled water in bowls, dog toys and treats as appropriate. We get a lot of "ATTA girls" from my business associates, friends and recognitions from business organizations and the media for our special kinds of loving attention to everyone.

So right now you have daycare. What about future? Do you have new locations planned or other kinds of services?

At this time, we are limited to dog daycare and grooming which we call Bow-Wow Beautification. We also offer obedience training out of our facilities, but that is sub-contracted through an outside organization we have built a relationship with over the years. We tried to incorporate retail, message therapy and pet photography but with little success at the time. It requires a different set of employees. Future ideas include camp Ruff & Ready for people and their dogs, private label products and perhaps overnight – all of which would involve major investments. We are also considering franchising. I like to make a difference and provide only the best. Of all the governing issues to me ethics and intellectual honesty are paramount. I've lots of ideas but without good people they can't be done. All that

RECEIVING THE GREATER PHOENIX CHAMBER OF COMMERCE'S SMALL BUSINESSPERSON OF THE YEAR FOR COMMUNITY INVOLVEMENT RESULTED FROM OUR SUCCESSFUL OUTREACH. OUR ANNUAL BOWL-A-RAMA FOR ANIMAL RESCUE RAISED OVER $650K FOR HOMELESS ANIMALS SINCE LAUNCHING IN 2003.

Eileen Proctor (continued)

is a part of my VISION. If you don't have a vision and stick to it you're subject to crash and burn.

If you were starting again would you change some of the actions you took initially, if so what would they be?

I don't believe in regret and that circumstances are the way they happen. You learn lessons you are supposed to learn because you make decisions. I live by understanding that decisions have results and that means some will be what I expect and some won't. Hindsight is always 20/20. So, I did what I should have done based on who I am. I learned a lot. If I had waited and researched more extensively, I would have experienced a loss of enthusiasm and it would have gummed up the works. I did it right because I pursued a passion rather than starting a business. I did it the right way for me.

Eileen your passion and animation caught my interest from the beginning. I'm always curious about defining moments in lives of significant people who have achieved. Those kinds of moments had profound influence on my life. Would you share some of your defining moments with us and would you say leaving the corporate world was one of them?

I have thought about this. There have been many — and yes leaving the big corporate world was one of them. But the most important one happened when I was 12 years old. It was the first night of Passover in 1969. We were on the way to the First Seder. We are not an overly religious family but some religious celebrations are important, as they are family oriented. We always celebrated the first two evenings with my grandparents who were in Brooklyn and my aunts, uncles and cousins who were in New Jersey. On the way we stopped at my grandparents' house to pick them up in Flatbush. My mom went to the bathroom and didn't come out. My sister, brother and I had gone up with mom. Dad was downstairs in the car waiting. You can't park in Flatbush, so he was double-parked. We were pounding on the door getting annoyed and hungry when Mom stumbled out mumbling and fell in the hall in front of us. We were scared and didn't know what to do, so I ran down and blubbered "Dad, something's wrong with Mom". He was annoyed, but came up. We later learned that she had had a cerebral aneurism. Over the next week she was in the hospital and had brain surgery.

DESPITE HER PHYSICAL, EMOTIONAL AND FINANCIAL CHALLENGES, EILEEN'S MOM VIVIAN HAS BEEN A CONSTANT SOURCE OF LOVE, SUPPORT AND INSPIRATION.

She had a stroke a couple of days later and became paralyzed. So us kids had to really grow up fast.

Dad was running back and forth from home to business and the hospital. He had started his own small business six months before, a frame company. He had no insurance so he was working 20 hours a day to make the business work and taking care of mother. We kids were ten, twelve and fourteen - we were food shopping, cooking and other household jobs. We learned how to be resourceful and interact with adults. We didn't have a mother for quite awhile so we became self-sufficient. I believe my life today and the way I face challenge has a lot to do with this defining occurrence. My mom is alive and lives in Florida. I send her the media and publicity and she is proud and gets great pleasure out of keeping up with my activities and achievements.

You've spoken some about family influence. I'd like to pursue this facet of your life a little more. Let's start with your father, OK?

The person I am is a great mix of my father and mother. My niceness, compassion and sensitivity are like mom, but I definitely got my father's can-do attitude and his way of being able to turn a phrase and communicate. He showed me that no matter what happens you can always find a way to succeed, solve the nastiest of problems — that nothing is without a solution if you turn your mind to it. Here's a guy with a sick wife, three young children, no insurance and a ton of bills to pay and a new business to build. To top it off he was a Korean War Veteran from the Choson Reservoir battle. He has lots of physical problems, but he taught me that if you really want to do something you can if you believe in yourself.

EILEEN'S BROTHER PHILL AND SISTER WENDY WEREN'T ALWAYS, BUT HAVE ULTIMATELY BECOME, TWO OF HER BEST FRIENDS AND STEADFAST SUPPORTERS.

My mom showed me that you can be a really good person and have bad things happen to you, but you can still go through life with grace and still have the faith. That God gave you more than he took away from you. My brother is one of my best friends and he too is an entrepreneur. He has tried many different businesses but definitely believes he has not yet reached his ultimate success. He is in Florida and is in printing. Dad is also in Florida but Mom and Dad do not live together now. My sister lives in Boston. She has no interest in business, just wanted marriage and a family.

With all but your sister in Florida, why did you choose Arizona?

Arizona had huge opportunity. It is after all, one of the most active entrepreneurial areas of the country. The other reason is I am in the prime time for all my entrepreneurial energies and certain family interests are not my interests. I can still relate well with my family and do for them without being right next door to them. I keep them informed and they enjoy sharing my successes.

Earlier in our discussion Eileen we pursued your ability to get publicity and notoriety. I sensed that you have developed a following in Phoenix and the Valley in general. Some of your projects have become exceptional contributors and influential. Let's pursue influences as they relate to benefits to community.

Eileen Proctor (continued)

Well first we were the very first of our type of business that was October 2000. We fill a need sorely lacking in Arizona. It is now a recognized industry and there are increasing numbers of competitors. In Arizona we were the pioneer. Our vision states that we will be the benchmark to which other daycares will aspire. Some have lasted six months to a year, then closed because they weren't able to maintain the standards we set for continuing quality service. We treat dogs as well and sometimes more luxuriously than they get at home. Our "regulars" look forward to the dog friends they live with in their daycare community. That is another way we are different. At this point I need to define who our customers really are. The majority of people we serve are working people. The economic range goes from blue collar, mid-management to high management. In other words we cross the economic spectrum. What they have in common is they consider their dogs to be family members. Some consider them children. They feel guilty leaving the furry kids alone all day when they are at work. People worry about their health, or leaving them outside in the yard where anything can happen. We provide a safe and enjoyable environment that provides exercise, water, companionship, play, places to rest and if the family wants it, beautification, like grooming, bathing and the like. Families can live their lives, do their work and not worry about their doggie kids.

> *"Our vision states that we will be the benchmark to which other day cares will aspire."*

Actually because of our publicity and community activism we are getting letters, emails, calls from people all over the country who want to replicate Ruff Life's success. I do take time, as it is available to me, to help some. At least help them to not make too many mistakes and also to suggest they need to do a lot of special amenities. I tell them we use padding at our facilities especially in many places so that in play they don't hurt themselves. There is constant supervision. We use filtered water in our premises and bottled water in water bowls. As to the betterment of the valley and the state I am very involved in the efforts like animal welfare. A portion of our time, energy and revenues go to organizations helping to save animals and find homes for abandoned animals. I'm on the board of the Pets 911 Auxiliary that works with 90 to 100 welfare organizations in Maricopa County. All my personal pets are adopted. Much of the work here is with grass root groups. I handle marketing for the adoption event, fund raising and PR. The big event is BOWL-A-RAMA which I started in 2002. We were able to bring together all these organizations in the summer and it has now become one of the largest annual fundraisers in the state. In 2005 we raised over $200,000.00 for a one-day event and helped over 50 different organizations with the money.

We also allow four abandoned dogs once a week to come to our facility and play free of charge. They are from the Arizona Welfare League. They have to meet the same criteria as our clients — just they come free. We also give them a bath so they go back looking and feeling great. It's our hope that people shopping for a rescue dog will find them attractive. We are also able to give the league helpful information on the dog's personality like can they be with other dogs? Are they afraid of men or like women? Do they like to chase or fetch?

I'm proud to be on the board of the Better Business Bureau for Central and Northern Arizona because I believe strongly in their ethics mission. Anyway I can help the community I try to fit into my life schedule, because at the end of the day, it is about creating a better world overall for people and their animals, a better business world as well and a better personal world for me.

What do you get out of all this Eileen?

From my perspective, I vowed when I opened my business to be the boss I never had. One who recognized and showed appreciation for contributions, ideas and loyalty, who could walk over to an employee and pat him on the back and tell him he makes a difference in my business and in my life. To provide an atmosphere that employees are happy to come to each day. I try every day to live up to this personal expectation. One of the beauties of being an entrepreneur is I can do what I want to do and make a difference in their emotional and physical well being. As I do this I am happier. We celebrate our successes. We don't grieve over our problems, we solve them. I get a great satisfaction out of seeing people learn and grow and see them acting as though it was their business and feeling the thrill of that responsibility. Cards and notes I get from people I have helped. The knowledge that I have made some things better in my community.

FRIENDLY, FURRY BLENDED FAMILY - EILEEN, SHERI AND THE KIDS BORDER COLLIE DIZNEY, GOLDEN RETRIEVER CASSIE, KITTY AUTUMN AND NEWEST DOGGIE ADDITION TRACEY.

With all you do Eileen do you take time to play or do hobbies, sports maybe?

When I play it is usually with my furry kids, Hi Disney, Hi Cathy and my kitty, Hi Autumn. When I'm at work, even though I'm surrounded with dogs, it's the various aspects of the business that get my attention so when I go home it is play time with my kids.

As to sports - not much. In my younger days, I was quite athletic. My brother played semi-pro baseball and he taught me how to check the angle of a ball off the bat and I was an excellent outfielder. He taught me how to throw a ball like a pro. I do enjoy spectator sports. I'm a good bowler and love to bowl. Hobbies? Well, writing ad copy and inventing promotions and yes, I hate to admit it, but I like to write song parodies and jingles. In late 2004, I wrote a songbook called the *Ruff Life Howliday Song Book* featuring festive photos of our fabulous furry friends. It really went over big and it got a mention in the Arizona Republic Biz Buzz.

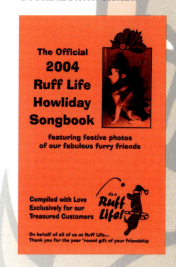

Are these kinds of inventive ideas the way you regenerate yourself?

It is more than that. I try to enrich the process of my business. Make it more intriguing and attractive. I'm always

EILEEN PROCTOR (CONTINUED)

aware that my clients, four-legged or two-legged like to enjoy their experiences as well as be served. I am quite dramatic and one of the other ways I use these skills is in local amateur and professional theater.

> *We all like to make work fun. Along with fun I pursue my passions.*

I'm aware of that flair from some of the many emails and PR releases I get from you. You put fun into your many promotions.

I do. We all like to make work fun. Along with fun I pursue my passions. I've also been mentoring entrepreneurs and do that as a side business. It will be the next of my creations. I've said to some, "If I can make money picking up dog poop, you can do anything in your life that is passion-laden and live a good life." I'm not rich in dollars and have a modest home and surroundings, but I am happier than I have ever been. Happier than when I earned six figures in corporate America with a fancy title to go with it. My title today is TOP DOG.

Are you grooming any one to carry on your business day to day or if something happens to you?

I regret so far I've not identified someone with the drive and passion to step in. We've created brand recognition but the business requires drive and commitment. That's not to say I'm resigned to this. More and more I'm working with some of the staff to create more leadership interest. I'm aware that to implement and expand my work with other entrepreneurs puts me in the position of becoming less of a doer more of a leader. A lot more reliance on staff. A lot more delegation and trust. I've realized that staff cannot grow if I don't put them in the position to do so. The other side of the equation is that I can't grow if I mire myself in nitty gritty. If I don't trust, we will never be able to duplicate success. I can always be the top visionary but not the driver. I must train and give away responsibility. There can be no progress with out that commitment on my part as the leader.

In your preliminary write--up you sent me, you projected opening a lot of It's A Ruff Life! centers. To date how many are open?

Two are open. The original plan was very expansive and called for five in five years. As it has turned out, I over estimated. Finding the people to groom proved harder and certainly the monetary resources. My enthusiasm far out stripped the potential of human and monetary resources. I was a little naïve. Finding the proper locations from zoning perspectives is still difficult and the ever present personnel difficulties. What I know is we did not hit breakeven our first year, but one month after 9/11 we hit it and it continued to increase since then. We then started an offshoot within our frame work here — The Fluff Life a Ruff Life Bow Wow Beautification Center. We started that at the second location as well.

If someone approached you and offered to buy you out, would you sell?

That would be a tough decision. Right now if the buyer was a major corporation it would be a really terrible emotional situation. I would get money but could almost guarantee you the business as we do it would disappear. They would convert it into a corporate structure which would eliminate the charm and loving benefit we created. They might even close it to get rid of it as competition. As it is for me, to call myself an entrepreneur or as you call it an innovator and changemaker is a person who has guts and heart and soul in a business. I'm still there!

These situations happen every day, Eileen. Creative people with amazing ideas burst on to the business scene, a few transition and mature their business as was the case with both Gates and Dell. Most eventually sell, often for money and the need for a new direction. Some buying organizations buy to obtain the creator and whatever ideas they have yet to produce. Let's go back to the period when you were most vulnerable putting more money and time in and feeling almost at a breaking point. What did you do?

I put in days of soul searching. Suffered a great deal of anguish. Even questioned my motives. Debated whether I even had an asset here that was saleable. Wondered if my energy would hold out. Thought about the people in my life who depended on me, like my mom. I have to help support her along with my siblings. I rationalized that I had other great ideas and did Ruff Life have its run or could I incorporate those into Ruff Life? Losing money hand-over-fist is pretty uncomfortable. At the lowest ebb, I confided my feelings to a good close friend who suggested I speak with a banker friend of hers. So I did.

And what was the out come of that meeting?

I told him my story and he said, "You know Eileen, there is no way you are going to make this business work. You don't have the money. You don't have the support of the community, obviously. You are just not going to make it. My recommendation as a banker and a friend is — fold."

At that moment I was almost euphoric. Somebody told me it was ok because it couldn't work because you can't do it. I was both crying and smiling at the same time. Someone was letting me off the hook. And as I got in my car my decision was made and I started driving home to set the stage to fold my Ruff Life — my dream. About three blocks into my drive, I hit the brakes and parked and suddenly my emotion welled up and I said out loud "who the hell does he think he is, telling me I can't make my business work? He doesn't understand my business. He doesn't really

Eileen's family joined in for a festive day with 50 clients and 70 shaggy sons and daughters for a cruise on the Dolly Steamboat.

EILEEN PROCTOR (CONTINUED)

know me. How dare he?" and I made up my mind then and there that if nothing else, I would bring Ruff Life to profitability so I could tell him I did it. Right? And that was a defining moment in my business! Not in my life but in my business. Nobody is going to tell me I can't make it work or that it is impossible. It didn't happen overnight but within two months we broke even and then hit the black. No one has the right to tell you what you are doing can't be done. The only person who has the right to tell you to quit is you.

So, Eileen what is your advice to an aspiring entrepreneur?

You have a choice to believe in yourself or not. Based on circumstances in your life on any given day, you can question your ability, your ideas or circumstances. I would ask you if you believe in your purpose. Have you explored every ethical avenue to achieve a successful result? There is always someone waiting to tell you to fold. Where you earn personal respect is when you have the guts to say to the naysayer, "Who the hell do you think you are telling me to fold?" I believe many people give up one inch before success is about to hit. Were they to take one more inch they would experience a different result.

I still have those days that challenge my resolve but then I remember that day with the banker. You will have a time in your venture when someone you trust or love will tell you to quit because they care about you or want to protect you - - but they are not you.

Eileen, you get it. Most people want someone to tell them what to do. Very few people have the guts to be their own person - who says only I can make that decision.

It looks like you have the end of the day checkout for your four legged clients. I will need to finish our exploration later.

Eileen, since our last session, you have continued to be the "media magnet", your phrase. My file of your public comings and goings has grown fat. Let's start with your possible expansion, ok?

Well, as you know, I had opened a second location in the northwest valley. It was in response to lots of inquiries there. As was the case with this first location, we were experiencing a time problem with breakeven. Splitting my time between there and here was frustrating. Again building staff proficiency and leadership was frustrating. I soon became aware that to expand needed more than my energy. I sold the second location as a test of whether or not the company could flourish with a licensing concept. I formed a separate company called Top Dog Business Builders and a

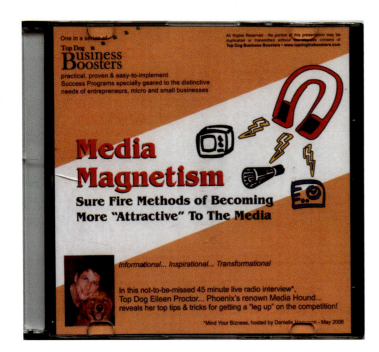

second off shoot called Top Dog Business Boosters. The builders concept was to franchise, the boosters was to market my know how for entrepreneurs looking for advice and help. The second grew out of the increasing demand on my time by people needing experienced advice and motivation.

Let's get back to Ruff Life. Where are you on that?

I reasoned that if I found someone who had the passion for an ethical business in day care for dogs, I could expand by tutoring them and at the same time provide a visible proven company. I would still be the face of the parent organization but they could build with my help.

Where is the process at this point?

I sold the location to a wonderful man who shares a passion for animals. Although he was excited about being It's A Ruff Life owner and taking over the proven procedures we offered, he was a typical entrepreneur as well. He started adding services and features that were inconsistent with my plan, such as doggie cams, probably good but if you are going to license you have to have a standard product or service. I agreed we cold test doggie cams, but then he wanted overnights. To make a long story short he began to change everything and so in July we withdrew his right to use the name. It is now a different place. We may do something about this later, but we announced in the Arizona Republic that the location had been sold as a first step to starting a licensing program.

Eileen, did you have a lawyer who specializes in licensing? There are a lot of intricacies and you need an iron clad agreement.

No, I didn't and I'm aware that it was premature on my part. I'm looking for a solution because It's A Ruff Life is a viable business.

Eileen, you need to move on this while the experience is fresh in your mind. I'd bet one or more of the legal firms here has someone you can work with while you are developing your other concept and overseeing the further development of It's A Ruff Life here on Shea Blvd. I've had some experience relating to franchising. Enough to know the pit falls. If you are serious don't wait. You will need someone on your staff who has experience with multiple locations, even after you get an iron clad contract. Are you working on it?

Right. I agree with that.

Eileen Proctor (continued)

Let's get back to Top Dog Business Boosters. How did all of that start?

It started with all the requests I got to share my business successes and skills with others. I began to realize that as I built an experienced team at Ruff Life, there was another avenue for me to achieve additional success. I had achieved credibility and notoriety and it could be put to the good of people not just my beloved dogs.

Introspection is a wonderful skill if properly used, Eileen. Is your flip here to altruism?

Well the human aspect of my skills has been front and center all along. Every bit of my notoriety has come from the actions and programs that had an under privileged aspect to them. Staying visible, raising money, having credibility. So it feels good and not strictly altruistic, but it is about helping other people discover how to pursue their passions, and be paid for it.

Altruism is not a bad word, you know? But are you ready for the challenge?

I don't think it is a bad word, Shirley. But I don't think it is mutually exclusive to enjoying a very full opulent life. They don't have to be two different things. I believe they can be combined. I've still my vision and passion to create, as I have, a profitable and ethically improved quality of life for dogs and the people who love them. I've just expanded it to experience, enjoy and pursue what I have done with like minded people. When I do speaking and motivating now my message is that I am an ordinary person who has done something out of the ordinary. I took the steps to pursue a passion and to step out of what was expected of me as a person. I want to give other people the license to do that and help them find the knowledge to do it. I have leveraged the Top Dog name which has come to identify me because people know me as that. The calls, questions and appeals for help began to come too often to continue to ignore them. I got calls daily some weeks. Then after some luncheon talks I was asked what my fee was. On one of those occasions, I said she should make a donation to an animal welfare organization. She did and I also received a note card that said, "Others are waiting to hear what you have to say." I was also asked by Susan Ratliff, a prominent woman business owner to participate with a panel group Marketing Mavericks at her Entrepreneurial Boot Camp. She encouraged me to help other people and insisted I begin to charge for the service.

Are you in a stationary or dynamic mode?

Definitely in a dynamic mode and have greater clarification of where I want my vision to go.

Good. Describe your future as you see it now?

For my life or my business? My life takes more than shooting from the top of my head. As to the business of Ruff Life, I've been developing experienced people and we are doing very well. I'm determined to be the guide – the **Top Dog** as my title denotes, and make way for people on my staff to develop as well. I'm buoyed up and my heart sings when I see people grow and develop. That is also why Top Dog Business Boosters really appeals to me as a great business as well. My impact will not just be on the lives of pets and their owners but other people who want to explore what is deep within them. That will help our creative society as well. And, as you said to me earlier, that when you leave this earth, it will be what you've helped other people to become that will be your testimony to what you have accomplished. I really do feel that way as well.

Eileen, you have a great heart and a way of expressing yourself. I truly wanted to give you an opportunity to tell your story. There were others I hoped would respond but they didn't seem to want to tell their stories. You have responded with great candor and eloquence. Why were you willing to respond?

Because, I wanted my story told. The good, the bad, the achievements and missteps. I want people to know it's ok to fail and to succeed. That is what my future is going to be about.

NOTE TO OUR LISTENERS

Since my interviews with Eileen she has gone on with TOP DOG BUSINESS BOOSTERS with success and has teamed up with Susan Ratliff for a weekly radio show on KFNN titled "The Small Business Power Hour."

Eileen has become a much sought after speaker and holds weekly seminars for small business people and those who want to tap into the ideas she generates.

In addition, she is editing a book her father has written on his experiences in the Korean War, specifically at the Choson Reservoir. Eileen says, he saw all of his buddies blown away at 18 years old. He had to kill people and has had horrible psychological and physical problems since. This journal is a way of helping himself by shedding his anger.

Whatever else Eileen tries, whether a success or not, it will be worth a listen.

The ULTIMATE Ice

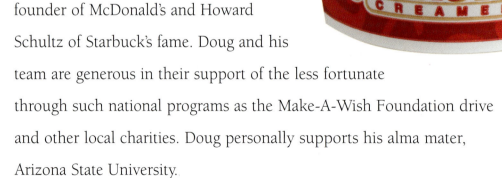

Doug Ducey is a unique guy. From the moment I first met him seven years ago, I sensed a man of quiet determination, an empathetic manner tempered by a reserved attitude. I've admired his drive to stay on message and succeed with a carefully crafted plan. He is acutely aware that one person cannot achieve a vision as defined as Cold Stone Creamery's is, and to lead without overpowering his growing worldwide army of entrepreneurial franchisees. His style is to accept criticism but attribute achievement and success to his bright headquarters team and the entire franchise organization. He admires the business perspective of the late Ray Kroc, the founder of McDonald's and Howard Schultz of Starbuck's fame. Doug and his team are generous in their support of the less fortunate through such national programs as the Make-A-Wish Foundation drive and other local charities. Doug personally supports his alma mater, Arizona State University.

Cream Experience

Cold Stone's goals are challenging which fits his personal competitive nature. He has spearheaded a comprehensive continuing education process, spliced with innovation to support the efforts of the franchises. He describes his leadership style as coaching.

Doug is not an easy person to interview as he is reticent to talk about himself. As I share with you my conversation with him, you will get a greater sense of his philosophy, competitiveness, planning skill and determination to convey how Cold Stone differentiates itself from other long term, successful ice cream purveyors. He is steadfast in his assertion that there is no bad ice cream, just differences in ice cream.

Doug, you were born and grew up in Toledo, Ohio. What brought you to Tempe, Arizona?

I was ready to go to college, maybe Ohio State University and my folks split up and mom moved out west. I was the oldest so I came west too. ASU seemed similar to Ohio State, a place I could establish residency and I really liked the atmosphere and excitement of Arizona.

As I recall, your special focus at ASU was finance, which I find interesting as you are very people-oriented and a business builder type, while finance is a business housekeeping skill. I've a double question here. Why did you choose a finance major and how did the real you get away from following a finance career in a corporate structure?

Umm, those are good questions. I chose a focus on finance because money was a personal concern when I showed up at school. I wanted to understand finance and money to ease my financial anxiety. As to why and how the change came about, I was fortunate to get a job in my freshman year with Hensley and Company, which is the number one

Doug Ducey (continued)

A WORLDWIDE BRAND, COLD STONE CAN BE SEEN IN MULTIPLE MEDIA OUTLETS SHARING THEIR SWEET SUCCESS.

Anheuser Busch distributor in the country. So, I was supporting myself in college selling beer and you know, everyone said yes. I grew to love selling and my career interests really began to go more toward sales and marketing. While I graduated with a finance degree, Proctor and Gamble hired me for sales and marketing and I enjoyed that more and never practiced finance.

Thanks for the explanation. I look at your core values as stated in your business plan and they are great examples of developing markets and interacting with people.

That would be true, Shirley.

So after graduation you took a job at Proctor and Gamble. Why there? Why not remain here in Arizona your adopted state?

Proctor and Gamble seemed like a great place to work. Their interview process was competitive. I interviewed with a number of companies but Proctor and Gamble was far and away probably the most sought after position on campus at that time and I accepted their offer and joined the Food Service and Lodging Division.

Food service would seem to have some linkages to ice cream. How long were you with P & G?

I think, about seven years.

Okay. About enough to know you wanted to do something to build your own company?

I think that is fair to say. Proctor was a great organization with great brands, great culture and when I joined it was not to spend a lifetime there, but over time, you have certain success and become a part of the system. What really awakened me was when Proctor had its first re-organization in its history. Although I was 28 at the time and the re-organization would have played in my favor, it was a disquieting eye-opener to me.

So, from there what direction did you take, Doug?

I was interested in a franchise. My brother, stepfather and I put up money for a Subway franchise but we got to meet

Don Sutherland, the owner of Cold Stone during our process of franchise investigations and due diligence and our timing was good. I wanted to get back to Phoenix. I wanted to live here and intuitively took to Don's and Susan's organization as a real ground floor opportunity.

LEFT: FOUNDERS DON AND SUSAN SUTHERLAND

BELOW: THE COMPANY IS BUILT ON STRONG VALUES.

What were some of the special factors that caused you to consider Cold Stone Creamery a unique opportunity?

Well, Don and Susan had been on an ice cream lover's crusade to develop the perfect ice cream desert and their efforts were enticing to me. They had invested years searching for ice cream that met their standards of quality and had finally come up with a program that satisfied them and had opened their first Cold Stone Creamery in Tempe, Arizona in 1988. I actually give credit to Don for convincing me and I was lucky enough to find Cold Stone in its embryonic stages, just before the beginning of franchising. I guess you could say, Don's love of ice cream was infectious and convinced me. It was a true business opportunity and Don's enthusiasm captured me. Don is now my partner and holds the title of Founder. The Cold Stone Creamery that we know today is a direct result of Don's driving passion.

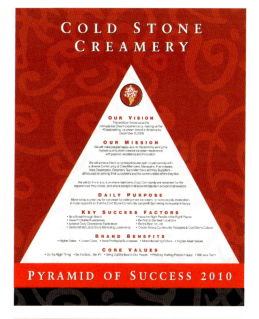

Tell us more, Doug.

In the early years of their quest the Sutherlands had noted subtle changes in the purchasing habits of our population. People had become more quality conscious and willing to pay more for quality. It fit right into their standards of quality flavor, consistency and variety. Their success came down to delivering fresh, personalized ice cream. For me that was a great opportunity.

Doug, your enthusiasm is infectious and we'll get back to the Cold Stone building process, but first let's talk more about you. What traits do you believe a person should have to be a successful entrepreneur?

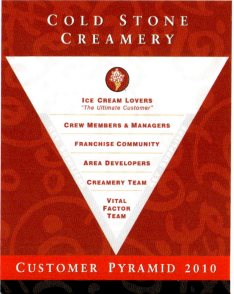

Doug Ducey (continued)

Well, there are a bunch of traits, I think like the ability to assess and overcome obstacles, the ability to think through and set goals, persuade others to believe in their vision and take ownership of that vision and help move it forward. Individuals who have these traits more often achieve success. You find these traits in the greats like Ray Kroc and Howard Schultz.

COLD STONE IS A MASTER AT TEACHING PEOPLE WHILE HAVING FUN.

And what about you, Doug?

I subscribe to these traits and work hard to apply them personally, and look for others who exhibit them as well.

Okay. What other special attributes do you look for in the people who surround you and support you? Your direct line team members?

I look for energy, enthusiasm and positive, can-do attitudes.

Are these the same attributes you seek when selecting franchisees?

Exactly.

Do you have any special ways or techniques you use to find potential franchisees?

We don't advertise or solicit franchisees. It doesn't work for us. Without solicitation we average at least 4000 people a month who seek us out and apply for a franchise. About one percent of applicants qualify and are awarded a franchise. We want them to sell us on why they are worthy and believe they can bring the added value to our organization that will ensure their success.

While we are on the subject of success Doug, a few years ago you shared with me some unique planning tools and a video. Two very complete visual pieces were your Pyramid of Success and Customer Pyramid. They show both a great from-the-top-down and bottom up plan for success. You gave me copies of both which I have kept. They tell me a lot about you and your system for success. Your focus and leadership. Can you elaborate?

PAGE 204 | CHAPTER 9 | THE ULTIMATE ICE CREAM EXPERIENCE – DOUG DUCEY

We still have them, and will provide the updated versions with a complete press kit. There are changes and I would love to have you see them. Our team reviews our plans and progress regularly and we update as we achieve.

The 4000 applications a month you mentioned is a huge total for a year. How many have you accepted and awarded?

Over the last couple of years we have accepted and awarded 600 a year. We have to build a successful business for franchisees over the course of time and stick with the mandate of quality rather than the turbulence of quantity with a lot of failures. Our franchisees are stakeholders and I am, in a sense, accountable to them. They have a substantial investment and we an obligation to see them succeed.

Doug, you have your own "university" where you train franchisees. I've been at your headquarters in the past when you had classes going for new franchisees. Do you have an ongoing training system that brings them further ahead in their local businesses as well as what corporate really wants to see?

Sure. We have training for beginners and a continuing program to improve results. We help our franchisees to address problems to maintain their forward movement. For Cold Stone to succeed and be profitable means franchisees must succeed and be profitable.

Are you interested in synergistic acquisitions?

I am interested in achieving our vision. As stated, "The world will know us as the ultimate ice cream experience by making us the number one, best selling ice cream brand by December 31, 2009."

Right. I know that, Doug. Are you saying, you are not interested in any acquisitions?

If I thought it could help us achieve our vision, I might be interested. I have not seen that kind of opportunity. We are in the business of selling ice cream, in the broader sense making people happy. That means we are in the people business.

DOUG THROWS THE CEREMONIAL FIRST PITCH AT AN ARIZONA DIAMONDBACKS GAME.

Doug Ducey (continued)

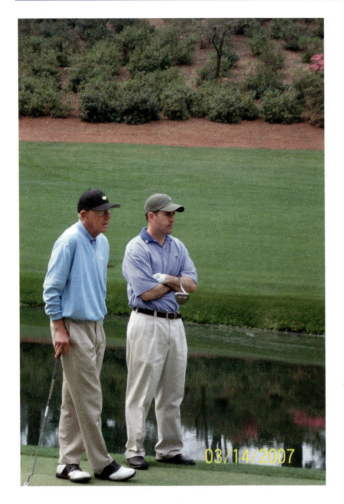

DOUG ENJOYS THE COMPANY OF LOU HOLTZ AT AUGUSTA GOLF COURSE.

Doug, Cold Stone Creamery has become a very visible company. You attract attention and interest because you are different. In particular, people want to know how and why you have achieved such visibility. That's why these questions are relevant. Some are hard, personal and often invasive. Especially about you as the leader. Here comes one now. Please describe the type of person you believe you are?

Eccentric!

I want to bring out the best in other people.

Or not, Doug. I sense you have hard time talking about yourself, right?

It has not been my habit to focus on me. I know what you are trying to accomplish here, Shirley.

What am I trying to accomplish, Doug?

Look, I like and am at ease talking about Cold Stone Creamery and the people here that have been responsible for our successes. I haven't wanted to or done a lot of talking about me.

You are the leader, Doug. Leadership counts. And people are always interested in the qualities of leadership. Can you share with us?

Ok. So what was the question again?

Would you describe the type of person you believe you are?

I think I am the type of person who wants to bring out the best in other people so they can reach their potential. I think I grew into this over time. Without a doubt, I always admired that type of person. Still do.

Possibly because of the life experiences you've had, Doug?

Could be doctor! I don't know.

What are the highly personal principles that you have that make a difference in your personal life – not your business?

I don't think I can differentiate, Shirley. The core values that underpin Cold Stone business are the same that I have at home. I think of myself as a leader, teacher, coach and student as well. So, I don't see a dramatic change from the way I would treat others or be treated whether at business or home.

Let's go back to the Pyramid. In looking at the core values stated for Cold Stone, are those you constructed or was the Pyramid and its contents a team effort?

It was definitely a team effort. I lead the effort and would say the only part I take full credit for is the environment created here that stimulates the efforts of our team. There is a good story that I think is worth re-telling. When we were going through the planning process to identify our vision, mission, and core values it was hard to keep on track. We had a lot going that is critical like phone calls, e-mails, stores to be built, potential franchisees to interview, it can seem like a waste of time to plan and identify who you are and where you are going. Sheldon Harris, our president was just an incredible contributor and performer. He kept us on track. He understood as a leader you need a plan to know where you are going. You don't want to tell folks that you don't have a plan, a vision, values and clear strategies. He made our team understand and pull together. To develop a specific easy-to-follow written road map. He without a doubt, brought us to the point we are today as an organization.

No question, Doug. You can't achieve a result or get to a destination without a map – a plan to guide you to your destination.

Some folks seem to, but we can't. Time will tell, Shirley.

Doug, time is already on your side. Your success to date is a good indication that your preparation and leadership is well-executed. If you were starting all over, would you change any of the actions you took? And if so, would you share with us what those changes would be?

LEFT: COMPANY PRESIDENT, SHELDON HARRIS

RAY KARAM (LEFT) AND DOUG DUCEY

Doug Ducey (continued)

Yes there are of course changes we would make in hindsight. Timing for instance. I would have brought on some of the great key people we now have much earlier. The first person I brought on changed our success pattern a lot. He was paid by the way, significantly more than me. This was a major and productive decision. When we started to bring on such key talent, and pay them well, they made great success happen. This process took two or three years to find, persuade and hire the talent we needed. So, knowing this now, I would recruit and pay the best talented individuals from the very start.

Very insightful Doug. One of the first lessons I learned from a wise mentor when I started in business was you don't hire someone like yourself. You hire someone smarter and better. Surrounding yourself with that kind of team makes you better as a leader. The smart ones push you and that's a tribute. They take a personal interest in not just being a part of the company but take initiative in the process of improving operations. What I have observed of your style of leadership is you stimulate everyone to treat Cold Stone as if it was their very own business. When I walk in here at headquarters, people are bustling, they are friendly, smiling and eager to help. They reflect your determination and style of leadership. Buying from your franchisees' shops, one experiences the same dedication plus the enthusiasm and charm of your youthful crews. It's what you have achieved that inspired me to want your story in my book.

Thank you Shirley.

Your career has been productive and varied with some challenges. Operating a franchise company with thousands of independent entrepreneurial franchisees is not for the faint of heart, Doug. Let's switch to the personal. You surely have had some challenges or defining moments in your life. Can you share a few with us.

RIGHT: HE AND HIS BROTHER, NICK DUCEY, WIN THE TOURNAMENT AT AUGUSTA GOLF COURSE MARCH 13, 2007

When my brother and I won the member/guest gold golf tournament.

That sounds tongue-in-cheek. Humorous and I see some smiles here in the room. Care to share? Perhaps we can include the picture you are referring too in the story.

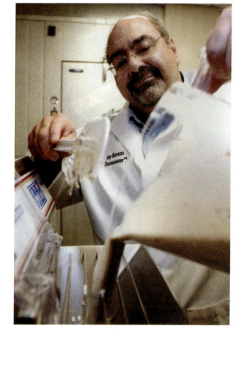

> "I've been very lucky and blessed with good parents and good health, a wonderful wife and kids."

My brother will like that too. In all seriousness, Shirley, I can't at the moment think of one. There are a lot of small, important personal occurrences along the way like being very lucky and blessed with good parents and good health, a wonderful wife and kids. And, I think really incredibly lucky to link up with the Sutherlands during the embryonic stages of Cold Stone's evolution and to know right away it was what I was meant to do.

You know Doug, many people listening would consider these few instances you have listed, as significant events, all relevant good and bedrock to your career and life. Smaller by your understated value, but certainly in the aggregate more dramatic than a single happening.

So, give us a couple of important Cold Stone milestones, please?

Sure. We had 74 operating stores in August of 1999. There were about four of us working here and we went on a retreat which was a special event. We knew we had an emotional connection with our customer base and there were lots of people knocking on our door to purchase franchises without our advertising for them. This was really special. We looked across the ice cream landscape which had 5500 Dairy Queens, 4400 Baskin Robbins, 3300 TCBY's at that time and said, "Let's have the world know us as 'the ultimate ice cream experience.'" The plan we put in place gave us 1000 profitable stores operating by December 31, 2004. Just having a vision and goal propelled us forward. The other important reason was how we assessed the ice cream landscape. It was us versus others who kind of looked like us, kind of smelled like us, claimed they started before us and wanted to taste like us but didn't. We made the decision that they were not our competition.

EACH EMPLOYEE LEAVES THEIR UNIQUE MARK ON THE CORPORATE HEADQUARTERS AS IT IS BEING CONSTRUCTED.

Doug Ducey (continued)

I would say that was one of the first big commitments we made, that we did not want to be placed in that same standard bracket. We decided to begin our drive to open units in premiere locations and really got good at that strategy and to lead all comers in unit development. We attracted the interest and attention of the public who wanted an ultimate ice cream experience. Time magazine wrote that we were doing to ice cream what Starbuck's did to coffee. CBS evening news said we were the clear leader in our ice cream category. True, or not, it gave us great momentum and set us on the way to realizing our goals. These were some of the little decisions along the way that have resulted in significant results.

You hit a home run here Doug, that will create some frustrating challenges for those with established business patterns. The press and media comments will be hard for them to digest. If you want to be enthusiastic, you have to act enthusiastic. If you want to be the big guy, you have to act as though you are already there. You have finessed these basics very well. You mentioned your family. Let's talk a little more about their influence on your career.

AN AVID READER, DOUG SURROUNDS HIMSELF WITH WISDOM OF ALL KINDS.

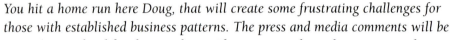

I think it was my upbringing. The set of core values they exhibited and taught me and their continuing support in every way possible in my life and career.

While we are on your early years, I'd like to go back in time to when you were young like, high school. What were your interests then?

Probably sports. I liked both hockey and football. I played football for a couple of years but hockey throughout high school.

What other kinds of interests?

Varied I guess. I liked school. Read a lot and still do. Especially about successful people like Ray Kroc of McDonald's, Howard Schultz

PAGE 210 | CHAPTER 9 | THE ULTIMATE ICE CREAM EXPERIENCE – DOUG DUCEY

of Starbucks and keeping up with what is happening in all areas of franchising. Ideas are important and I look for them.

When you relax or play what do you do? You surely look physically fit. Your PR man Kevin says you run ten or twelve miles a week.

I like to run. I guess it is an extension of my early sports years. I play golf, but not as much as I like. As a father of three boys, I give a lot of time to them. That is play time and relaxing for me.

Something else comes to mind that influenced me greatly early in my life. I took an entrepreneuring class at ASU during my college years. It was taught by Claude Olney, a great professor. He brought in a number of local entrepreneurs. I remember he said something that has stayed with me. "The only experiences that will make your life different ten years from now are the people you meet and the books you read." I have found a lot of truth in that. Some of the books that have been meaningful to me from a business perspective have been Peter Guther's books on being an effective executive, Jim Collin's books on "Good to Great" and "Built to Last" and Peter Drucker's many writings.

Absolutely good advice and information Doug. The books you mentioned help when every one around you loses faith and presses your attitude in a negative direction.

Amen, Shirley.

Let's talk more about your varied influences on Cold Stone Creamery and through the business, your products and franchise activities on a larger group of constituents. Your employees and franchisees, their communities, the industry and the many countries you now serve in. That is a large sphere. Aside from each individual within the Cold Stone family touching special local issues and needs you have the very visible campaigns that receive great exposure such as Cold Stone's Make-A-Wish promotion. Very impressive. Please elaborate?

THE COMPANY EXTENDS THEIR SUCCESS TO HELP MAKE A WISH AND MODELS GIVING BACK.

DOUG DUCEY (CONTINUED)

Thank you. I appreciate you saying that. I think it starts with our focus as the ultimate ice cream experience. That's a focus on being the best. I often ask our team at headquarters, "Do you know why I am here?" Then I say, "Because Don Sutherland, our founder, needed help and wanted me. And, you are here because I need your help." Philosophically, attracting, motivating, training incredibly wonderful gifted, talented and enthusiastic people is a good thing for the communities we serve and in turn the success of Cold Stone. We engender a culture that believes in and supports the five core values that you see on our Pyramid of Success. Those values grow projects like Make-A-Wish, and Best First Job, how we treat and support, franchises, consider them partners spiritually, in the equation and bring customers into our values in support of community and country. We believe, just like the first eight words of our mission says, "We will make people happy around the world…" From our base the definition of happiness for a franchisee is being successful and profitable, for a crew member it's pleasing the customer, for the customer, the best, ultimate, quality ice cream experience. Our headquarters job is to make the conditions right to keep all those contributors happy and it starts with me and all or leadership team.

From your perspective, what makes Cold Stone strikingly different within your industry? You've talked about it as a goal. Where are you in this transition now?

Several key ways make us different. We have a comprehensive selection process in granting franchises followed by an ongoing training program. As to product, our ice cream is made fresh every single day on site. We make our own waffle cones. We provide a wide variety of candy, fruits, toppings the buyers can select from. A marvelous experience for people to create their own delightful desert. Our crews also differentiate us. They

not only create and mix what you select on the cold stone, but they entertain you as they do it. Our testing team is always experimenting with new ideas and product so that we always keep people returning and enjoying new and unusual delights.

Please describe a couple of the most difficult problems you have encountered and how you have solved them?

That is a great question. To start with, originally Carnation was our ice cream supplier here at home base. They shut down giving us three weeks notice. It sent us on the hunt to find a national supplier that could make a consistent ice cream mix so we could make ice cream fresh each day inside each store. So the problem turned into an opportunity. We get the same smooth, elegant ice cream wherever there is a Cold Stone, be in Toledo, Ohio, Times Square, Tempe, Arizona or Alaska. Another milestone problem had to do with concept location. When we were beginning our growth mode I was trying to apply some of the Proctor and Gamble thinking. Back in the 80's, Phoenix was thought to be a great test market. It was a growing, transient market. We tested here on home base. Once we were secure we needed to go to the biggest food service market in the world, Los Angeles. No matter how hard we tried, we weren't making a lot of headway. At that time, headquarters staff consisted of only four people. We had people who actually came to headquarters once they filled out an application. One of those people was Dan Farr who came in and was in the lobby. He snuck back to my office. Big guy, six foot four, looked like you would imagine an Alaskan entrepreneur would look like. He said to me, "Hey, you have some time for me Coach?" I was like, how did this guy get back here? He was very persuasive and charismatic. He said that it was time for us to go to Alaska. I said to him we were interested in Alaska but wanted to open Southern California first. I felt we didn't need Alaska right away, but he said, "Come to Alaska, if it doesn't work, it will be a speed bump for you and if it does work, you can tell the

Doug Ducey (continued)

world that Cold Stone can sell ice cream to the Eskimos." Long story, Dan's store was our number one store in volume for 18 months. We put it in a very mediocre location because Dan owned the small shopping center. Lesson learned for us, bet on people before locations. A huge learning process. We began to concentrate on bringing in really excellent people both in the field and home office. With both these experiences we solved the two greatest problems. We got the right product and learned to focus our efforts on the right people no matter the territory.

"By picking the right people with our great product we have prospered no matter the territory."

By picking the right people with our great product we have prospered no matter the territory.

Doug, Cold Stone has won a lot of awards that are noted in you PR packet and your web site. Do you have a special one you like best?

The only award I want to win every day is a customer saying that their favorite place to go for ice cream or a special occasion is Cold Stone.

Doug, your first major goal was to have 1000 profitable franchises. You achieved that by 2004. How has your vision changed?

We now want to become the number one best-selling ice cream brand in America.

And then Doug, the world?

One step at a time, Shirley.

It would be valuable for someone contemplating starting their own business to know if you have special advice on keeping their enthusiasm up. We all have those occasions when we get in a funk. Can you help here?

I would say the first thing is as a leader, you have to avoid those funks as best you can. And, if you do get one you need to use every way possible to reverse it. For me, I may leave the office for awhile. Sometimes I take a couple of days off. I sometimes go in to see Kevin, our PR guy and chat with him because he has a very uplifting manner. But as the person who holds the leadership role, my effect could be detrimental. I would tell you, Shirley, I take preventative steps and so I don't face a lot of those bouts of pessimism. Our whole organization believes in the beneficial power of the good and positive attitude. Lou Holtz spoke at one of our annual franchise meetings. It was a real

highlight having the legendary coach of Notre Dame. He gave such a great presentation to our franchises on the power of a good attitude versus a bad attitude. It was an inspirational highlight for us all.

Do you have something special you might convey to someone who is interested in starting a business or being entrepreneurial?

Sure. If it is something you have a passion about and a vision for what you want, you should do it. Also, if you have an opportunity to become a part of an entrepreneurial start up, not your own, I'd say – go for it!

LOOKING FORWARD

Since our conversation with Doug, Cold Stone's dynamic growth precipitated the need for a new strategy that would enhance the value of the franchisees investment. On May 11, 2007 Cold Stone entered into a merger with the Kahala Corporation which had twelve food brand concepts. Doug believed the merger would bring cost savings and increased opportunities for franchisees to grow revenue. In late September, Doug took leave from his role as CEO at Kahala Cold Stone. Like many inveterate entrepreneurs he will eventually pursue the process of inventing new ventures.

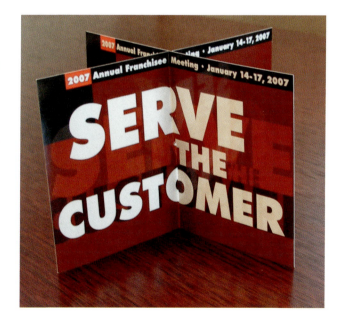

What Now?

You have invested in our "talking book". My name is on it. I've been called an inveterate do-gooder. Maybe so – but I'm a lifelong work in progress with miles of adventure and years of experiences to share. A font of good ideas used and some rejected. A developer of highly successful innovations that changed practices within the industries I served. Bad ideas I inherited, willed to some success that eventually collapsed. And as a futurist, concepts and programs twenty years ahead of their time, rejected at the onset as absurd, and now reappearing as exciting and as important to the field of business. Well – that's a big win. I take heart in the comment made by Albert Einstein. "If at first an idea is not absurd, then there is no hope for it." I have been redeemed by hope.

We will explore here some of the special lessons the previous 9 chapters of wonderful stories told by our selected entrepreneurs in their own words. We'll underscore their suggestions and ideas shared with you, the reader, seeking to take charge of your future. And, by request of my friends and advisers, a short biographical, experiential look at a few of my own lessons and views, which you may find beneficial perhaps provocative.

WHO QUALIFIES TO BE AN INNOVATOR, CHANGE-MAKER, ENTREPRENEUR?

Stand on any corner, drive down any street or highway and look at fliers and advertisements you get in your mail. You will observe entrepreneurial activity, advertisements emblazoned on vehicles, buildings and signs. They offer us services and products for every possible need we have and some of these hardy individuals and organizations want us to want. Where do they all come from? Are they special and born to be entrepreneurial?

They are all of us. Friends, relatives, neighbors, strangers and they come from every possible source. In my view and experience **nurture** outshines **nature** in giving birth to entrepreneurs. Anyone could be an innovator and changemaker, **you gotta wanna**. Every person does something innovative at some point in their lives and many catch the inspiration and continue. You hear nurture at work in the Ananda Roberts story as her father taught her from childhood to want to be in business and be ready to achieve. There has been a misconception for years that entrepreneurs are born and are creative. That nature anointed them with powers others did not have. Gosh, if that were entirely true we would not have tens of thousands of the small businesses and many larger ones today serving our needs and wants along with new innovative products and services.

There is a lot of chatter, incessant noise and printed clutter we are subjected to every day by press, media, books, educational institutions, etc., pushing the myth that only college or well-educated people can be entrepreneurs. Some even say that techies and scientific types are the only true entrepreneurs. That's just plain bunk! Those of us who have taken the brass ring and been through the adventure have an obligation to assist others eager to start an entrepreneurial venture and carve an independent future for themselves and others. Through these actual stories, you hear many of the events, failures and successes these innovators weathered to achieve success and the best for them is yet to be. There is no ending to any of these selected stories, as they daily move ahead in their planned future.

Since you invested in my book, I assume you are in a start-up business or have ideas you feel have economic value — or know someone who does. For sure, we are living in a fast-paced, tumultuous and sometimes dangerous world. Still anything is possible and nothing is certain. Here are a few questions to ponder. They can act as a personal audit of how far along you might be in your decision to try or test your preparation.

- Have you a personal vision? One you think suits your lifestyle and goals?

- Are you presently employed? If so, do you like what you do?

- Have you treated your job as though you owned the company looking for ways to improve the business without being instructed to do so?

- Have you taken the initiative to share with the owner or manage your ideas to improve the company?

- Have you some ideas you think may be marketable for you to start your own venture?

- Do you have some reserve cash or a source of monetary resources you can tap? Could you support yourself for a year or will you need to borrow?

- Would you need to start your business and work part time as well?

- Have you made a list of your interpersonal skills? Starting a business depends on working well with both employees and customers or clients. You need to be persuasive and communicate. I've learned and confirmed over my career that people don't work for companies so much as they work for other people. Sure pay comes into play - but recognition, trust and respect are more attractive and persuade and ensure people stay and help build companies. And you will need other people. What does this have to do with entrepreneuring? Well – you can start a company – that's easy. But you can't build it without inspiring people and getting work done through people. Every story here illustrates how much these individual innovators realized the importance of the humans who worked and helped them achieve. Without employees you are only a one person show. You can't grow.

- Are you risk tolerant? Are you inclined to take calculated and strategic risks? Putting off strategic decisions and waiting can result in losing. There is no long term winning unless you are willing to risk short term losing. John Ridgway's story is dramatic illustration of risk as a winning strategy.

May 3-5, 2006, The Club of Amsterdam held a summit at HES School of Economics and Business in Amsterdam. The summit's focus was on the importance of taking a risk in innovation. The conclusion was "without risk taking, there is no progress, no growth and no prosperity." Entrepreneurs are the engines to rebuild and strengthen any nation's economic infrastructure. Without increasing effort from people willing to risk the innovative base will begin to crumble. The United States needs increased entrepreneurial activity and support. The rest of the world is catching up.

- How's your tolerance for stress and challenge? Stress is often characterized as bad for general health, however facing down a challenge can produce good stress. The more you tackle and win the better you become. Don't get stuck in what I call the "fear gear!" The Marcia Veidmark and Ananda Roberts stories are marvelous examples of innovators who accepted risk, challenges and failure with the help of their faith and persistence to go forward to new achievements.

- Do you understand that being your own boss requires you to perform the most menial of tasks and that you will work harder than ever you did working for someone else? Gregory Torrez as a student, started at dawn, attended school, and at the end of the school day, was responsible for cleaning all the bathrooms in the family business compound, even though he was a son of the owner. Forget the glamour and status stuff. That's an earned long-term benefit.

- How do you rate your ethical principles? Perhaps you have heard from some people in business, "The means justifies the end result we need. We can fix the situation later." Bad ethical mistakes can't be fixed. Best advice here is don't patronize that kind of business. The corporate environment isn't trustworthy. Complete honesty and ethical principles are absolutely necessary in starting and building a business. For sure, with business as in life, a bad first impression is most often irreversible.

As you read the stories of our entrepreneurs you have copious examples of how the ethical practices, programs and caring treatments attract good people as employees and encouraged everyone to perform acts of service for their communities, as well.

- Are you a problem solver? Starting and building a business of any kind usually has new or different instances that need immediate answers or fixes each day. Some so unusual they require inventing a solution. That's both a challenge and with the right attitude, the most satisfying fun of owning and building a business.

- Is your product or service for a recognized existing market or a completely new cutting edge approach where no special market has been identified?

In the stories of Gregory Torrez, Marcia Veidmark, Ogbonna Abarikwu, Carol Den Herder/Kristin Rezler, Doug Ducey and Eileen Proctor each first served an existing market as they reinvented products and services that were better than their competitors and then raised the bar by creating whole new solutions and conveniences though exciting new products and services.

Breaking into an already served market where there are companies with long term histories takes challenges that involve showing you have a better more viable commodity. Creating a market for a product or service where none ever existed presents a different set of challenges. The John Ridgway, David Kravitz/Eileen Spitalny, and Ananda Roberts stories dramatically show the unique challenges of convincing clients they have solutions or products never available before. And you learn how they achieve success.

- Do you think you have the right stuff? There is another crazy myth still floating around that only outgoing people make good entrepreneurs. That myth is bunk too. There are no special types of personality that succeed better than any other. Your passion, desire and self confidence helps. The strength of your ideas is important. Start by accepting preparation is a must. Accept that no task or job is too lowly and be prepared to be a dedicated learner. Accept that founding and building a company is **not a 9 to 5 activity.** The work days are clockless and timeless.

ARE YOU NOW OR CAN YOU BECOME ENTREPRENEURIAL?

You make that judgment. You have these few audit questions. They may just be reminders of steps you've already taken. What follows now are a few key areas I've covered in classes with budding entrepreneurs, techniques I used in my early preparation for career, some cautions and ideas. They are in no hierarchical order as they are all equally important.

- Anticipate surprises and problems. Practice using the "what if's." List the worst case possibilities and look to neutralizing as many as you can in advance. One, often the first noted is the "naysayers" amongst family and friends. There are others. They are inevitable. Preparing for them should challenge and galvanize you to move on. Communicate with those close to you, and seek their support.

- Solve problems as soon as they occur. Be aware that what seems a problem at first may just be a sign of a deeper real problem. Tackle problems by looking for the root cause. When you perceive you have a problem, ask yourself why and how did this happen? Get to the root cause because avoided or smoothed over problems bleed energy, morale and money. I'll cover more on this subject later.

- Expect to adjust to virtual change and plan ways to stay nimble and comfortable with change. Keep current with all the advances in your industry, government, technology, world affairs and the economy. They are intricately linked. Cultivate business relationships with people who have knowledge in these areas. You can't know everything but you can build reliable sources.

- Hire a lawyer and accountant. Set up a structure for your company immediately. Expect to have to cope with the frustration of past and archaic laws and practices. A high percentage of our body of law, especially regulatory law is 50 to 100 years old. Some go back to Teddy Roosevelt as relates to tariffs - - and their purposes do not remotely fit this century's fast paced change and the global market place. Even a large portion of infrastructure that affects power and communications doesn't fit or respond to present needs. And, the IRS is never friendly.

- Be a promoter. Being persuasive is a leadership tool. An entrepreneur's necessity. If you feel a little weak in this skill consider a public speaking course and/or a sales course.

- There is an ageless faculty you can draw on when challenges come along, it should be your first resource in strategizing. **intuition**, that isn't covered in business texts, is now considered a prime requisite for hiring executives and an absolute necessity for innovators who are creating and building businesses. Some define intuition as instinct or gut feeling, hunch or horse sense. Whatever you call it you will know the symptoms, as it is a deep bone and gut kind of feeling that transcends reason and logic, defies understanding and yet can point you in the direction to take or caution you. Where does it come from? A combination of knowledge, trial and error, failures, successes, practice in following clues to solve problems and develop ideas, observations of people and events puzzling through dilemmas in which you have the urge to run away or ignore. In short, being sensitive to people, events and over-all participating - not avoiding the working world. It can smooth the way to making decisions that require risk. Absolutely essential to innovating. You heard examples of intuition at work in every one of our entrepreneurs' conversational stories. And, as they moved forward they learned to listen to that feeling.

So far, you have been privy to the stories of these selected evolving entrepreneurs. Their stories have very clear defining elements and should inspire and help you find your possible similarities. Again keep in mind these innovators still have decades to go as they raise their bars and expectations. Their quests are still on track.

The potential "achilles heel" of innovators is to grasp and then evolve the role of doer to leader. To learn to gain thrills from others achievements and be energized through leading, motivating and teaching others. A large percentage of entrepreneurs sell out because they are unable to broaden their domain of creativity and soon miss the thrill of creating and ideating in a pure personal environment. In these stories you hear and see truly talented people going through this transition from doer to leader in different ways. You experience the process with David and Eileen at Fairytale Brownies, Carol and Kristin at Identity Marketing and Eileen at It's a Ruff Life. It is a process that takes consistent, dedicated effort. The conundrum is you have to move yourself from being the total doer, as founder, to the respected leader but not forget that you still remain a doer at the leadership level. Here is where the process gets sticky. You've got to show and teach employees how also to take leadership responsibility while performing their jobs. The success of any organization is best ensured when you achieve the true balance. Leadership must go from the top down and come from the bottom up. Unless you have this kind of innovation moving from both directions you do not have a fully dynamic company.

I've been instrumental in building some significant organizations through building people. The ideas and innovations were mine but my true success was through the people I selected, taught, motivated and lead to believe in themselves. Never lose track of the realization that we are in the people business. We don't build companies. The only asset that counts in any business is people. Not money. Not functions, not buildings, not equipment and not even ideas. They are tools when in the hands of willing, committed people, build companies.

WHY SHOULD YOU LISTEN?

You may be wondering about my credentials and why you might profit by listening to me. I'm the senior entrepreneur here. A pioneer whose story starts back in the 20th century. When planning for this book, all the people I assembled for ideas and to check out the value and feasibility, strongly urged that I share my personal adventure. While reluctant to do so at first, the wisdom of that suggestion finally overcame my hesitancy. In the sharing, you will have a fairly short overview considering the length of my career and the adventure it was. The world of my youth and career covers America's history from a struggling depression era to an emerged world power. I have led an innovative and exhilarating life.

The way I've seen myself has gone through copious iterations, so I'll do some short biographical scenarios. Incipient visioning for me started in college. It wasn't until then that truly serious soul searching seemed appropriate. It didn't come easily and I found getting a guidance system in place for my unruly personality took personal and external persuasion. Nina Murphy, a professor and department head of girls physical education, triggered it. As I look back, she was well ahead of her time, both philosophically as well as the field of physical education. Nina was empathetic, brilliant and admired by the many young women she influenced. Each year, to this day a group of us attend an event called The Murphy Girls, to remember her contributions to our lives. But, back to my story.

The year was 1945, my freshman year. Our class was made up of young people who had been born in the great depression, grew to adults during World War II and its sweeping societal changes. The way Nina Murphy handled us and her counseling helped me to get hold of my running wild in all directions and seek some structure. Toward the end of my year of graduation in 1949 and during my first year of teaching at Mesa High School in Arizona, the potential opportunities weighed heavily on my mind. The desire to achieve my own independence. From what I had experienced as the ordained role of a woman through my early formative years certainly wasn't the life I had in mind.

Another event occurred that accelerated and changed my career time frame. During my late high school years, college and early teaching year, I played competitive sports. My special activity was women's fastball with a team of very talented women athletes, the PBSW Ramblers. I sustained a severe knee injury and soon could not compete at the level required. After a short period of self-pity I turned my competitive spirit to full emersion in my career efforts.

As I searched the events in my life, I looked at the positives first before owning up to the negatives. A super home, the oldest of six. A strong mother, a brilliant father and a life influenced by growing up through the 30's of the last century in semi-rural Pennsylvania, with no indoor plumbing, we grew most of what we consumed. One year in a one-room school, then I walked over two miles to a consolidated elementary school and four miles to high school until my dad could afford a fairly decent used car. He dropped me off each morning on his way to work. When war was declared, my father who was brilliant in metallurgy and design was tapped to help design and build a state-of-the-art aluminum plant in a small western town called Phoenix, Arizona. Its mission was to supply aluminum for the warplanes being built in California. We were transferred and then transported to Phoenix on a troop train around 1942. A truly defining event in my life.

The differences between the environment, weather and the societal practices of the east and west in that era were substantial. Another invigorating new learning experience. I graduated from high school, my family moved to Richmond, Virginia for my father to design systems for a state-of-the-art facility there. I stayed in Arizona and enrolled at Arizona State College (now ASU), worked my way through college with numerous untraditional jobs. Graduated in 1949, taught at Mesa High School, but couldn't live on that income so I left to sell World Book Encyclopedia on commission. Another major change requiring sweeping re-education. To understand the change here, is to understand that very few women undertook such positions in the 40's and 50's. I took the company's sales course, but after great bouts of failure and hard earned success determined that I needed far more education and understanding of business if I were to succeed. I made the decision to leave my teaching position that did not pay me a living wage. I decided to make a career of sales and set about creating a timetable for my advancement. I designed a self-education program which with work kept me busy day and night. I read copious books on sales and philosophy of persuasion. Selling throughout Arizona, a sparsely populated state in the late 40's and early 50's required some resourcefulness and planning. Much of my profitable territory took me to the mining areas where there were no overnight facilities for women. This challenge is one which is historical in nature. There were no hotels or motels, only facilities for single men and company houses for families which forced me to spend only one day in many areas. One of my territorial locations was at Bagdad, Arizona, the site of one of the largest open pit copper mines. I made a sales call on the mine superintendent's wife. To save me from going all the way to Prescott for the night, she arranged for me to sleep in the bookkeepers private room located near the bunkhouse which was at the bottom of the pit. My instruction was to get down there before sunset and out before the ore trucks began to move at sunrise. My trips there were once every month on payday and now I could stay for two or more days which provided more sales opportunities.

From 1950 through 1954, I progressed up the field management ladder. During that time I began to assess my future. No one set my schedule, I did. By this time I was recruiting and training sales representatives and my reading changed to more specialized material about industry, planning markets and dealing with upper level management. I felt the need to broaden my ability for social interaction. So, along with the "meat and potatoes" reading I added some classical explorations. My fun reading had always been history. American history to begin with and then into the ancient civilizations which took me to classical explorations into philosophers such as Plato and Socrates, Alexander Pope and others. I was intrigued by Pope whose essay on man had many lessons for me. Lots of phrases we use in everyday language come from that essay. The essay helped me understand human complexity. I also read some of the political thinkers. My favorite was Friederich A. Hayek's, "Road to Serfdom." I enjoyed poetry. Rudyard Kipling actually helped me to understand how to evaluate decisions, which I will discuss later. So how does all of this strange combination help as a defining time in my career? This reading diet provided insights on people, events, and philosophies. I began to develop a comfort level with social interaction and became more than this ambitious kid in her 20's. I wanted to eventually be on my own. As it happened, many of my training systems attracted the attention of executive management in Chicago. I had started thinking about creating my own company to offer training. But, at the end of 1954, the company promoted me to Division Manager. I became the youngest person to be promoted to that level at that time. What an ego surge. Really defining for me. Go on my own as I wanted to - - or take up the challenge and learn more.

If I accepted, it would require me to enter Canada as a landed immigrant, design a plan to open the province of Quebec and the Maritime Provinces and office out of Montreal. A truly entrepreneurial challenge, with full authority. The company would finance the operation with advances of funds, provide product, let me design all the systems and a long-range plan. Sort of like having my own business complete with "banker" and top ranked product. What was the catch? Had to be some, right? You bet! I'd be selling an English language encyclopedia, written, edited and printed in the United States in a largely French speaking territory, with the potential of personal cultural shock. I accepted, in what turned out to be another substantial re-education.

Two months prior to leaving Arizona, I subscribed to both the English language paper and the French one. That provided me vital information on cultural events, sports, daily news, attitudes and in such a bi-lingual and hotly political process, pitfalls to avoid. Another defining event.

The five years invested in Canada gave me a broad look at the thinking of people outside the U.S. Canadian history takes an opposite view of the American Revolution. Its history, culture, value beliefs, government structure and other services, and educational systems are very different. While the U.S. influences Canadians they hold steadfast to their basic beliefs. I designed new materials, plans and systems for the use in Canada and truly enjoyed a different environment and became more international in thought and behavior. My success caused the world headquarters of Field Enterprises to bring me back into the U.S. as an executive in the Chicago office. During the next few years, I redesigned the company's sales materials, wrote all new sales manuals, redesigned the training programs, made sales films and records, created training materials for schools using World Book and at the same time served on the team of selected nationally recognized professional writers who produced the training guide for the National Association for Training and Development. I also helped write, direct and participate in the company's international sales conferences that were produced annually where hundreds of field based people attended.

During this time I traveled extensively across the U.S. and Canada teaching managers and field people – thousands of them. My travel schedule was in the following format, two weeks out in the field, one week in the home office. I worked in every state except Alaska and every Canadian province except Newfoundland. My last assignment at Fields was to design the executive training program. One where we brought five to ten candidates and their families to Chicago for one year to get them ready to open and manage divisions throughout the U.S., Canada and the off shore world. The Vice Presidency I expected failed to materialize so I accepted one with a competitor and as one of five top people, we redesigned product, sales materials, field offices, etc., competing successfully with all other publications. While my former organization still remained the dominant player in the subscription books industry, Compton's became a force to be reckoned with.

Then came another defining moment. Upon the death of the owner, former Senator William Benton the incoming management of the corporation, in turmoil, put Compton's under the management of Encyclopedia Britannica, abandoned Compton's field based organization and effectively reduced the program to zero.

Time to move on and try the road to independence. With an adventuresome colleague, Bobbye Young, we formed a company with two divisions, which turned out to be an overly ambitious undertaking. It was a combination of portable bookstore and children's publisher. My partner and I managed a small stake, but soon ran out of funds. The ideas were good but the timing was bad as the country was suffering an economic turmoil and bad inflationary times. The banks would not deal with a two woman company without the addition of a moneyed third partner spelled "male." The double standard was unacceptable to us. We closed up, paid our bills and I accepted position and went to work for ITT's publishing division as the executive in charge of Bobbs Merrill Educational Publishing, a subsidiary that was in deep trouble. It took seven years, and new salable publications to bring it to profitability. At that point the corporation made the decision to sell off the units and product lines while they could demand top dollar.

What next? Each of the defining events over my career had built for me an international reputation as an innovator, a results driven changemaker and futurist. I took delight in challenge – rejected the word impossible – looked for probable targets for solution, tackled sensitive issues and in every career move ended up reinventing the business, it's products and systems. But more importantly doing it through developing people. My strong belief was always that building the human asset is the secret to every success or conversely without it failure.

My vision for me, had always been to be a builder of business not as housekeeper of already built business structures. I had experience in fixing organizations and reinventing them, which is truly hard work. Through the years I had been described with a variety of terms – perfectionist, stubborn, uncompromising and pushy. In my mind tactfully persistent and satisfied with only the best is a better description. I had long come to understand how history, political systems, social patterns, great tragedies, divergent ideas, inventions and complicated value systems played a part in the environment in which one sets their personal vision or alters it. Over the years these influences had tinkered with the plans I set in early life. I had become entrepreneurial within the established systems of the chaotic world of the 20th century. In my thinking the tired, "big-is-better" systems and companies of the 40's, 50's, 60's and 70's had narrow insular focus and did not serve to produce innovation for the last part of the century. In a lot of what I had done was to build units within companies as if they were stand-alone and had always taught employees to treat their job as if they owned the company. Time again to refocus my vision.

While working on the retooling process, I received a call from a former colleague and friend, Frank Balzano. He had gone to work for a very small company with a unique product concept operating in a couple of midwestern cities, Detroit and Chicago with smaller operations in other places. The company was initially started by an entrepreneurial husband and wife team with a desire to build a national company and take it public. Through a series of discussions, I agreed to join them as the Vice President of Sales and Market Development. The key deciding chip was my international reputation as a mover and shaker.

The challenge, to move the company quickly and aggressively into the national and international arena. Over the next ten years working with a talented, innovative group of young people, and with the understanding, supporting and giving nature of the family, received the freedom to build an organization that dominated the industry largely created by Hughes and Sheila Potitker. The company, Entertainment, became a public company, provided stock ownership to all its employees and became a merger target. The subsequent merger created wealth for everyone within Entertainment.

For me, again time to recast my vision and while doing so, over the next year, I assisted others, more or less as a freelance consultant and investor. My thinking turned toward education. My experience, especially during my years with Bobbs-Merrill, I dealt often with universities– through their academics, especially in colleges of business which did not exist in my early youth. In contracting with academics writing books while at Bobbs-Merrill, I was struck with their lack of respect for small business and their narrow course focuses on what I call the "housekeeping" positions within major corporations, accounting, finance, management, supply chain, etc. After some research, I determined to contact my alma mater with a proposal to start a program for small business and budding entrepreneurs – and having a few bucks in my jeans, offered the money to create and implement the program.. I also offered my extensive experience and ideas in building business to design and support the curriculum to meet the needs of developing entreprenerism in generations to come. That was in 1991-92 and this part of my story will cover that last decade of the 20th century and the early 21st century, so it is not ready to tell. May even require another storyteller to evaluate and write about these experiences.

I have taken these few pages, galloping through the highlights of over 50 years of my exciting, often turbulent, some times disappointing and often gloriously successful and fulfilling career of innovation and changemaking. Along the way I made international history as a woman who entered and achieved in basically male dominated arenas. The balance of this chapter is devoted to a few selected helpful concepts and ideas for those in search of answers or a helping hand. Pick and choose as you like.

What I can do first is to share a few comments which deal with process and attitude as opposed to rules and rights. There are some points that relate to my philosophy and style of behavior. Some opinion which would be hard for me to avoid. Take each comment or recommendation as they are meant only to be helpful thought starters. To share some of my beliefs and evolution with you in this short chapter has not come easily. I'm basically a very private person.

My business style is to race forward to meet the future head on – not have the future over take me. Early in my career, I discovered that practically all setbacks and obstacles were of my own hesitant, unprepared making. That I was not a victim of circumstances, rather unsavory circumstances were my creation born of hesitation and unpreparedness. Through trial and error, risking, reconstructing and doing a better job of studying the effects of actions, the light bulb of wisdom came on. With these experiences I learned to plan for the unforeseen. Those are the challenges and you will face them.

So, how did I do what was needed? First step was attitude born of envisioning. Success was never about money – it was about achievement. Money to me was then and still is a result – not a goal. What I set out to do was never about status, it was about being the best I could be. Never about recognition. Always about successful completion of goals and tasks I set for myself. Never about authority but about responsibility to self and others who depended on me. Always about honor – never about fame. I ran into a lot of dead ends and walls. Failed more often than I achieved – but achieve I did.

None of what is shared here is theory. It is based on discovery and it worked for me and might help you. I know that applying what I learned helped me prevail when others in my competitive world of equal and maybe more talent did not survive or prosper. After attitude adjustment comes process for getting a handle on planning for vision and its impact on the future. The past is prelude to both the present and the future, but deadly if we play only by the rules that evolved during the past. The past can only help understand how you got to the present. I learned to discipline a portion of my time and used my immediate past performance and results to mostly identify what needed improving. The objectives are one – don't repeat mistakes, and two – enhance the productivity of your time. Makes present activity more productive and less frustrating, clears the mind, reduces stress which allows one to imagine possibilities for the future, by doing better in the present. Engenders a positive spin to one's attitude to continue. I suspect you each have some personal system of evaluation so this may not be a new concept. Relying on one's experience alone is not the answer. Extensive repeated experience – so often used as a measure of value can be suspect if it narrows your envisioning process. You need an open mind to change, rather than a fixed paradigm. There is little to be gained if you must struggle to fit a new problem or potential opportunity with yesterday's experience or tools. That is not to say all paradigms are bad, they can be helpful to process routine work. This is just a caution to prevent them from mesmerizing creative thinking as new opportunities need fresh approaches – new problems fresh solutions.

Back to process for tracking yesterday with today to dream and plan for tomorrow. I've a title for this process. ANTICIPATORYRETROSPECT. That phrase-word became my memory jogging tool number one. The past is baseline and the foundation for the present which portends the future. The future is rooted in the past but can be influenced by the present which can be changed. My second memory jogging tool is to record each day as it occurs. I write a one page report to myself at the end of each day. Covers people, contacts, highlights, special results, actions and emerging problems or opportunities. I use these either to alter the next day's plan or take actions if needed. These summaries are invaluable in reviewing the past at the end of the year to plan or alter plans for the next year. Aside from its value to business, it has become essential to preparation for my taxes each year. In general, multi year planning becomes much easier and forecasting more accurate.

Next stage of this process in decision making and prioritizing opportunities and timing on problem solution and activities is to support each with a timetable. Here's where my early historical studies, reading the great philosophers, poets and authors came in handy. The poet-author Rudy Kipling enabled me to make analyses of opportunities as well as problems. In his Just So Stories there is a verse that goes like this:

"I keep six honest serving men

(They taught me all I knew);

Their names are WHAT and WHY and WHEN

And HOW and WHERE and WHO."

I started using the genius and wisdom of this verse early in my career with great success. Not just for business per se but in special activities involving elementary school children, high school students and sales training classes.

At World Book and Compton's I helped design a service program to use in follow-up of purchases in the schools. These classes were taught with the teachers present. We had workbooks, club pins and certificates for this program called Look-It-Up-Club. The program was to teach research skills. In my opening, I used the verse from Kipling and the work we did with the kids followed the six serving men. I also did some TV teaching and videos for high school students using the six serving men. The classes were taught within live settings and taped for future use. In that time, these were new concepts and ahead of the curve.

The six serving men system is exceptionally helpful when applied to a strategy or new product idea as you can winnow out strengths and weaknesses and ultimately access the feasibility of an idea, a plan, a product. The system is essential when puzzling through the development of a vision.

So far, every element mentioned is good sense and good relations. Now let's talk about the ground floor of readiness. There is an old biblical proverb "Where there is no vision, the people perish." Good caution for you personally and your business. vision is the ability to see the unseen future you want in a world of people intent at looking at where they are not where they can go. Deadly for an aspiring entrepreneur. A personal vision becomes your commitment to yourself, to act on behalf of the future you want, not the future ordained by someone else or just chance. Your exciting pledge for your trip through the life you want. After you decide your own route to the future and are comfortable with the fit – designing a business vision is easier. It should help deliver your personal vision. Your work should fit the future you plan for yourself. Sounds easy in words – but it ain't!

SO WHAT IS VISION?

Vision is a mind picture of one's dream for their future. So visible that it can sustain your resolve and can help create a story for you of what you want. So compelling that you can't wait each day to achieve. It drives your energy output to reach the exciting promise it portends. So sustaining that it causes friends, family and associates you share it with too help you – even go along for the ride into the world you envision. Does that sound too dramatic for you? Maybe, but you need all those people to want to be with you on the trip – because you need them and they need your vision which adds adventure ahead, starts and keeps your adrenaline pumping each day as you commit and pursue that special adventure. Don't forget your commitment and cause it to be a chore every time you hit an inevitable bump in the road. Look at the vision journey as a challenge by continually inventing ways to get there.

A vision has some special components. A sense of worthiness, inspirational, inviting and intriguing to others to share. It should be clear and understandable yet not easy to achieve. You've got to have stretch. Set your mental picture high. It's a picture of a process not a rigid structure. An open highway – not a wall. It's best if it assumes others will be with you. So flexible to allow inclusion not exclusion and gives room for it to evolve as your life progresses and your relationships increase and change. Once you get this far in your mind quest you need to capture its essences in a fairly understandable statement. There is a need for a visual, literate record for both you and your companions in your special quest. Not too long and yet not so short that it is non-directive. Not a garble of words that it can neither guide nor inspire, which is the main reason to articulate a vision in the first place. You can subsequently put fuel in the vision with a series of missions, goals and hard strategic drivers, designed to give locomotion to your vision.

Avoid buzzwords or generalities. Words that are really results of a vision with missions. Money, growth, reputation are not vision words. They are cosmetic and the results of vision with missions which help you to assess your progress. Vision should not be impersonal. It needs to relate to you, so those you share it with are influenced to help you. Has to be inspiring perhaps have the seeds of picturing a story about who you are and what you believe. Can be translatable into stories that showcase what you value. Stories that can move your heart. And, as you travel forward in life, stories of your accomplishments that can interest, inspire, involve and change others. Actually create believers who go along with you.

Well, how do you begin? First stage, look into your past for clues about yourself – good or not so good and assess their influence on your present. Some may have been life changing. In each of our Innovators' stories, they have shared some of these private episodes that changed them and gave us clues into their philosophies, opinions, internal guidance systems and deep beliefs. They were willing to open their private episodes and show how they often snatched success from daunting tragedies and competitive circumstances.

Look for some of your own life milestones to help you elucidate your vision. In visioning worry less about your experience or what you are doing. More about who you are or have become through your life experiences. Then step into your future and take a stand on who you want to be and where you want to go. Not how you intend to get there. Save your list of competencies, skills and education for your missions, and strategies. They can be tools to get there. You need a personal vision before you design a business vision. Chase it now and you will make a pledge to yourself and others opening the door for support from friends, family and others along the road of your life. Once you have established your personal vision you are ready to fit your entrepreneurial venture with its ideas and business purpose into the vision for a company. The elements are similar. The process is the same – but the business dream forecasted needs to benefit others as well as you. You need to envision the values derived by the market place and your employees, and then encapsulate into a statement much the same way as you do for personal vision.

For your entrepreneurial venture you follow vision with mission. To achieve a specific immediate action and result and an operating statement to inspire and involve your employees in the excitement of the venture and at the same time remind them of their essential role in achieving outcomes. One of the best crafted examples of this process that I've seen is from the National Space Society. Here it is:

VISION STATEMENT
People living and working in thriving communities beyond the Earth.

MISSION STATEMENT
To promote change in the social, technical, economic and political conditions to advance the day when people will live and work in space.

OPERATING STATEMENT
AD ASTRA

"TO THE STARS"

Pretty exciting – pretty directing. Easy to understand and relate to.

Through two plus years, hours and hours of extensive interviews with the outstanding, selected people whose stories you listen to here, their daring, creativity, courage and impact was awesome to me.

The Carol Den Herder, Kristin Rezler story is especially rich in the challenges of mother and daughter innovators achieving success as a team. They share their intimate human occurrences that shaped their road to success, especially the painful tragedy of losing a child and sister. A marvelous example of two entirely different personalities coming together to form a driving vision in more than one business. What is incredible is how they make their differences work. An example of tolerance, love and commitment, delivering success and teamwork.

Gregory Torrez' eventful youth in the early shadow of two towering entrepreneurial parents. His willingness to listen, learn and through faith persist to form a vision that would honor those parents by his being successful in business, a recognized humanitarian and influential business leader and spokes-person in his state. You feel the dramatic awakening of Gregory as he expands his vision of supporting his parents creations to realizing he has more to offer and launches his career expansion through personal sales skills and drives forward to create his own success and still honor his family name.

Marcia Veidmark whose amazing vision and the enormous faith it contained supported her family business through unspeakable tragedies and inspired her employees to stay the course to prevail with her through enormous economic set backs. And, at the same time, grooming her sons to take over the business and providing them the room to grow. Her generosity in making community support an intricate part of her vision.

Eileen Spitalny and David Kravitz whose vision of working together started in grade school and never wavered. Inspired their families to work hard to help and support them through their darkest hours. Their vision inspired them to utilize David's mother's wonderful brownies recipe and through their dedication propelled them to international fame in competition with the world of cookies. They call their success their 'Fairytale Journey'. Fairytale Brownies are on everyone's list of elegant gifts today.

Ogbonna Abarikwu is an immigrant intent on being the best possible American. Whose staunch patriotism and ethical, moral approach to business and community inspires his staff and has earned the respect of authorities and municipalities to win prize engineering assignments in fierce competition with larger engineering firms. His broad and eclectic vision is to create other companies continues to drive his actions and benefits the communities, education and other entrepreneurs.

Ananda Roberts, whose entire life has been devoted to serving the non-profit sector so they can better serve the country. A courageous, empathetic individual whose corporate vision is to develop and maintain the most powerful public sector software tracking solutions in the world. To empower each of their client non-profits and government agency partners so they each can better serve the public at large. It's hard to find more dedicated, commitment, drive, bravado and courage.

John Ridgway whose vision began early in his youth and took him into influencing the lives of three quarters of the world's population. His dominance of the audio and visual persona of television, radio and entertainment organizations is legendary. He finds time to support and teach universally in his chosen field, so that young people aspiring to rise in these areas have access to his knowledge. That effort is worldwide as well as in the U.S. In his vision, the U.S. is just another country.

Eileen Proctor is always in transition from one idea to another – a serial ideator. Personable and charismatic, her dramatic style captivates those she encounters landing her almost daily in the press, on TV and radio. Her ideas, fame and energetic manner place her on the demand list for those seeking stimulation, excitement and motivation.

Doug Ducey has a knack of leading without overpowering. He possesses a quiet drive, an ability to stay on vision message and motivate his diverse and talented head quarters team. Together they select and support a growing worldwide army of entrepreneurial franchises, in their quest to become the ultimate top-of-mind ice cream experience.

None of these changemakers just happened into their success. No luck here! They all made it happen through strong enduring vision. The world they influence is and continues to be a better place and change because their visions are put into actions. Their guts and imagination propelled by great infusions of faith, persistence and generosity in sharing their talents makes it hard to think about a world without their visions and thousands like them. Their impact is huge locally, nationally and internationally. They represent the monumental potential of entrepreneurs who start, build and grow – the millions more in the world and the future tidal wave of innovators and changemakers can bring.

There have been thousands of people over the last 60 years whose lives I've touched in some way and still do. Many have gone on to successful careers, and yes, have become successful entrepreneurs. Out of the many skills and activities needed to innovate, I've selected for this chapter, those I know to be most crucial for long term commitment and a solid foundation for success.

If you question the power of vision rethink and envision your own. Your life will be better for it. You may exist one day at a time - but don't bet your future on that premise.

EPILOGUE

"Know then thyself, presume not God to scan;

The proper study of mankind is man"

Alexander Pope: An Essay on Man

WHERE TO NEXT? YOU CHOOSE.

Pope's essay points up the quintessential importance and complexity of human capital, something not often, if at all taken into honest consideration by businesses over the last few decades.

This concluding section will round out the intent of our conversational exploration into the heroic activities, adventures and contributions of these selected entrepreneurial builders. The great difficulty has been extracting from hundreds of recorded pages of conversations with our selected innovators, those cogent nuggets and episodes without losing the flavor of their exciting stories. We could easily have a book on each. Each story highlights the pursuit of individual quests that contain an elegant combination of faith, persistence, ethics, creativity, guts, imagination and determined visions. Their forthright willingness to also share failures, disappointments and tragedies as well, made these stories worth the telling. All through the two years of interviews and compilation, I thought of a phrase I read in a small weekly newspaper called the Huerfano World, "Fear is a reaction; courage is a choice". They choose courage. They have all provided their web sites should you wish to contact them and learn more. We encourage you to make contact. They are all good guys.

As knowledge and technology has advanced exponentially, ethical and moral behavior has dissipated equally as fast. Tough moral choices have given way to rationalization and expediency often covered by the phrase "the means justifies the end," or "it's a competitive world out there," or "a dog eat dog world".

It will take innovation, foresight and concomitant actions to move toward a wiser less acrimonious future for this world of ours. The battle is daunting faced with the images that jump at us from the Internet, books, TV, radio, theater screens, magazines and newspapers. Most of it not very objective or uplifting. The revisionists have maligned the founding fathers and their courage with sordid warped examples of "political correctness" and spawned malaise and angst rather than positive values. These corruptive forces have tainted our businesses, priceless institutions of religions, governments, education and charities, invaded our sports and theater, turned our special holiday celebrations into ridiculous effigies and circuses and worse turned our political scene into an open confrontation of lies, half truths and personal character assassinations. They harm us all. What is dangerous is these infections to our nation have produced a tidal wave that is washing on to our young people - our future legacy. Is it a fact that the worst of human behavior sells better than the good?

Whatever happened to our wonderful children's stories such as the Horatio Alger stories, the amazing truthful history of our country, ripe with examples of courage, faith and leadership? How is it that the heroism of determined pioneers building an amazing nation from east to west, north and south suddenly became passé? What happened to neighborhoods where caring, concern, safety and good deeds could be found most everywhere? Have we lost our sense of direction - our daring to do? Are we losing our precious heritage? Where did all this destructive venom and complacency come from? If there is any, where is the good stuff hiding?

Innovation has been the soul of this country from its very foundation. Entrepreunerism and perspicacity the bedrock of economics, capitalism and the early structure of our society. Freedom to build and create was not impaired by general negativism. Countries all over the world are catching the entrepreneurial spirit and creating their own economic and social miracles for their societies. Are we losing our momentum while others are gaining it? We have the human capital and all it needs is a little faith and leadership. The people featured here represent a variety of personalities and backgrounds. They daily change, for the better, the world they serve. I have a passion as do they to tell their stories. My associate Norma Strange has the creativity to illustrate so you would have visual and words to get the full flavor of their contributions. And, through the activity of my scholarship foundation we are building a small brigade of new young talent to swell the ranks of entrepreunerism. We're focusing on the good stuff.

Every day is born fresh and presents us with a bundle of choices and challenges. What we each do with these resources adds another positive or negative building block in the person we continue to become. Each individual is a unique creation. One person can change the space he or she inhabits. All we need is millions, each doing their part as the twelve entrepreneurs whose stories grace these pages have done. We drop the curtain on our Epilogue again with the question: Where is the good stuff hiding? The answer is all around us. Will you make a difference? The following is a poem with food for thought:

CHOICES

We all have choices. We can
Choose to laugh or cry
Tell the truth or lie
To ourselves and others.
Choose to help or hinder
Be good or bad
Smile or frown – be happy or sad.

The choices we make
Make us what we choose to be.

Choice is conscious or unconscious
Depending –
Whether the choice has been made
So often that it has become habit –
Or it's a first time choice.

Habits form patterns and traits
That exhibit the character
We have or lack.
Our character makes us attractive –
Or unattractive.
Whichever we consciously
Or unconsciously choose to be.

The choices we make
Make us what we choose to be.

We attract or distract
Make friends or lose friends
Or worse – not better
We repel or alienate
Anger or harm – not help.
Making enemies who are
Active or inactive.

We give or take
Lose what we gave
Or take away or leave behind
What we found
Continually adding and subtracting
From ourselves.

The choices we make
Make us what we choose to be.

We create and mold ourselves
Continually choosing and changing
For the better – or the worse
Every second we choose
And become that choice
Sometimes understanding
Sometimes not understanding.

So does each of us go on
For our lives choosing what we become.
Even after death
Having impressed or depressed.
Causing remembrance or
Because we have chosen to be forgettable
Are forgotten.

We each possess
An abundance of talents
Have chosen consciously
Or unconsciously
To use them
Abuse them
Or not use them.

Use or lose
Fail or succeed
You have a choice

The choices we make
Make us what we choose to be.
Choose to stretch for success
In all of life's choices.
Choose to help others and
Others will choose to remember you.

— Shirley G. Schmitz

2007 Shirley G. Schmitz Foundation Scholarship Recipients. Photo by Donna Kesot.

SHIRLEY G. SCHMITZ FOUNDATION, INC.

Set people on course to reshape the future of business

The Shirley G. Schmitz Foundation, Inc., a 501(c)(3) non-profit corporation, provides scholarships for education and training leading to starting and operating a business. Acceptable programs include formal college courses offered by accredited universities and community colleges.

The Foundation provides scholarships as incentives rather than rewards for achievement. Proven achievers, by in large, will tend to continue. We enlarge the spectrum by assisting ambitious talent and interceding to shape it.

Each year the Foundation Board determines how many scholarships will be awarded. The awards are paid to the scholarship recipient directly and can only be used for tuition, training, and books.

Any U.S. citizen who demonstrates ability and motivation is eligible. Special attention is accorded to those with entrepreneurial goals as part of their future. Recipients must have a high school degree or equivalent and must be enrolled in an Arizona school during the school year for which the scholarship is awarded.

For more information, please send inquiry to:
Shirley G. Schmitz Foundation, Inc.
11445 E. Via Linda, Suite 2 #442
Scottsdale, AZ 85259-2638

ABOUT THE AUTHOR

Shirley G. Schmitz has been described as a strong small business proponent with an entrepreneurial brain. She earned an international reputation as an accomplished business "house builder" in an era when women were an anomaly in business. Thousands of people during the last half of the 20th century and the first decade of the 21st century, have benefited from her firm direction, teaching and guidance. Especially known for bold, activist approaches to solving tough business issues and her skill in anticipating future trends. Possesses extensive experience in strategic planning, budgeting, market development, sales and acquisitions. A proven profit generator.

For information on her many achievements, awards and businesses you may turn to her listings in:
- Who's Who in the World
- Who's Who in America
- Who's Who in Finance and Industry
- Who's Who of American Women

ABOUT THE DESIGNER

Norma S. Strange's nearly 20-year career as a proficient graphic artist, branding and marketing strategist suits her entrepreneurial, problem-solving, quick-witted personality. She truly loves to encourage and educate others to accelerate their own success. She has a natural willingness to engage in conversations, public presentations and mentorship. Her practical business balance comes from her grasp of mathematics and her ability to envision unlimited possibilities. She was a math major before she embraced her artistic gift and gained a bachelor of fine arts degree. Her desire to solve challenges and create a superior customer experience that results in financial profitability keeps her in the center of various business ventures. You'll find her delivering business training while her generous heart listens for ways to help the people she encounters along her journey.

As for what captures her heart, first God, then the man that made her Strange, her husband Greg, and their two angel girls, Casey and Jessica. She's especially grateful for her friendship with her 77-year old mom. Norma views each day as a gift, encouraging everyone to be present and live it fully. She feels privileged to meet interesting and inspiring people each and every day.

COMMENTS ABOUT THE AUTHOR

"I worked with Shirley Schmitz for years and have always been proud to call her my mentor. Her ability to analyze situations, anticipate the directions going forward and teach the process has benefited me in the pursuit of my business." — *Paul Sollicito, President/CEO, a la Carte, Long Island, NY*

"On the chain of entrepreneurial thinking Shirley is a welcome link. She is like the spark that makes a mighty flame. Her philanthropic and entrepreneurial contributions have impacted many lives and her examples have created new directions in thought. The joy of knowing her is seeing life through her lenses." — *Theresa Mendoza, Senior Advisor, Campus Advancement Programs, Office of the Chancellor, Long Beach, CA*

"Shirley Schmitz exemplifies the qualities of a successful leader. She has a powerful message that offers insights for all of us and especially for the emerging leaders in today's business world. Her focus is more about building a solid business foundation and providing quality leadership than on the bottom line. Shirley's past roles and experiences in corporate America puts her in a 'who's who' category all her own. She is an extraordinary individual with an uncanny sixth sense about how to build strong, sustainable businesses. Shirley has a profound understanding of what it takes to be a successful leader today and, more importantly, is willing to share that wisdom with all of us." — *Barbara Malone, Visions Unlimited, Tempe, AZ*